C000044891

HIT THE
GROUND
RUNNING

By the same author

WHAT THEY DON'T TEACH YOU AT HARVARD BUSINESS SCHOOL

WHAT THEY DIDN'T TEACH ME AT YALE LAW SCHOOL

SUCCESS SECRETS

THE 110% SOLUTION

HIT THE GROUND RUNNING

THE INSIDER'S GUIDE

TO EXECUTIVE TRAVEL

Mark H. McCormack

CHAPMANS

Chapmans Publishers
A Division of the Orion Publishing Group Ltd
Orion House
5 Upper St Martin's Lane
London WC2H 9EA

First published by Chapmans 1993

ISBN 1–85592–683–0 hb
ISBN 1–85592–630–X pb

A CIP catalogue record for this book
is available from the British Library

Photoset in Monophoto Photina by
Datix International Limited, Bungay, Suffolk
Printed in England by Clays Ltd, St Ives plc

To my trusted personal assistants, secretaries and associates – especially Laurie Roggenburk, Sarah Wooldridge, Fumiko Matsuki, Penny Thompson and Michelle Lane, who tirelessly worked throughout the year to make sure that I 'Hit the Ground Running' wherever I might be in the world; and also to those who have filled these roles during the past thirty years including Mary Wenzel, Ayn Robbins, Nancy Grey, Doris Jones, Judy Chilcote, Vicky Micatrotto, Jean Barnes, Sally Anne Pickard, Elaine de Spoelberch, Penny Clark, Mary Ann Badalamenti and a host of others.
Finally and especially to my father, Ned Hume McCormack, who taught me the first things I ever learned about travel and who showed me how enjoyable it can be.

Acknowledgements

Writing this book would have been impossible without the help of many people. My gratitude and thanks:

To John Meyer, Jose Luis Ferrando, Todd McCormack, Steven Flanders, Eric Drossart, Michel Masquelier, Ivo Cozzini, Fred Adams, Peter Townsend, Tony Barry, Laurence St. John, Alastair Johnston, Peter Henke, Jacques Heyer, Marc Biver, Breck McCormack, Richard Avory, Timo Lumme, Cino Marchese, Kappy Flanders, Cliff Minshull, John Beddington, David and Jeannie Evans, Leslie McCormack, Erik van Dillen, Lars Sternmarker, Jim Curley, and Kazuo Kondo for their knowledge of what is excellent and true in various ports of call around the world.

To Hervé Houdre, Mike Baverstock, Michael Gray, Bob Anderson, Marvin Bush, Sir Christopher Lewinton, Ian Wooldridge, Michael Parkinson, Sir David Frost, Gino Santin, Anton Mosimann, Bill Fugazy and Melvyn Hartzel for sharing their personal travel secrets.

To Gretchen Mayfield for her fleet fingers at the word processor.

To Digby Diehl, an insightful and responsive collaborator, without whom this book could never have been completed.

Contents

Preface
Less Haste, More Speed

A series of commercials ran on American television a few years ago for Hertz rental cars showing the great American football star, O. J. Simpson, no longer in helmet and pads but impeccably attired in suit and tie, sprinting through a crowded airport terminal, dodging travellers, hurdling luggage, all in a frantic last-second effort to get to the rental counter, pick up his car and get to his meeting. It was a vivid image of speed and dynamism.

But there was a twist. As Simpson rushes up to the counter, he's greeted by a smiling Arnold Palmer (Hertz's longtime spokesperson) who is calmly picking up his keys (because he had the good sense to use Hertz's then-revolutionary express check-in service).

For some of you, the title of this book may conjure up an image of a dashing executive, with tie and briefcase flapping in the breeze, doing some nifty broken-field running through an airport. I can understand how people are seduced by that vision of energy. But I'm less impressed with the disorganized frenzy it implies. People who are always running for the plane or the rent-a-car may be enjoying the kind of exercise that gets your heart rate up, but they are not going to last long as serious business travellers.

My concept of *Hit the Ground Running* is derived from the carefully planned, precisely executed landings made by Allied paratroopers during World War II. The soldiers practised for months, studied the terrain, reviewed their plans of attack in detail, made pinpoint parachute jumps, stayed in communication with each other and re-formed their units rapidly to maximize efficiency and surprise. They hit the ground running to win battles in the European and Pacific theatres and, eventually, the war. They knew where they were going, what they had to accomplish there, and how to do it. O. J. Simpson might not have made the flight.

I always make the flight – well, almost always.

One of the reasons I decided to write this book is that over the past twenty-five years, my friends and associates have noticed that I not only get to flights and meetings on time in cities all over the world, but I get there ready to do business. I leave my running for the tennis court. In fact, I still look forward to every trip as an opportunity to help my company – and to expand my own horizons.

Over the years, other executives often have asked me how I avoid 'travel burnout'. Associates always call me for tips on hotels and restaurants when they are heading to new cities. And colleagues have pressed me for my 'secrets' of efficient travel. At some point in the history of our company, I started collecting some of this hard-won advice in a company manual, telling our executives, for example, 'How to Travel in Tokyo'. We have done this for three dozen cities where we maintain an office. You'll find some of these secrets in this book.

A far more important reason for this book, however, hinges on one irrefutable fact: Over the past thirty years, I have seen travel become the key to success in my own business life. Our company, International Management Group, began with one client (Arnold Palmer) and one small office (in Cleveland, Ohio). Today, IMG represents sports, music and entertainment celebrities all over the world, including Nick Faldo, Gary Player, Ivan Lendl, Alain Prost, Greg Norman, Andre Agassi, Martina Navratilova, Chris Evert, Monica Seles, Jim Courier, Joe Montana, Wayne Gretzky, Kristi Yamaguchi, Jean-Claude Killy, Alberto Tomba, Jackie Stewart, Kiri Te Kanawa, Itzhak Perlman, Sir Neville Marriner, James Galway and Michael Parkinson.

IMG has been retained to manage various commercial

activities for many of the world's foremost sports events, including both the 1992 Winter Olympics at Albertville, France, and the 1994 Olympics at Lillehammer, Norway, Wimbledon, the British Open golf championship, the America's Cup, the Australian, Italian and German Open tennis championships, and various World Cup skiing championships.

We also organize and present sporting and cultural events around the world, everything from the ATP World Championship tennis tournament in Frankfurt to the Johnnie Walker World Championship of Golf in Jamaica to the Grand Prix of Cleveland motor race to 'An Evening with Jose Carerras' in Bath. In between, there are cricket tours in New Zealand, badminton championships in Hong Kong and snooker tournaments in Dubai.

From a one office–one client establishment in the 1960s, IMG has grown to become a multinational enterprise encompassing sixty-one offices in nineteen countries with about 1,500 full-time employees.

The Importance of the Global Perspective

I tell you all this not to brag, but to impress upon you the fact that travel and the broadened outlook it engenders will become increasingly important to all companies in the coming years. For years, people have paid lip service to the concept of an emerging global business environment. Well, you can erase that word 'emerging'. The global market is here – now! The businesses that will survive and thrive into the twenty-first century must take an international perspective.

All of us are dealing constantly with other cultures and other vocabularies. Even when the language is the same, as is the case with Britain and the United States, the means of expression can be very different. A British friend of mine told me that although our house in Orlando, Florida, was very big, it was nevertheless very homely. I was not offended; the man was paying me a compliment. In England 'homely' means comfortable and inviting; in America it means ugly.

Another Englishman once described a golfer's putt as very 'nervy'. 'Nervy' in Britain means 'nervous'. 'Nervy' in America means 'gutsy'. They're total opposites. George Bernard Shaw wasn't wrong when he said that Britain and America are 'two nations separated by a common language'.

These are just two tiny examples of the shades of meaning that occur between cultures. To understand what's going on in business and in life in general, you have to catch the conversational nuances, which are highly variable from one part of the world to another. Although you can study books on business etiquette in the Far East or social customs in France or Italy, it's like learning to play tennis by reading about it without ever getting on the court with a racket in your hand. There's no better way to become more global yourself than by travelling and immersing yourself in another culture.

I think that doing so gives you a leg up on business dealings with people outside your geographic area and indeed on life in general. You don't really understand other people until you've been in their environment, talked to them and learned from them. I'm always learning as I travel, not just from business associates, but from cab drivers, bellboys, and headwaiters.

Because of IMG's worldwide reach, I've become one of a new, rapidly growing breed of traveller: *the global commuter*. I have learned how to feel 'at home' in many different countries – and in the air. A sedentary month for me means that I fly fewer than 10,000 miles, the equivalent of four trips between London and New York. Last year I logged over 225,000 miles on business travel – just as I have for each of the past thirty years. I have eaten meals in more than 5,000 restaurants on six continents and stayed in hundreds of hotels in every major city.

Unlike the many journalists who write books about travel, I have paid my own tab – always seeking the best value for me and for my company. My travel is always arranged with the practical aim of accomplishing business. I am certainly not a promoter or an apologist for the travel industry, as you will see in the following pages. However, I am not a dewy-eyed sentimentalist about the 'good old days of travel', either. In almost every area, the travel experience has improved in both comfort and efficiency over the years I have been on the road.

The 'Good Old Days'

Thirty years ago is far enough back for many people to think of them as the 'good old days'. However, in travel as in other areas of life, rosy memories obscure the fact that for the travelling executive, those 'good old days' weren't very good at all. When I started travelling on business, the flight from Sydney to Tokyo on an Electra prop-jet took twenty-six hours. We had to stop in Darwin and in Hong Kong, where we had to get off the plane for about five hours.

For those who have not been through as many take-offs and landings as I have, I'll try to describe how far we've come since those first twenty-six-hour airborne marathons, and how much easier those last 225,000 miles were for me than the first 225,000 I racked up. Travel is a very change-intensive industry, and the speed of that change has been accelerating. It is very different today than it was even five years ago. It has changed, and by and large it has changed for the better.

Even taking terrorism into account, flying is a lot safer than it used to be. The equipment is more reliable, and computers help airlines establish regular maintenance and replacement schedules. Travellers are also far less vulnerable to the vagaries of weather systems and other natural phenomena.

I remember trying to get an appointment with John DeLorean when he was the head of Chevrolet. He was a friend, but his schedule was tightly booked and he was very hard to see. My schedule was very busy too, but finally we set up a meeting in Detroit. I flew to Detroit from New York, but when we got there we were told that the airport was fogbound and we couldn't get in. We landed in Chicago instead.

When we finally got in I called DeLorean, of course. Since there were no phones on board back then, until I called and explained, he thought I'd stood him up. And although he understood what had happened to me, he had no openings in his agenda for a long while. Our meeting had to be postponed for several weeks.

Today that just doesn't happen very often. With the advancement of technology in flight routing, instrument landings and aircraft design, weather is much less a factor than it was. Bad weather, which commonly affected about 20 per cent of our flights, now only rarely causes delays.

The airports themselves have become far more user-friendly. Not long ago they had all the appeal of a dingy bus station, oriented far more towards accommodating planes and baggage than people. The newest terminals are light, airy places that can handle large volumes of passengers quickly. Airline frequent flyer clubs are very pleasant and offer wide-screen televisions, conference rooms, bars, complimentary drinks and hors-d'oeuvre, and a chance for some real privacy in what can be a very public place.

Baggage comes off the plane more quickly than it did, and preferred baggage usually gets there even faster. Although it is most assuredly far from perfect, the computerized reservation process, including the ability to request a particular seat and/or a special meal, has become more efficient over the past few years. Clearing Customs is usually speedy now and no longer the brutalizing experience of just a few years ago.

Hotels have changed as well. The grand hotels have always been remarkable, but I believe that the experience for the average traveller has become better, because the quality of an average hotel room has improved dramatically. Now there's twenty-four-hour room service, pressing service, shoeshine service, everything you need for maintenance on the road. In the 'good old days' before I could afford to stay in better hotels, it was not uncommon for the rooms to be dirty and fitted out with plumbing and electricity that worked fitfully, if at all.

There is also the new, enlarged role of the telephone in

business life. Thirty years ago telephones were almost prehistoric. An international call was an adventure, and not a pleasant one at that. When we first began representing South Africa's Gary Player, I tried to place a call from Johannesburg to the United States. There was no such thing as direct dialling. You had to call an overseas operator, and they were always engaged. It would take hours to reach one. Once you got one, you had to book a time to make your phone call. In effect you had to make an appointment with the operator to call someone, something no business person would put up with today. The connection, if the call actually went through, was often dismal.

The Specialness of Travel

The one good thing that too many of us seem to have lost from the 'good old days' is a sense of the specialness of travel. In the past, a large part of that specialness was the sheer wonder that you could do it at all. Except for entertainers and athletes, frequent business travel was relatively uncommon. It used to be that a trip was something that you saved up for vacation. A family stayed at home all year and went on one or two eagerly-awaited long trips a year. However, the vacation experience did not truly begin until they arrived at their destination. People lived in a state of suspended animation while *en route*. The travel itself *wasn't* part of the experience.

Today the rigours of the past are long forgotten, and the business-as-usual nature of travel, for business and for pleasure, is both what's right and what's wrong with it. Travel is so commonplace that people no longer look forward to it. Too many travellers start anticipating the hassle with the baggage, the hassle of standing in line, the delays, the uncomfortable seats, the lousy food. They don't compare their experience to the way travel used to be, but rather to the comfort and convenience of staying at home or in the office.

I firmly believe that expectations create their own reality. Those who constantly measure the adventurous experience of travel against the comfortable familiarity of staying at home are doomed to disappointment. People who approach travel wringing their hands with trepidation in effect sabotage themselves. Because they are not looking forward to their trip, they don't plan adequately for it. Their shortsightedness and joyless explanations go a long way towards guaranteeing a bad experience.

On the other hand, if you look at travel as an invigorating or exhilarating possibility, that has a self-fulfilling (and positive) effect too. Your outlook helps you to turn what could be drudgery into an experience that you can remember with pleasure.

Unlike many frequent flyers, I still genuinely enjoy travelling. I'm travelling at least as much as I'm at home. I look forward to it, and I plan some joy and positive experience into each trip. I travel for a living and in a sense I live to travel. I'm not Pollyanna, but I've never lost that sense of the specialness of travel, and that's one of the reasons why I still love life on the road.

The Positive Aspects of Business Travel

How do you approach every business trip with a positive attitude? First you have to realize that going to see someone is in and of itself a positive thing. Everyone appreciates it when someone makes the effort to visit them. It doesn't matter whether it's across the Atlantic Ocean or from London to Paris, or from uptown to downtown. In all of my previous books – from *What They Don't Teach You at Harvard Business School* to *The 110% Solution* – I have emphasized the importance of that person-to-person contact. In a global business environment driven by fax machines and cellular telephones, the Personal Touch takes on even greater value.

Far too many business travellers counterbalance that highly positive aspect of a trip by thinking about the negatives – the hassles of travel itself. Business travel can be fun, enjoyable and relaxing, even as it accomplishes its business objectives. I believe that putting some enjoyment into business travel makes good business sense.

Hit the Ground Running is designed to help the executive traveller make travel, which is essential, a positive experience. Let's get started.

1 Travel Should be a Life-Enhancing Pleasure

Travellers are always discoverers, especially those who travel by air. There are no signposts in the sky to show that a man [or a woman] has passed that way before.

Anne Morrow Lindbergh

I can still recall the thrill of travelling with my parents on long train trips as a child. My father was in the publishing business – farm journals and magazines. We lived in Chicago, but Dad travelled frequently on business to New York and Topeka, Kansas, and occasionally to Washington, DC, to see Senator Capper, who owned the publishing company, Capper Publications, for which he worked. My mother used to take frequent vacations every year and would often plan out her trips years ahead. She knew what she was going to be doing every minute. She would figure out which hotels were the good ones and which rooms in those hotels were the quietest. She knew what tours she was going to be on and where she would eat. She was an amazing traveller.

Whole worlds of new sights and smells, new people, new experiences opened to me on those trips with my parents. I switched from watching the American landscape flashing by outside to studying the other passengers on the train with equal fascination. I returned from each journey like an explorer – laden with treasures and filled with exotic tales. At home, when my parents would begin to discuss another trip, I always reacted with enthusiastic excitement.

Travelling beyond the narrow confines of our own homes and neighbourhoods is a childhood thrill that most of us remember with great pleasure. But for many adults, years of hectic, repetitious, mandatory business trips have taken the pleasure out of travel. The majority of business people regard travel as an unpleasant duty, a drudgery that comes with the territory. You can see their long faces at boarding gates and luggage carousels all over the world.

Contemporary Travel Is No Bed of Roses

There is a lot of evidence to support those who feel that business travel is a misery. Long periods away from friends and families, packed highways, crowded airport terminals, uncomfortable aeroplane flights, bad food, lack of exercise, impersonal hotel rooms, stressful schedules, hostile 'service industry' personnel, sleepless nights, shrinking expense accounts – the litany of legitimate complaints goes on. There are some real impediments to enjoying business travel!

There are impediments to enjoying other aspects of life, too. However, I enjoy my life, my business and my frequent travel. Perhaps that is because I constantly re-examine my goals and objectives to be sure of where I am headed, and to enjoy the satisfaction of accomplishing those goals. I design my life, my work and my travel to be enjoyable. Sometimes that means redefining impediments, problems or hassles as 'problem-solving opportunities' which challenge my resourcefulness. Sometimes that means redistributing my work or travel load over a longer schedule. Sometimes – much as a corporate executive hates to admit it – that means spending extra money. Ultimately, I find that enjoyment in almost any area has a lot to do with my own attitude.

Attitude Adjustment

If you are reading this book, you are already committed to finding ways to make your own travel more effective and pleasant. I want to show you how this can be done at all levels of business experience. I will demonstrate how modest adjustments in your goal definitions, your thinking, your scheduling, and your travel strategies can reap big rewards in satisfaction and efficiency. There's no magic to my methods. In fact, much of what you will read in this book is common-sense judgement that could be applied to many areas of endeavour. In my book, *What They Don't Teach You at Harvard Business School*, I pointed out some of the simple ideas that get lost in the abstractions of marketing theories and management techniques. The same common-sense approach to planning your business travel works, too. You just have to apply it.

Willingness to change, to learn, to adjust old attitudes is always more difficult than you think. You may have to consider the possibility that you are setting yourself up for misery with your present travel techniques. You may have to confront the fact that, like most people, you waste valuable time that could be better used. You may have to consider that you have stuck yourself in an unpleasant rut. So get ready to examine your attitudes towards travel, to reorganize your travel planning, to maximize your travel efficiency, to add some new experiences to your schedule, and to take responsibility for making your business travel fun again.

The Six Most Common Complaints About Business Travel – and How to Deal with Them

In surveys of business travellers worldwide, the same complaints appear year after year. I suspect you will agree with most of them. I certainly do. But after we grumble together, let's consider how the expert traveller deals with these problems.

- Separation from home, family, and daily routines.
- Stress of unfamiliar surroundings and hassle of life on the road.
- Time wasted in transit and standing in lines.
- Discomfort of aeroplane seats and hotel accommodation.
- Bad food.
- Expense account pressure.

The 'Dorothy' Syndrome

Most of this book will deal with getting the most out of business travel by attacking items 2–6 on my list, but I believe it is important here to address the number one issue – separation from family.

As Dorothy discovered in *The Wizard of Oz*, even the most magical travel experience is unpleasant if you miss your home and family. According to a study of 700 business travellers conducted for Hyatt Hotels by Harvard University psychiatrist Barrie Greiff, separation from home and family is one of the primary dissatisfactions of life on the road. Everyone misses their loved ones, and even grown-ups are subject to homesickness. The study found that the conflict between career and family is difficult for most people to handle.

Because my wife, Betsy Nagelsen, plays professional tennis and I am able to determine my own travel schedule, I'm fortunate that she can accompany me on many of my trips. For executives with young children, however, I realize that this is not possible. Although repeated long absences will strain family relationships under almost any circumstances, there are ways for the travelling executive to **take a little of home with you, and leave a little of yourself at home**.

Schedule Your Trips Carefully

Marvin Bush, the son of former President George Bush and an investment banker in Washington, DC, plans his travel to avoid family dislocations. 'I travel about five days a month, but I don't like to miss things at home,' he says. 'I've got two kids, aged seven and three. There is no meeting that's more important to me than an event that's important to my children – a birthday, a school play, the first soccer game. Unless it's *really* something that can't be changed, I tell colleagues that I just can't be there at that time. Nine times out of ten, the meeting can be rescheduled. That way, when I do go away, I can leave with a clean conscience.'

No Surprise Departures

The real travel benefits come from planning ahead. This advance planning also benefits family members who will stay at home. Kids do much better adjusting to the absence of a parent when they have time to anticipate that absence. **Announce your trip to your family as far in advance as you can.** Especially with small children, mention your trip repeatedly. Use your trip as a way to teach them about things they will learn in school:

● Count down the weeks and days on a calendar.
● Get out a globe or an atlas and show them where they live and where you are going.
● If you are travelling overseas, show them your passport and foreign currency.

One dedicated dad even lets his kids help him pack, but I don't advocate this for everyone. A child's packing certainly won't win any awards for efficiency or neatness, but it doesn't take much manual dexterity to put shoes into a flannel shoe bag, take a prefolded shirt from the laundry and put it in the outside pocket of your carry-on bag, or make sure that your toothbrush and toothpaste are in your toilet kit. Psychologists suggest that by helping with packing, children become used to the idea of your departure – and of your eventual return.

Pieces of Home

Although spouses and children must cope with the absence of a loved one, don't underestimate the potential effects of homesickness on you, the business traveller. Take a small album of family snapshots along, and keep it updated. I have an associate whose wife always puts a going away card or other memento in his luggage – somewhere. From time to time the location is obvious, but more often she's very cleverly hidden it. She also has their daughter make a card for dad and tucks that into the suitcase as well.

Pieces of You

In the same vein, a travelling executive who is also a mother leaves little reminders of her own eventual return in unexpected places – a new set of crayons in a kindergartener's lunchbox, a good luck charm in a basketball shoe or ballet slipper, a note in her husband's sock drawer, a tape-recorded message to 'clean your room' in an older child's Walkman. Most travelling parents bring back presents for family members. These don't need to be extravagant – some business travellers find a collectable item such as a doll or baseball cap and begin building a collection that they add to with each trip.

The most personal piece of yourself that you can give to your family while you are away, however, is your voice. Before leaving, **make a date for a phone call**, and make sure you keep it.

Rethinking Time away from Home

There is no doubt that separation from home, family and personal contacts is a far more emotional issue for business people than concern about being away from the office. Parents, particularly parents of young children, are already filled with guilt about not spending enough time with their kids. Working couples often resent how work keeps them apart, and travel will only exacerbate this problem. Unmarried young professionals are more susceptible to homesickness, the need for contact with friends, and simply the comfortable surroundings of their homes, than they would care to admit.

There are many ways to ease separation anxieties, to bring some of the comforts of home on a trip, and to continue friendships while on the road – and I will discuss them in detail in the coming chapters. However, the more fundamental issues of goals, objectives and attitudes need to be addressed first.

Although family and friends come first, career is an important part of most people's lives. And a career that requires business travel can share space with those personal connections, if you have a clear assessment of your objectives in life and design your life to attain them. If travel makes you more effective in your work, then that same travel makes you a more effective breadwinner with a more secure future for your family. The well-balanced business traveller sees his or her time on the road as part of a life plan that has room for many objectives.

Opportunities for Personal Growth

I'm in my early sixties now and I have already lived a very active and interesting life, but there is not a day I can remember when I haven't tried to learn something new. Sometimes, new insights arise from the daily flow of information and people I encounter in my travels. Sometimes, my natural curiosity will lead me into a new area. Sometimes, I am taken by surprise in some new – and, I hope, pleasant – way. But most often, I learn something new every day because I plan to.

For example, over many years of travelling to New York City, I have developed a list of favourite restaurants I return to regularly. I enjoy the food and service, and the restaurant managers have come to know me. But I realized a few years ago that this comfortable rut was keeping me from having new dining experiences in a city with thousands of restaurants. So I made a private rule that, for every time I went back to one of my old favourites, I had to try three new restaurants.

Have I had some disappointments? Naturally. I have also had many new dishes that I never tried before, seen new wine lists and enjoyed a variety of unusual restaurant ambiances. A few of those new places have even been added to my 'favourites' list. I don't even regret the disappointments, because usually I learned something new about what does (or doesn't) make a restaurant work.

I believe in the value of business meetings over meals. Seeing your business associates in surroundings outside their offices often gives you a different relationship with them. You can tell something about a person by how he or she orders a meal or deals with the social amenities of seating at a table. By going to restaurants that I have not tried before, I take a bit of a risk. But the opportunity to combine a new dining experience with a business discussion gives 'added value' to my life.

There are dozens of other examples of how travellers can enhance their lives while on business trips. I try to arrange a game of golf if I am travelling to a destination with a particularly good golf course. I'll seek out information about theatres, concerts or other shows in cities where I am doing business. Sometimes I just want to take a break in my business routine for a quick visit to a historic or cultural monument. I have a friend who tries to visit the zoo in whatever city he is in. Does that sound silly for a grown man? Not to me. This opportunity for self-fulfilment gives him a bit of exercise, a break from the stress of a hectic schedule and something to look forward to in every destination.

Breaking Routines, Creating Small Adventures

For those who have trapped themselves in an unpleasant routine, one of the best exercises I can suggest is to define pleasure for yourself. Try making a list of the things that you like to do and see how they might fit into your travel plans.

Some suggestions:

- Reading a good novel.
- Listening to music on a CD player (not the airlines' ten channels of muzak).
- Writing a journal.
- Playing video games or computer bridge or doing cross-word puzzles.
- Seeing some architectural high points of a city.
- Looking up old friends or classmates.

At this point, I can almost hear some of my readers objecting: 'My company doesn't send me on trips to enjoy a tourist's vacation. I don't have time to entertain myself. I barely have time to get to all of the meetings I must attend in a day!' Possibly so. However, when it comes to busy schedules, there are few people who can surpass me.

I own my company and I want to maximize every business opportunity I have. I also know that I will have a more positive attitude if I have given myself a late morning half-hour to stroll through a historic neighbourhood *en route* to a business lunch. I know that I will arrive more refreshed, more alert, more relaxed than if I had just come from another business meeting. To me, that is time well spent – and all too many people who think that they have busy, efficient schedules waste valuable time that could be devoted to such moments of self-fulfilment.

Finding Precious Hours

Business people who complain that there is a great deal of wasted time in the travel process are correct. And, usually, they are to blame for the waste. Even the most capable business people lose time, energy, money and opportunities for personal growth and pleasure on the road because they are not nearly as effective and efficient while travelling as they are at home.

The most common cause of wasted time is poor planning. Managers who know how to keep a tight schedule in their office seem to fall apart on the road. In Chapter 2, I explain the basics of planning and suggest some time-saving tricks that have worked well for me. For starters, however, let's spell out the business traveller's golden rule: Never Stand in Line.

Never Stand in Line

When friends complain about how much time they waste standing in lines at airports or hotels, I can only shake my head in amazement. With sensible planning, there is no reason a business traveller should ever have to stand in line. Before you depart for the airport, you should have your tickets and probably your boarding passes in your pocket. Ideally, you have packed everything you need in carry-on luggage. If not, on domestic flights, use the kerbside baggage check. Have a tip visible in your hand. Service will be quick.

If there is no alternative to bringing luggage or identification documents to the check-in desk – cases or passports for an international flight, for example – you will need to be a bit more creative. In later chapters, I will give you the details of how business travellers can take advantage of frequent flyer clubs and airlines' Special Services divisions to avoid the long lines of tourists at the main airport ticketing desks. However, my point is that there are a variety of ways to deal with this hurdle, and you must consider them before you embark or you will be left standing there while the entire Berlin Philharmonic checks in.

Long before you arrive at the departure gate for your flight, you should have confirmed your seat assignment through a travel agent or a call to the airline. If you are not already a member of the airline club, your travel agent can often arrange for you to be admitted on a one-time guest pass. There, you can check in, have a cup of coffee and wait for your flight in the civilized atmosphere of a lounge hidden from the noise and chaos of the gate waiting area. Also, the club desk will issue boarding passes if you don't already have them. If you have extra time, in the club business areas you have easy access to telephones, computers or fax machines to continue doing business.

Excuse Me, I Think You're in My Seat

In general, I prefer to board the plane as soon as possible. I always enquire with the airline about preboarding privileges. Sometimes preboarding is routinely offered to first class and business class travellers; sometimes, the Special Services division can assist. This allows me to be certain I have possession of my assigned seat, to let the flight attendants know about any special requests I might have, to get organized for the flight and get to work. Other experienced travellers tell me that they wait until the rush is over and board at the last minute. They avoid standing in the jetway (if they have not been able to arrange preboarding), but they risk the possibility of finding another passenger holding a boarding card with the identical seat number sitting in their seat. How this happens as frequently as it does in the computer era is difficult to explain. But it happens, and you don't want it to happen to you – in this instance, unfortunately, possession is nine-tenths of the law.

Forget the Red Carpet

The same travel strategies I use in dealing with airlines apply to hotels. Check information about the location and facilities of the hotels in the city you are visiting. Make direct arrangements with the hotel desk. Make sure that the hotel knows who you are, what you want in your room and that you will have 'express check-in'. Almost every hotel is familiar with the business traveller's complaint about long check-in lines, and most of them are prepared to get you in and out quickly if you provide them with credit information in advance. Sometimes, this entails joining the hotel chain's 'frequent guest club', usually at no cost.

Solving Life's Little Puzzles

I certainly don't like to find myself in potentially time-wasting situations any more than the next person, but I have learned to react to them as one of Life's Little Puzzles. Instead of getting angry – which might be a reasonable enough reaction in a travel hassle – I find myself searching my memory bank, alerting my mental resources, preparing to meet a challenge. Keeping cool and coming up with unconventional solutions to those annoying problems has proven effective. I remind myself that I have already avoided many pitfalls of the travel-ler's life. If I can deal with this glitch, my trip will continue smoothly. And generally it does. What enables me to solve this sampling of Life's Little Puzzles more calmly and effi-ciently than the person with steam coming out of his or her ears? Attitude. I'm confident that I have the resources and the know-how to come up with an answer. I'm on a roll of positive travel experiences. I'm having a good trip, and one overworked desk clerk is not going to get in my way. Don't Get Angry: Get Creative. (Trying to Get Even with a belated letter of complaint is rarely satisfying.)

Set Your Own Agenda

Ultimately, you are in control of your own travel experiences. If you establish the self-fulfilling prophecy that your next trip will be a hectic misery (just like all the rest), there's no doubt that a cloud of gloom will follow your footsteps. However, if you would like to make your next trip fun, enjoyable and relaxing – even as it accomplishes your business objectives – then you've come to the right book. I'm going to urge you to take charge of this area of your life, to set your own agenda, and to see how putting some enjoyment into business travel makes good business sense. I'm going to show you how to 'personalize' your travel and to let your friends in other cities improve your business. I'm going to force you to think carefully about when to enjoy travel luxuries – and when to skip them. I'm going to demonstrate how you keep your focus on your business objectives on the road, despite distractions. Most of all, I'm going to teach you about detailed, meticulous planning – the not-so-secret weapon of my success.

2 Planning the Trip

People don't plan to fail. They fail to plan.

Good travel planning can avert many disasters, but there is often little that even the most agile executive can do to salvage problems created by poor or incomplete planning. Sadly, many executives believe they've 'planned' everything once they have airline tickets, a hotel reservation and ground transportation. However, virtually no input of their own has gone into the decisions about what airline they are flying, what flight they are on, what hotel they are staying at, what room they receive, or what ground transportation they will be using when they arrive. Most executives rely on secretaries or aides who book reservations for plane trips, hotels, and rental cars and type out an itinerary. For the savvy business traveller, this is far from sufficient. **Do you hit the road, or does the road hit you?**

This chapter demonstrates exactly what comprehensive planning for a trip entails, how to gather information and do your spadework before leaving, how to know which travel arrangements can be delegated and which details to handle yourself. It will also discuss how to avoid being a travel victim by forcing others to be prepared – how to schedule meetings for your own convenience, how to schedule time for personal reward and enjoyment, and how to pack. I also discuss a bit of how to get a better price break on some aspects of travel, but I'll deal more with that in Chapter 7.

The business traveller is a successful executive who has

learned how to delegate authority. In making travel arrangements, however, many executives err by leaving the details of their trip to lower-level staff or to unsophisticated travel agents. In this electronic age, many executives have never *seen* their travel agent. A corporate travel office is a little more concerned, because they are more readily held accountable, but often its staff are not nearly as knowledgeable or demanding as you are yourself.

Travel planning is not trivial or menial – it's the difference between a grim trip and an enjoyable one. The executive traveller knows that choice of hotel rooms and flight times should never be left in the hands of someone who is not getting on the plane and who may not be familiar with the executive's preferences and destination. For example, someone who has never travelled to London's Heathrow Airport on an overnight flight doesn't realize that many of these flights land at the same time in the early morning. There could be a thousand people waiting to go through immigration. There are, of course, ways to beat this problem, but many travel bookers aren't going to be familiar with them.

How to Plan a Trip

Know Where You Are Going

The first rule of trip planning sounds obvious but is all too often ignored: **know something about where you are going**. The executive traveller maintains an active interest in travel in general and in his or her most frequent destinations in particular.

I make a point of maintaining an up-to-date library of travel guides from a variety of sources. Most larger cities have bookstores which specialize in travel guides. I regularly read newsletters and magazines such as *Frequent Flyer* which keep better tabs on rapidly changing conditions than guidebooks that are updated annually at best.

I also keep a 'go to' file for each city I visit, whether it's New York, London, Calgary or Singapore. When I see an article about a hotel I'd like to stay at or an interesting new restaurant, I either clip the article or make a note in the file.

Block Out Your Time

The second rule of planning a trip is the one that is most often overlooked: **block out your time.** Too often, overburdened executives don't start thinking about where they are going until they are on the plane. But if you organize your days on the road before you leave, you can meet all your business objectives and plan some fun into the trip. By 'fun' I don't mean a boozy good time in the hotel cocktail lounge. Fun to me means something which nourishes and enriches you personally, on the inside. It may be culturally rewarding, such as taking in a new play in London, or educational, such as taking in a tour of Monet's house at Giverny outside Paris, or pure relaxation, such as tacking on an extra day to a trip to San Francisco to enjoy the Wine Country.

I can visualize a lot of you shaking your heads at this – there's no time for this kind of activity when you travel, and to do these things is somehow 'cheating' the company. Wrong. That's what real executive travel is all about. There is time for these activities if you plan them into your trip, if you are efficient in the use of your time during the business day, and if you know how to avoid being a victim at the airport and hotel. This enables you to conserve your most valuable resource, your time, and make it work to your own advantage.

The Ten-Minute Time-Saver

Time saved in small increments all adds up. For example, our New York office is located on 71st Street between Madison and Fifth Avenues. Madison Avenue heads north, Fifth heads south. If I'm going to an airport, ordinarily I'd have the car or cab wait for me in front of the building I'm going to leave from. But our front door in New York is thirty yards west of

Madison Avenue. If the car pulls up in front, it has to circle the entire block – i.e., go down to Fifth, wait for a light, get into the Fifth Avenue traffic, wait for another light, go down 70th Street to Madison, wait for another light, turn into the traffic – in order to be headed in the right direction for the airport. It can take as much as ten minutes just to get back to where you were before – and all for thirty yards! For that ten minutes, it's worth it to me to go downstairs, walk the thirty yards and meet the car heading north (towards the airport) on Madison Avenue. With that extra ten minutes, I can stay in a meeting a little longer, make a couple of phone calls, or finish dictating a memo. If I can engineer a few more of these ten-minute time-savers into each day, I can get in a little tennis, some worthwhile leisure reading, or take a nap.

Long before you step on the plane, you should have made your choices about the use of your time. You should have made a calendar for yourself of your activities during your trip, including all your meetings, lunches and dinners.

The first thing I try to do when I know I have a trip is to prioritize the people that I really want to see. Some are hard to get hold of, so I get in contact with them first, and let them know when I'll be in town, as far in advance as possible. I put people that I really want to see but who generally are more available next, followed by people who it might be nice to see, and by people on our own office staff who can work around my schedule. I do this weeks, even months, in advance of my trip.

Use Who You Are

Rule number three is one that business travellers perhaps don't realize or fully understand: **use who you are**. Many executives underestimate how much clout they have with hotels, airlines and restaurants, in part because they leave the details of their trip to aides who have little clout themselves.

Let me make it clear how much power you have. As a business traveller, you are the very customer that airlines, restaurants and hotels value most. Business travellers are repeat customers, and repeat customers are highly prized, especially in these difficult times. The effort to secure repeat customers is at the foundation of any frequent flyer or frequent stayer programme. It's an attempt to establish your loyalty to a particular airline or hotel chain.

You really are number one, not just with Hertz but with everyone else in the travel industry. Executive travel is the industry's major profit generator. Without the business traveller, hotels would be largely empty Monday through Friday, better restaurants would go belly up, and airlines would be stuck trying to turn a profit on deeply discounted economy fares for families of five in plaid Bermuda shorts. Only about one-fifth of the passengers on a full flight sit in business or first class. These passengers, however, bring in as much as two-thirds of the revenue for the airlines. Your position as the preferred customer gives you added clout when making reservations, but it's your job to know how to use it.

Making Reservations

Using a Travel Agent

Most people, even sophisticated business travellers, don't really understand how travel agents work. Just because you don't have to pay agents a commission doesn't mean you're getting something for nothing. In travel as in most other endeavours, there's no such thing as a free lunch. Travel agents have to make their money somehow. If the traveller isn't paying the agency's commission, someone else is.

Who? The airlines you fly and hotels where you spend the night. In most businesses, it's customary to believe that you work for the people who pay your salary or commission. Travel agents are unusual in that they work not for the vendors of travel services who pay them, but for clients – business executives and other travellers – who don't. Because agencies make their money from someone who is not their client, they sometimes forget who they work for.

With the highly complex airline fare system, even 'independent' travel agents are dependent on computerized reservation systems. These systems are owned in whole or in part by various airlines, and many have a built-in bias in favour of the flagship carrier. If you call a travel agent for information about an early flight tomorrow from London to New York, and the agent informs you that the first flight out is a British Airways flight, it's a pretty good bet that their agency computer is hooked into the Galileo system, which is owned by British Airways and which most agents in the UK use. With US travel agents, if the first flight mentioned is a United Airlines flight, it's probable that their computer is part of the Apollo system, which is owned by United Airlines. Likewise with American Airlines, which controls the Sabre system. BA's Galileo, United's Apollo, and American's Sabre reservations systems list their own flights ahead of competitors' flights leaving at the same time. When an agent starts reading you a list of options, these are the flights that will be at the top of the list.

With daily (and sometimes hourly) changes in airfares, and a plethora of new hotels and travel destinations, staying on top of the travel game has become far more complicated in recent years. The days of the one-size-fits-all travel agent who can book a cruise, a family vacation in a big city, a week touring the Maya pyramids in the Yucatan, a convention in Sydney, *and* your next business trip to Milan are over – or should be. However, too many travel agencies still try to serve all kinds of travellers.

Pick Your Travel Agent Carefully

You should audition a travel agent like a doctor before surgery. How does the executive traveller find a good travel agency? As a minimum, your agency should be a member of ABTA (the Association of British Travel Agents) or ASTA (the American Society of Travel Agents), and should be fully automated. It goes without saying that it should specialize in business travel – you wouldn't see a neurosurgeon to remove a wart, or a gynaecologist for a coronary bypass. You're not going to get the kind of service you need from an agency that specializes in cruises or in adventure trips to remote destinations. When you find a business-orientated travel agency, let them know your standards and how they must perform. If you're a volume traveller, the agency needs to know what you will and will not accept, and what the conditions of your continued business will be.

No matter what the credentials of the agency, remember that your travel agency is only as good as the agent who is handling your account. There should be just a couple of agents within a firm handling travel arrangements for your business, unless your company is large or your travel plans are very intricate and change frequently.

Two Travel Agents Are Better Than One

It is best not to rely on one agent exclusively. A cruel fact of the travel business is that agent turnover is ferocious. Having more than one agent who knows your business is good self-defence. However, if your agent moves on and someone unfamiliar is handling your account, you have every right to question him or her closely to make sure they are experienced enough to do the job. If the new agent is unsatisfactory, talk to the manager and ask to be assigned to a more seasoned travel veteran. Failing that, take your business elsewhere.

Good travel agents are part tightwad, and know how to navigate the maze of fares to get you the best possible flight at the best possible rate. Get to know your travel agent, and make sure he or she has a computerized up-to-date personal profile of your travel preferences and dislikes. Give your agent feedback when you return from a destination you've never visited before – not just if something went wrong, but if things were terrific, too.

The very best agent for the executive traveller is also part bulldog, part geographer, part artiste, part computer genius, and part mindreader. That agent knows whether you meant Portland, Oregon, or Portland, Maine; the Plaza or the Plaza

Athenée; Paris, Texas, or Paris, France; Orly or Charles de Gaulle; Perth, Scotland, or Perth, Australia; 8 a.m. or 8 p.m.; Cambridge, Massachusetts, or Cambridge, England; Gatwick or Heathrow; *or knows enough to ask if the instructions are unclear*. Because these kinds of misunderstandings are not uncommon, **always look at your tickets before you leave the travel agency**.

Booking Your Flight

You Are Your Own Best Travel Agent

Having said all that, I must confess that I don't use travel agencies myself, except in a very limited capacity. If you are truly serious about executive travel, your best agent looks you in the bathroom mirror every morning. By and large I have nothing against most travel agents. However, it's only human for them sometimes to put the best interest of the traveller slightly behind the best interest of the airlines whose computer reservation systems they use, especially when the airlines, among others, are paying their salary.

I am my own best travel agent. The more I travel, the better I am at doing it myself. By being my own travel agent, I am free to expand or constrain the range of options open to me – my personal profile is constantly updated, always up-to-the-minute. I can see whether going a day sooner or a day later makes more sense than my original target flight date. I can determine whether flying through Vienna rather than Frankfurt will save me a couple of hours. I can choose whether I'd prefer to take the Blue Train overnight from Johannesburg to Cape Town or sleep in a hotel and catch a plane in the morning.

Although I am a demanding traveller, I am probably the easiest client my travel agency has. All they have to do to earn their commission is issue my ticket. I choose the airline, flights and seat assignments myself or through a staff assistant. When you make your own reservations and plan to be ticketed by a travel agency, the most important thing to remember is that you get your locator number from your airline. This is generally a six-letter or six-letter-and-number code. Once you give that code to the travel agency, that's all the information they need to write up your ticket.

This means that all you have to do is pick up your ticket and boarding pass at the agency – without standing in line. Again, however, **always look at your tickets before you leave the travel agency**. The time to discover a ticketing mistake is as soon as possible after it's been made. If a staff assistant or family member is picking up the ticket, make sure that they know what the ticket is supposed to say before they walk out the door.

The OAG: The Executive Traveller's Best Friend

I often find my preferred flight in the OAG, which is the executive traveller's Best Friend. OAG stands for Official Airline Guide, and no business traveller should be without it. It lists all commercial flights of all airlines, from anywhere, to anywhere, and is available in both North American and worldwide editions. It also shows seating charts for all commercial aircraft, so you can see how the plane is configured, how many seats there are in a row, and how much leg room there is. When you're on the road, there's an OAG *Pocket Flight Guide* to carry along. I keep a full-size version (both domestic and international) at my desk, and always travel with the pocket-sized editions. The OAG is available only on subscription and it isn't cheap, but the first time the OAG gets you out of a jam at the airport when a flight is delayed, it's worth every penny.

The OAG gives you power because it gives you control over information about potential flights and frees you from dependency on travel agents. All your choices are in front of you. Studies have shown that most travel agents never get past the first computer screen when offering alternatives to their clients. With the OAG, I don't have to ask the travel agent what time the flights are leaving, I tell them what flight I want. How do I know which flight I want? Very often, I'm not entirely sure.

Don't Be a Victim of Airline Scheduling

I'm a great double booker of flights, or triple or quadruple booker. For executives, celebrities, and other travellers with uncertain schedules, it's an act of self-defence and quite common. On a recent trip to Los Angeles, I wasn't sure when I would be able to leave. I thought I was leaving on Thursday morning, but I also booked myself on a Thursday noon and Friday morning flight on a different airline. I often use different initials or slightly different spellings of my last name so they don't pick me up on the computer if I've had to book on the same airline.

Airlines hate this, of course, but business travellers continue to do it because from our perspective it's better to double book than to get stuck or not get the flight that you want. It's a matter of attitude: the executive traveller plans ahead to use airlines, hotels and restaurants to suit his or her own convenience, rather than being trapped as a 'victim' of procedures and policies designed for the convenience of service providers.

Schedule requirements narrow the choices of which airlines I fly to particular destinations, but they are not the only considerations. Think creatively, for example, about where you clear Customs. In America, almost anywhere is better than New York. If you are a US citizen returning to the north-east or north central United States and need to make a connecting flight, you are far better off flying into Canada and connecting than flying into Kennedy and connecting. Canadian Customs from Europe is much easier and quicker. For our staff returning to Cleveland, Ohio, it's about the same timewise to fly London/New York/Cleveland as to fly London/Toronto/Cleveland. However, Toronto Customs is much easier than New York Customs. It's a much more pleasant place to fly into: Toronto considers you a transit passenger. Moreover, having been a transit passenger in Toronto, you are now cleared by American Customs when you land in Cleveland as if you were coming from Canada rather than coming from Europe. It's a much smoother homecoming.

Some Gates Are More Convenient than Others

I can also save a lot of time and avoid unpleasantness by picking the airline with the most convenient gate and terminal location. If I'm flying into O'Hare in Chicago, I'll use Delta because their gates are about sixty yards from kerbside. Those assigned to United and American can be almost a mile away. If you have to change planes, it's worse. It always seems as if someone with a sadistic sense of humour has maximized the distance between your arrival gate and your departure gate – arrival Concourse H, Gate 12; departure Concourse K, Gate 16, about half a mile away. In New York's La Guardia, Delta and Northwest have their own terminal, as does USAir which recently opened La Guardia's newest and most efficient terminal. The baggage claim is quicker and more modern. If you are being met, pick-up at the exit is also much more convenient.

Fly the Flag

On international flights, my general rule is: **fly the flag**, meaning the airline home-based in my destination. For over-taxed foreign airports, it makes it more likely that I'll escape one of my pet hates – being bussed to or from a plane whose 'gate' is in the middle of the tarmac. When you think about it, it's just common sense. Air France will have more pull at Charles de Gaulle than British Airways. Coming into Tokyo, Japan Airlines will almost always have a better gate than Delta. These factors pay time benefits for the executive traveller, factors that aides and travel agents don't ordinarily consider.

Fly Against the Hub

Within the United States, however, it doesn't follow that you'll get better service at an airline's hub airport. In fact, my general rule within the US is **fly against the hub**. The Hub Theory of airline management is designed to cut personnel costs for the airlines. As such, it works to their benefit, not necessarily to yours. Often, too many flights from a single airline converge on a hub city at the same time. Frequently there aren't enough baggage handlers to process the luggage from all flights expeditiously. You are usually better off on an airline that doesn't have tons of flights coming into a particular city than on one of eight flights landing at the same time. You have a much better chance of getting your bags sooner if the baggage from your flight is the only luggage being offloaded.

Fly Alternative Airports

The OAG also gives you information about alternative airports. I'm a big fan of alternative airports. They are generally less congested, and are often more convenient to your ground destination. I can get to Hollywood or Beverly Hills a lot faster from Burbank Airport than from LAX. Often it will be quicker into downtown San Francisco from Oakland International than from SFO. Depending on what time of day you land, Newark can be a better choice into New York than JFK. We'll discuss alternative airports in greater detail in Chapter 7.

Aisle v. Window

It's fine to leave the actual process of making reservations to your staff, if they know your preferences. It's your job to make your preferences known. I know many travelling executives prefer aisle seats. It's easier to get up and move around, and you can sprint for the exit and be the first one off the plane.

Nevertheless, I always ask for a window seat. It's a lot more private. No one is leaping over you during the flight. You can get yourself settled and stay there. There are no ringing phones or other interruptions. I sleep on planes a lot; it's a habit worth developing. I couldn't maintain my schedule if I didn't. For me, it's better to lean against the window than to start to fall asleep and end up on the shoulder of the person seated next to you or falling over into the aisle.

I think the window seat also promotes clear thinking. Some business travellers think that if you've seen one cloud, you've seen 'em all. But for me, looking out over the clouds can create a mood of contemplation that channels creative ideas to the forefront. I've had some of my best thinking sessions on planes. Jim Biggar, recently retired Chairman and CEO of Nestlé Corporation in the US, says the same thing. 'I find that I do a lot of my most creative work when I'm up there in the sky with nothing around but daylight. My mind is more open somehow.' Sir Christopher Lewinton, Chairman and CEO of TI Group Plc, says, 'I like being in that calm environment up there. Telephones can't reach me. It is a time when you are detached but your brain is engaged. Very rarely do I talk to the chap next to me, and I don't want him to talk to me, either.'

Getting a Good Fare

Everyone is ready to negotiate today. If you and others in your firm travel a lot, you are in a great position to negotiate with airlines for blocks of tickets at a discount. Our headquarters in Cleveland generates 500 trips a year to New York. We can strike a deal with Continental or US Air to buy tickets in bulk for use by our staff at maybe half the going rate.

Buying tickets in bulk also gives you a relationship with an airline that helps put you in contact with its Special Services personnel, who can be enormously helpful. Remember those long immigration lines at Heathrow Airport in London? Not everyone has to wait in them. Some arriving passengers are more equal than others. If you have a relationship with British Airways, one of their Special Services representatives can arrange to meet you at the gate and escort you through a VIP immigration line.

You don't think your business is big enough? You never know until you ask. People are trying desperately to get business these days, especially business that can grow. Airlines and others in the travel industry are willing to negotiate and they are willing to make accommodations with you in anticipation of future revenues.

Having a block of tickets in hand is also the best defence pricewise against the possibility of a last-minute trip. Airlines structure their fares by proximity to departure. The closer to leaving you get, the more expensive your seat becomes. Buying a ticket the night before for the first flight out almost always means paying a premium for your seat. However, if you've already got a prenegotiated ticket in hand, all you need is a reservation.

Booking a Hotel

If you ask a travel agent or a company travel representative to book you a room, that's exactly what you'll get – a room. Will you get a good room at a good rate? Not necessarily.

You Are Still Your Own Best Travel Agent

My first rule about hotels is **do the initial research yourself.** If you are going to stay at a hotel for the first time, it will pay great dividends to make a personal call and find out something about it. Most guidebooks will give you the bare minimum facts about a hotel. A few will go into greater detail, but it's often surprising that much information useful to the executive traveller is omitted. Are there blackout drapes? Is there soundproofing between rooms? Does the hotel serve brewed decaffeinated coffee rather than those vile crystals? (Brewed decaf is almost universal now in the United States, and in Europe it is easier to find these days than it was five years ago. In Asia and Latin America, however, it is still a relative rarity.) Are there complimentary terry-cloth robes in the room? If so, are they generously sized? (All too many of them are skimpy.) Is there a health and fitness facility? If so, where is it, and what's in it? (This last may be a letdown. In some hotels a small corner of the basement has been fitted with a treadmill, a stationary bicycle, two barbells, and an old Jane Fonda video – voilà! The fitness centre.)

Is there 24-hour room service? Is there a concierge? Is there limousine service available for guests? If so, how many cars does the hotel maintain? (One car for a 600-room hotel is a joke.) Is there an option for voice mail? (If it is there and you have no choice about it, that can be very good or very bad depending on your point of view.) What facilities are there for receiving faxes? What newspapers can I get in my room? Where are the phone jacks? Can one comfortably use a laptop computer with modem in the bed? Hotels vary widely in their capacity to accommodate modern portable business equipment.

How Many Telephone Lines?

For me the most important questions of all have to do with the telephones. I do a lot of business from my hotel room by phone. It's important for me to know where the phone is in relation to the bed. I prefer to have the phone to the left (as you're lying on your back). I'm right-handed, and that way I can cradle the phone and still take notes without having to deal with a jumble of wires. I hate phones with short cords, and phones on desks in hotel rooms. Rarely do you find yourself sitting at the desk in a hotel room. The phone on the desk looks nice and 'professional', and I am sure some decorator thought it was convenient, but to my knowledge not too many business travellers ever use them very much.

I also need to know how many lines (not extensions – lines, with distinct telephone numbers) are in the room. It's important for me to have at least two lines. Frequently my wife is travelling with me, and with two lines we both can make calls. Even when I'm travelling alone, however, I want two lines. This is not only for my own convenience but for the convenience of people trying to reach me.

When you are trying to contact someone in a hotel room, for most of the day they are not going to be there. You have just a couple of windows of opportunity. There is one in the morning, from whatever time you dare call them until about 9 a.m., when they leave for the day. The second window is in the evening at cocktail time, before they go out to dinner. In both those instances that's exactly when the people you are trying to get in touch with are going to be making calls themselves, calling home, checking in at the office, making dinner reservations. That second line is very, very important to have. Without it, you are at the mercy of the hotel telephone operators, dependent on them to get your message through to the room.

Some of what the business traveller wants to know, however, is what I call 'perishable information' – what's true on one visit may not be true the next. Has the hotel been renovated? If the hotel is a splendid old dowager of a building, it can be a wonderful place to stay, but not if the plumbing is still original and there's no hot water to shower with after 7 a.m. Is the hotel still being renovated and will my room be subject to construction noise? Is there a big convention booked into the hotel at the same time I plan to be there, so that hotel facilities will be hard-pressed to keep up with demands by a large number of guests?

To find out this information, call the hotel directly. Waste no time with any toll-free centralized reservations numbers. The people who answer those phones are not physically located at the hotel where you will be staying, and may never have seen the hotel you're asking about. It's much better in any event to establish a personal rapport with the manager or other high-level hotel staff representative and to develop a reputation as a demanding repeat customer.

Be Demanding

That, indeed, is my second rule: **be demanding**. This is not the same as being a pain, but you have every right to expect a hotel stay to be a positive experience. Remember your status as an executive traveller. Good hotels keep records on the preferences of their best patrons, so they can meet your demands, but they can't do that if they don't know what you like. Unfortunately, many business travellers are reticent about making their preferences known. I assure you that even the very top hotels have less desirable rooms that are next to the elevator, over the loading bay, or over the discothèque. Someone may stay in them, but it doesn't have to be you.

When you call the hotel, find out how extensive the room choice is. Ask what kinds of rooms are available. Get rather elaborate descriptions of the rooms and what floor they're on. Are all the floors the same? Has one been refurbished and the others not? Is one quieter than the other? Is there a balcony? Is there a view? Are there some corner rooms available with two views?

Getting a Good Rate

How do you get a good room at a good rate? There are many ways to do it, and I'll go into detail in Chapter 7, but here are a few ideas. You must think creatively. Consider the possibilities for tradeout or barter agreements between your company and the hotel.

At IMG, we've made all kinds of barter arrangements for travel. We named the Claremont Resort Hotel in Oakland as the official hotel of the Bank of the West Tennis Classic, and we made a similar arrangement with a limousine company. These kinds of barter arrangements aren't limited to the sports and entertainment business. Anything from computer hardware and software to legal services can be negotiated.

I know – if you manufacture ball-bearings or jet engines, you probably don't have much to trade, but you can still get a great room. If I were the CEO of the Wichita Widget Company and I was planning a trip, it's not stretching the truth too far to have your secretary contact the hotel's convention manager and say, 'Look, I'm making a reservation for my boss, the CEO of the Wichita Widget Company. He will be staying at your hotel on business now, but he is also thinking about doing a sales conference sometime next spring. He's looking for a venue to do it. We've heard you have a nice spa and tennis facilities.'

That call places you on a whole different level in the view of that hotel. Suddenly you could mean extra business for them. You're going to end up getting a better room, possibly a better rate, certainly better service, but a secretary or a travel agent will generally not think that way.

I also make a habit of booking a longer stay than I think I will ultimately need. Once I've checked in, it's more convenient for me to say I'm leaving early than to try to extend a stay in a hotel that might be booked up. On some international flights it's worth it to me to book the room the night before I arrive as well. An unsophisticated traveller arrives on an overnight flight with a Tuesday reservation and assumes he will be able to walk into his room at 8 a.m. when the prior guests haven't checked out yet. In many hotel lobbies, particularly smaller ones in Europe, it's common to see weary travellers and their baggage strewn all over the place, waiting for their room to clear. If I know I'm going to want a nap as soon as I arrive, I'll take the room for the prior night in order to make sure that my room is ready when I arrive. Often I don't even have to pay for it unless the hotel is completely booked up.

Booking Restaurants

Do you eat lunch in the same restaurants every time you travel? You shouldn't. You should go to different places in a city. Get yourself out of that rut. Many people are insecure when they travel. When they get to where they're going, they're not really there. To enjoy travel, you've got to make the experience a little fresh for yourself each time. You've got to have something to look forward to. You have to be adventurous.

You must ask yourself, 'What am I trying to accomplish with this meal?' If you need a security blanket for a particular lunch or dinner, fine. Go where you are known and the service and ambiance are reliable. Otherwise, experiment. If you travel at this level, you are already a successful executive. You didn't get to your position without taking risks. You learned how to gather information, listen to advice from peers and colleagues, and take the calculated risk when it was called for. Travel is the same. Most of the time, informed risk-taking pays off in enhanced enjoyment.

Restaurant knowledge, even more so than data about hotels, is highly perishable information. Star chefs can be highly mobile. Many restaurant kitchens nose-dive when their superstar moves on. On the other hand, some celebrity chefs have become restaurant entrepreneurs. When they open new eateries, they are likely to be not merely branches of the original but innovative new restaurants in their own right. The restaurant scene in major cities changes quickly. If you took the hundred most cosmopolitan executives of twenty-five years ago in New York, London or Paris, and had them make a listing of their favourite restaurants of the time, today more than half of them would no longer be in business. Of the half that remain, half of those would have deteriorated or gone to other management. Even a five-year-old listing of favourites would be dated and would leave out the trendiest places.

Guidebooks tend to be a little behind the times on restaurants. Magazines and newsletters are more helpful. Better yet, use your personal contacts in town to find out the names of interesting new venues. If you have chosen a restaurant to make your client happy and he is well known there but you are not, ask his help in getting a good table.

People Who Live There
Will Always Know More than You Do

Sometimes, not using your personal and business contacts to select a restaurant can be bad for business, especially if it reveals your ignorance about the city you're visiting. Marvin Bush describes the problem well. 'People like to show off their cities. What I like to do is rely a great deal on the people I'm dealing with to select a suitable restaurant. They know why we're meeting. They know what the tone of the meeting should be, that there ought to be a quiet and serious environment where we can sit down and talk. I've always felt it was rather strange when people came to Washington to see me and said, "I'll be in Washington next week and I want to meet you at The Palm." My first reaction is, "Who the hell is this yahoo?" He wants to go to the busiest restaurant in Washington, with waiters who won't leave you alone, where you can't talk without screaming at each other. It's completely inappropriate for a business meeting.'

How to Get a Great Table at '21'

For years 21 has been one of the classic power restaurants of New York, where the titans of finance, industry and show business can dine well, with the confidence that they will always be recognized, shown to their favourite table, and be coddled by a familiar staff. For regulars, 21 is a private dining club that happens to serve the general public, too. Although I have dined there many times, I would be flattering myself if I suggested I was a regular. I'm not. But my friend Herb Siegel, the Chairman of Chris-Craft, is definitely one of their great customers. If Herb Siegel and I are planning to meet for lunch, I often ask him to take me to 21 – because he gets the best table, the best service, and of course by extension so do I.

In fact, if I wanted to dine at 21 without Herb Siegel, I would still ask him to make the reservation – in the hope that he would introduce me as his friend and suggest that I be well taken care of. This isn't an imposition. It's a winning tactic in three ways: It's not unflattering to Herb Siegel who surely must derive some tiny but distinct pleasure in demonstrating his power on behalf of a friend. He also gets credit – in the form of the restaurant's continuing gratitude and goodwill – for bringing in a new customer. And I get treated royally at an establishment where I am not that well known. I'm a visitor in Siegel's power base, but I don't hear anyone complaining.

If a friend has more clout than you at a tough-to-book restaurant, let him make the arrangements. You are doing yourself and your friend a favour.

Never Book a Table for Fewer than Three People

When I book a table, I always make a reservation for three people, even if there are only going to be two of us. I don't like tables where everyone is too close together, and often tables for two are lined up so that diners are elbow-to-elbow. If I want to say something over dinner that is moderately confidential, I don't want people from the next table, who are actually physically nearer to me than is my companion seated across from me, to be in on our conversation. A table for three gives more personal space. I prefer corner tables for the same reason. With walls on two sides, the setting is far more private.

When you book the table for three, you must be sure to maintain the fiction with the waiter or waitress that the third member of your party is expected and is surely on the way. It's always a good idea, however, to clue in your companion about your charade, lest he or she inadvertently blows your cover. When your associate blurts out, 'Who's joining us? I thought we were going to work out the details between the two of us before the meeting!' you'll find yourself with a great deal of explaining to do, both publicly and privately. Remember to 'give up' on the missing phantom member of your party if you want your food to appear. Many restaurants will wait to take your order till the third person arrives.

Make Contact with Management

If you are going to a restaurant on the recommendation of a good friend or business associate and that person is not accompanying you, be sure to mention his or her name to the owner or *maître d'*. You will get better service as the 'friend of a friend' and your business contact may even get better treatment on the next visit as well. For example, one of my favourite restaurants is La Marée in Paris, and I frequently recommend it to others. Eric Trompier, the owner of La Marée, told me, 'I can't know how to help someone if I don't know who they are. I'm always grateful if customers introduce themselves to me. I'm especially anxious to help them if I know they are coming from another friend that I know. I pay special attention to them because I know that here is someone who is likely to become a good customer. I also know that here is someone who is going to go back to the person who referred him here and tell him about his experience at La Marée.'

To get a better table on your own, tell them you're scouting a location for a function in the near future when you book your table. Ask to see their private facilities. It gives a restaurant a little more incentive to do their best on your behalf.

Use a Fancy Suite for Lunch – Without Paying for It

If you are making plans for a larger group at lunch, be creative. The fatal error that most people make is that they don't think very far in advance and they think in very limited ways. A business lunch doesn't have to be in a dining room or restaurant. Use the full range of services your hotel has to offer. A business meeting with lunch served in an otherwise unoccupied suite is potentially much more impressive than one held in the hotel restaurant. Since the room isn't booked, often the hotel will not charge you for the use of it. The suite is likely to be far more luxurious than any of those 'banquet' rooms, which tend to be devoid of both charm and windows.

For groups of six or more, consider pre-ordering the meal. Very little business at a standard business lunch gets conducted until the coffee arrives. If there are eight people around a table, the first time the waiter comes by, I guarantee you that some of the group won't be ready to order. By the time he returns and starts explaining the specials to each person as he goes around, you've wasted over half an hour. Pre-ordering shows that you are efficient, that you think ahead and can anticipate what people's desires might be.

Planning Yourself Out the Door

Check and Double Check

Even the most careful pre-travel arrangements need some follow-up on the day you leave and the day you arrive. It helps for the executive traveller to have some standard travel-day procedures that staff members can perform automatically.

Establish a regular routine with your support staff for your travel days. Set a 'standard' time when you will check in for your messages, and a window when other people will be able to reach you at your hotel.

Ask your secretary to call your hotel the day of your departure to confirm your arrival and booking arrangements and to get the name of the desk clerk she speaks with, even before your plane leaves the ground. Make certain you are carrying a fax transmittal with your confirmation number on it. Be sure to contact your hotel prior to 6 p.m. if you will be arriving later than that time, so that they will hold your room. If you're still in transit at that time, make sure that someone else will place that call.

What is the one piece of advice that almost always pays off? **Call your airline before you leave for the airport to make sure your flight is on time.**

Even though you should always give the airline a local phone number so that they can call you in case there's a problem with your flight, don't depend on airlines to let you know there will be a delay. I can't tell you how many times I've been on flights that have been delayed or cancelled. I *can* tell you how many times the airline has called me in advance to give me this information. I remember these occasions very clearly – both of them.

The Joy of Packing

Are your personal belongings organized for travel or do you have to put yourself together anew each time you leave? Do you have a toilet kit and some standard business attire packed and ready to go? Do you have an onboard care package – bottled water, eye-shades if you use them, a personal pillow – that's already assembled?

I try to think through what I'll wear every day and every night that I am going to be gone. Obviously, you try to match your shirts and ties and socks and all that with your blazers and suits, but if I'm going to have to wear a blazer for a few days, I'll pack the one that isn't going to wrinkle too much.

If I know I'm going to be doing some shopping, I'll pack a soft empty suitcase inside a larger one to be able to bring other things back. If I know I'm going to take a short side trip from a longer trip, I'll put a small extra suitcase inside a big one. This time, however, it won't be empty. I'll throw in a toilet kit, a shirt and whatever else I'll need so it's prepacked before I leave.

Carry-On, Business-Style

Baggage snafus are among the worst problems of air travel. The three main problems are misrouting, damage and theft. To deal with the first difficulty, carry anything that really matters with you in the cabin – jewellery, furs, important papers, anything electronic. Frequent flyer Jay Leno jokes that it's better just to throw your bags away rather than to check them in. On a short trip, almost every seasoned business traveller will try to fit all of his or her needs into carry-on pieces. It's tried and true advice.

Luggage Appearance and the Appearance of Luggage

Nevertheless, taking the carry-on rule to extremes isn't useful. I used to try to get on the plane with a hanging bag and two or three briefcases, but that got me into trouble with the airlines because I was over my carry-on limit. Airlines are getting more and more stringent about enforcing these limits. It was also bad for my back.

Sooner or later, the executive traveller has to deal with the need to check baggage. Some travel experts give you a great deal of advice about what brand of luggage to carry, but my ego is not tied up in the appearance of my luggage. My main concern is that the luggage *appear* on the baggage carousel.

Leather luggage is stylish and durable, but it's also extremely heavy. If you're an international traveller carrying leather bags, you're most of the way towards being over the excess baggage limit before you've even packed your underwear. Serviceable soft-sided baggage made out of some lightweight synthetic fibre is a reasonable alternative, but the most popular brands of this kind of luggage look pretty much the same. It's a good idea to make your luggage look different or distinctive so that it's harder for other people to pick your bag off the carousel by mistake. Mike Baverstock, a Special Services agent with British Airways in London, recommends adding a colourful ribbon or baggage tag to suitcases to make them easier to spot. 'It's so easy to misidentify a suitcase. So many people have baggage that looks similar, but the chance of you putting the same ribbon or colour around the handle as another passenger is remote.'

Junk the Trunk

Designer luggage, although it looks chic when new, often can't stand up to the abuse that airlines dish out. From many years of watching that carousel go round and round, I can assure you that baggage handlers do not heave Vuitton luggage any more gently than they do the flimsiest cardboard suitcase belonging to the person holding the cheapest ticket in economy class. Vuitton and other expensive designer bags are great for crossing the Atlantic on the QE2, but if you fly, abandon the steamer trunk mentality and opt for practicality.

Don't Worry About the Wrong Thing

People who are afraid that someone will steal their luggage from the baggage claim area (as opposed to someone picking up their bag by an honest mistake) are by and large worried about the wrong thing. Most passenger baggage items stolen at airports are not stolen off the baggage carousel but before they get there, by people you can't even see. As often as not, thieves are people who have infiltrated the ranks of behind-the-scenes baggage handlers at the gate.

To would-be thieves, designer luggage like Vuitton and the aluminium-sided Halliburton stuff all but screams out 'I'm valuable. My contents are precious. Steal me.' Most of the time thieves don't steal the bags themselves. They steal items *from* bags. Baggage locks are no real help. Basically they are a fraud and do little more than announce that you are worried about the contents of your luggage.

Thieves will either pop the flimsy locks or 'accidentally' rip soft-sided luggage to get at the contents. It's a relatively risk-free occupation. Why? Because when you're at the carousel and your bags come off the plane, you never open them to see if anything is missing. On the contrary, you are so happy and relieved to see that your bags have arrived that you jump into your car and get on with your trip. When you get to your hotel and discover that something is missing, it's too late.

Bad Luggage Is Good Luggage

The best way to foil behind-the-scenes baggage thieves is to lead them to believe that you have nothing worth stealing. Travel with the most unassuming luggage that you or the person who picks your clothing and cares about your appearance will permit you to be seen carrying.

For some hard-core travellers, modest luggage is not enough. They choose not unpretentious luggage, not undistinguished luggage, but disgusting and hideous luggage – luggage that looks like it escaped from a fire sale in the bargain basement of Moscow's GUM department store.

An associate of mine was landing at La Guardia airport one night on a flight from Chicago. Standing next to her at the baggage claim was the Italian fashion designer Emilio Pucci, wearing an impeccably tailored suit. While waiting for the bags, she found herself speculating on what kind of luggage Pucci travelled with. She was expecting perhaps Vuitton, possibly Gucci, or maybe something custom sporting one of his trademark prints. She was shocked when he retrieved what must surely have been the homeliest suitcase in the world. How homely was it? Vivid yellow naugahyde. It might not have been chic, but he'd never lost it. On the other hand, someone as stylish as the late Mr Pucci gave his yellow naugahyde a cachet all its own. It was his version of the personal touch in travel.

3 The Personal Touch

A major component of enjoyable executive travel is doing it with the Personal Touch. That touch is manifested in two ways. One aspect is bringing some of your own creature comforts along with you (or making sure they are waiting when you arrive). Just as car rental agencies track the make and model preference of recurring customers, better hotels keep records of the preferences of frequent guests. The business traveller knows how to make travel arrangements that optimize both comfort and operating efficiency, and how to make support personnel aware of his or her likes and dislikes.

The other facet of the Personal Touch is getting the most out of airline, hotel, and other travel personnel by providing them with the positive stimulus they need to make them put their best foot forward on your behalf. Sometimes this stimulus is financial, but even more often it is the dynamic personal style of the executive traveller. The business traveller knows how to motivate and empower someone to provide an extra level of service, above and beyond the call of duty. With this empowerment, airline ground personnel cheerfully try to solve your booking problem; without trepidation a waitress asks the chef to prepare something special that is off the menu.

The Personal Touch on Board

Life Support on Your Flying Island

A good hotel should be able to supply all the comforts of home. On an aeroplane, however, these creature comforts may be harder to come by. Think of an aircraft as a small desert island flying through the atmosphere. What's there is available for your comfort, efficiency and enjoyment. If it's not on the plane, however, that item is not available at any price. What the executive traveller wants on board the flying island is the same thing he or she wants on the ground – control of the environment.

Bring Your Own Creature Comforts

The executive traveller maintains this control by packing his or her own collection of travelling paraphernalia, the small things that make you comfortable while in the air. Most savvy executives keep this airborne care package stocked and ready to go. All that has to be done is to grab the bag and go.

Everyone's assortment is different. Pioneering travel writer Temple Fielding used to bring three jars of his favourite mustard to augment (or perhaps to mask) the flavour of airline food. My wife, Betsy, brings along her own pillow. It is a lot more substantial than the little flimsy ones provided by the airline, which have a tendency to slip down between the seats or get wedged between the seat and the window. She's covered it with a bright pillowcase so she doesn't forget it. Others bring earplugs, eye-masks and inflatable neck braces. Neck braces support and cushion the head upright as you sleep, so that it doesn't flop over as you nap, creating a particularly painful stiff neck. (You also avoid the embarrassment of sleeping on the shoulder of the passenger next to you.) One publishing executive brings a Walkman, with his own selection of music or books on tape.

The Importance of Water

More and more business travellers have chosen to bring their own bottled water on board, such as Evian, Perrier or San Pellegrino. It's a truly smart move. Most frequent flyers know that it's important to drink as much water as possible while in the air. It's your body's best defence against dehydration and also helps to reduce the effects of jet lag.

The water on board your flying island, however, may have come from a multitude of sources. If you're travelling on an international flight from Los Angeles to Paris that stops in Chicago, the plane's holding tank is not drained in Chicago and refilled; it's topped up with Chicago water. This is not in and of itself bad. However, this procedure is likely to be repeated when that same flight continues on from Paris to Hong Kong, stopping in Cairo, Calcutta and Kuala Lumpur, where water quality can range from unpalatable to unhealthy, and bacteria counts may be far higher than in Europe or North America. Airlines that test their water will add chlorine if the count is too high. This may kill off the bacteria, but the water will then have a taste resembling household bleach. Too much chlorine can be as bad as too little. Water that is overly chlorinated may also destroy healthy, naturally-occurring organisms in your own system, causing gastric distress.

Even water that started out as good-quality drinking water can develop a high bacteria count if it has stayed in the holding tank long enough. You have no way of knowing how long your flying island's water has been in that tank, where it came from originally, or when the tank was last cleaned. The safest advice for the business traveller is to bring your own water or drink only name-brand bottled water served by the flight attendants. Don't be fooled by the frosted silver pitcher. If you don't see the bottle, don't drink the water, at least not cold. Hot beverages like coffee and tea are safe to drink because the water has been boiled. Ice is safe to consume, since it was made with purified water, not water from the holding tank, and was recently delivered to the aircraft.

Eating on Board

Many executive travellers pre-order special meals. Most airlines now have a wide variety of such meals available. Selections include vegetarian, kosher, low fat, salt-free, and diabetic, but you have to give the airline fair warning, usually at least twenty-four hours. To make sure that you get what you want, book the meal when you book your seat, but don't stop there. Remind the ground crew of your special meal when you check in at the gate; make sure that your meal is shown in their computer log for your ticket. In addition, remind the flight attendants when you board the plane.

With regard to Business and First Class meals, you should be aware that the elaborate meal service that most airlines offer, especially on transcontinental or overseas flights, tempts you to indulge in something that most health experts advise you not to do – which is to eat heavily and consume alcohol on a plane. It's easy enough not to eat the unidentified flying omelette or other cruel and unusual nourishment on a one-and-a-quarter-hour hop. It's a lot harder to say no to a glass of chardonnay, grilled swordfish with macadamia nuts and mango chutney, followed by chocolate raspberry torte, between Los Angeles and Sydney. Nevertheless, the overwhelming advice from doctors and business travellers is to eat lightly on board, and to avoid alcohol, including wine.

Some executives control their diet by bringing their own food on board, sometimes from home, more often from a favourite restaurant. Anne Rosenzweig, chef and owner of Arcadia, one of my favourite restaurants in New York, caters her on-board meal from her own restaurant kitchen. She has a wonderful meal, of course, but she also has to fight off the envious glances of other passengers.

Pack a Picnic for Your Flight

You don't have to be Anne Rosenzweig to do this. It's easy enough, if you plan it in advance. A day or so before you leave, call the restaurant or deli and ask them to pack you a meal to go. When you get your car or taxi to the airport, allow a little extra time and ask them to make a stop on the way. (Of course, meals packed for early morning flights should be picked up the night before.) It's not that unusual a request. Any restaurant that can pack food to go, whether it's for lunches at a board meeting or a picnic at the Hollywood Bowl, can equip you with food for a plane trip. Harrods or Fortnum & Mason in London, Balducci's and Dean & DeLuca in New York, Il Fornaio in Los Angeles and San Francisco, and other restaurants and gourmet food emporiums around the world pack in-flight care packages for their customers all the time. Many better hotels are also beginning to provide the same service for their guests.

What should you eat on the plane? I'm not that much of a stickler about following any kind of formal anti-jet-lag diet. I generally eat lightly. Often all I eat is the first course of the meal. However, my advice is to do what works for you. One of my associates makes a point of visiting Coesnon, one of the best *charcuteries* in Paris, before returning to Los Angeles. Coesnon packs him an in-flight feast of *foie gras* and an assortment of pâtés and terrines, accompanied by a baguette of bread from Poîlane. Because these foods are not canned or processed, they can't be brought into the United States. However, it's never a problem because they are always consumed before landing, often with a good bottle of French wine, frequently with the eager assistance of other passengers. Does this violate almost all of the advice about what to consume on a flight? Absolutely. Does it make his jet lag worse? Perhaps, perhaps not. Does he have an enjoyable travel experience? You bet.

The Personal Touch at Your Hotel

Training Your Hotel to Serve You

When you stay at your regular hotel in a city you visit often, do the 'welcome' flowers in your room make you wheeze and sneeze? Is the phone cord always too short? Does room service invariably bring regular coffee when you drink only decaf? If so, you need to revise your hotel's dossier on you. Many business travellers visit the same cities over and over. Better hotels monitor the preferences of their frequent guests, and strive to have everything in order for their arrival. At a good hotel on your first visit, you should be able to get almost anything you ask for. On your second visit, it should already be there waiting.

For this to happen, however, the hotel has to know what your preferences are. For some reason, many executives who have no difficulty making their wishes known in the office are reticent about making requests when on the road. It is a tendency which innkeepers worldwide deplore.

Michael Gray, general manager of the Hyatt Carlton Tower in London, says, 'Give us as much information about your visit as possible. Arrival times are important, so we can plan which rooms to allocate to avoid having people waiting in the lobby. Give us information about the number of people in your party. If we suddenly find that a party of two has turned into a party of three and we're not prepared, you may not get nearly as spacious a room as you would have had if we had known in advance.

'Our front office manager noticed that many American guests arriving early on Monday morning were football fans. During the fall season he now gets the scores late on Sunday night and has them available for new arrivals, who are tickled to be able to follow the San Francisco 49ers or the Dallas Cowboys even in London.

'This is the kind of service we are delighted to provide. Hotels *love* to be able to do something extra, personal, thoughtful. If we can find out things like what particular food or drink you prefer, or what you dislike about any-thing – soft pillows, hard pillows, bed boards, or whatever preferences or idiosyncrasies you might have – please tell us, or get your secretary to tell us. It makes us feel good. We're constantly seeking out ways we can really make the visit a personal one, to make the guest feel they're not just another number.'

The Crillon Will Keep Your Cigars

Hervé Houdre, manager of the Hôtel de Crillon in Paris, concurs. 'When you are new to the hotel, we keep track of your requests. The next time you visit, we will know what kind of cigar you smoke or which newspaper you want to read, so you don't have to call us and ask. However, a good traveller needs to convey what he needs. Before being upset with anything which doesn't suit you in the room, call reception and speak with the reception manager as soon as possible. Always go to the top person if you can. We can't assist you if you don't make us aware of what your needs are.'

What can you have waiting for you? Two phone lines. A fax machine or a portable computer to use in your room, or a fax and modem interface for you to hook your own equipment into. Restaurant reservations for the duration of your visit. Theatre tickets. A secretary. Voice mail. A treadmill, exercise bicycle or Stairmaster in your room. Your favourite newspaper. Your favourite Scotch in the minibar. Your choice of flowers, or no flowers at all.

The Crillon and the Carlton Tower pride themselves on taking excellent care of their clientele and anticipating their needs, but this kind of meticulous service happens not just there but at better hotels all over the world. Most American hotel chains keep similar if less comprehensive records. Even if they don't, you should keep a list of preferences (and – sometimes more important – aversions) on file with your travel agent, in-house travel service or secretary. When they book your room, they can tick off the listings as they make the reservation. The important concept is advance planning – give the hotel time to do what you want them to do.

Getting Others to Give You Personal Service

How does the executive traveller get others to extend themselves to the utmost on his or her behalf? By using the

Personal Touch. The Personal Touch is an extension of my business philosophy. Many executives have already learned to use it within their own corporate structure and in their business dealings, but it can be extended into your travelling relationships as well.

Make Yourself Known

The Personal Touch is not something you can delegate. When you see the same faces over and over, make a point of learning the names that go with them. Build your own relationship with them. Ask about their health and family – let them know you are interested in them as human beings. As you develop these personal relationships with people, even if you are only kidding around with them, somebody will end up giving you more service or extra help.

It doesn't take much, in part because surprisingly few people do it. If you've developed a friendly rapport with the elevator operator in your building, the next time you're taking stuff from your apartment and he's got two other people in the elevator waiting, he's going to be more inclined to make them wait for you and your stuff than to make you wait till he's taken them downstairs and come back up.

Get to know the secretaries of your business associates – a secretary will control access to her boss more often than not. When you phone, it may make the difference between 'He's not in. I'll take a message', and 'He's not in, but you can catch him in the car on the car phone, and here's the number.'

The key is empowerment – giving people in offices or at the airlines, at the hotel or in a restaurant, the belief that they can really be of service to you, and making them want to put themselves out on your behalf.

How do you do this? The basis for the success of the Personal Touch is that everyone likes to feel important, and everyone likes to show their authority. A great deal of it is public relations and establishing a genuine rapport with the people you meet. It works with your travel agent. It works with the airlines reservation agent at the boarding gate. It works with the desk clerk and concierge at the hotel. It works with waiters and waitresses in restaurants.

How to Be a VIP at Your Favourite Restaurant

You have to be a major-league power broker to become a big deal at, say, The Ivy or Le Caprice in London, the kind of big deal who can stroll in at a moment's notice and be confident that your favourite table will be waiting for you. The same is true of power restaurants such as 21 or The Four Seasons in New York. But it doesn't take a lot to become a big deal in your favourite local restaurant, with your own favourite table.

What's important to a restaurant is not how big your company is, not how big your title is within the firm, but how often they see your face for lunch or dinner. **Plant your flag**. Make yourself known to the owner and the *maître d'*. If you have a favourite waiter who gives you excellent service, ask for him by name.

How many visits to a restaurant does it take to make yourself known and become a regular customer? It may not take as many as you think. You don't have to be a weekly habitué of a restaurant to be a regular; however, this kind of loyalty should certainly get you special treatment in almost any restaurant I know. I am a 'regular' at La Marée in Paris, even though I only get the chance to eat there three or four times a year. I made myself known and developed a special relationship with Eric Trompier, the owner. Because I've been treated extremely well there, I also make a point of sending a lot of my friends to his restaurant.

You'll find that most restaurants will hold visiting business patrons to a much gentler standard than local residents in order to qualify as 'regulars'. An owner or *maître d'* can't help but be flattered knowing that you patronize his or her establishment each time you're in town, but he won't know to be flattered unless you tell him.

A Lesson in Diplomacy for Jack Nicholson

If you remember Jack Nicholson's classic restaurant scene in the film *Five Easy Pieces*, it never would have happened if he'd used a little diplomacy and the Personal Touch. Let me give you my version: The luncheon special in a run-of-the-mill restaurant says, 'Soup, salad, breast of chicken. No substitutions.' Fine, except you would like pasta instead of the chicken. If you peremptorily announce to the waitress, 'I'd like the luncheon special but make it pasta instead of chicken', you're going to get a hard time. The standard 'Sorry, we can't do that' is probably the best you can hope for. If, on the other hand, you put yourself at the waitress's mercy and ask her, 'Do you have enough influence with the chef to get him to substitute pasta for chicken?' the answer may be quite different. The request is not unreasonable. It's not as if there isn't any pasta back in the kitchen. What you are doing is acknowledging her importance and deferring to her power. You are letting her exercise and display her authority to help you. Likely as not the response will be a smile and 'I'll see what I can do'.

It is the same when you get on a lunch flight on a plane. You know that, depending on where you're seated, by the time they get to you one of the meal choices is likely to be gone. If you greet the flight attendant warmly as you board and ask what the lunch choices are, she may tell you there's an orange salad and lasagne. It's easy enough to ask her if she'll save you a salad. If you are even moderately civilized in making the request, she will do it.

It helps to do it with a smile and a sense of humour. I have made it clear to the doormen in my New York apartment building *never* to ring my bell when a hired car comes to pick me up. I'll know the car is there if I've asked for it. Half the time a car I've requested at 8 a.m. is there at 7.40, at which time I'm in the bathtub. No one likes to get out of the tub to answer the bell. I tell all our doormen on the different shifts so they know not to ring me when the car comes. It's just a small thing, but I make a point of not being officious about it. It's just a matter of explaining to them, 'Hey – I'm in the bathtub', which is something any human being can relate to.

The Personal Touch – Japanese Style

The Personal Touch works on me, too. When the 1972 Winter Olympics were held in Sapporo, and I was in Japan travelling with Arnold Palmer and Jean-Claude Killy, I had the chance to meet and become acquainted with Yoshiaki Tsutsumi, who owns the Prince Hotel chain. Some years later, he invited me to dine with him at the Tokyo Prince Hotel, in one of their private *teppan* grill rooms. For the hotel this was the equivalent of Lee Iacocca spending the afternoon at a Chrysler dealership in Des Moines. It was a huge deal for them. The hotel called my office three separate times asking what the licence number was of the car that would take me to the hotel. I couldn't figure out why until my car pulled up at the kerb and the doorman opened my door saying, 'Good evening and welcome to the Tokyo Prince, Mr McCormack.' I was a guest of their CEO and the hotel staff wanted to greet me personally. I was impressed.

The Fine Art of Tipping

Tipping is perhaps the most obvious manifestation of the Personal Touch. Many business people handle tipping awkwardly, but the business traveller knows how, when and who to tip to achieve the desired results. There are three general purposes for tipping. Never lose sight of what you are trying to achieve.

- Are you tipping for something you want to make happen immediately?
- Are you tipping to show gratitude for something that's already occurred?
- Are you tipping to set up a smoother visit or a better table the next time you come?

Tipping is a custom that varies widely from one country to the next. In Japan, it is not generally expected. On the other hand, small gifts are appropriate for people who serve you frequently. In Eastern Europe, a tip in a hard currency, such as dollars or Deutschmarks, is appreciated far more than a gratuity in the local coin of the realm. In Europe, most restaurants include a service charge in the bill, but a modest additional tip is considered in order for service above and beyond the ordinary. How do you know what's appropriate? Ask around. Ask your local business contacts for advice. A good concierge will know what cabbies and waiters expect in his town. Many of the better guidebooks will also provide guidelines for tipping.

Tips in Advance

Keep in mind that the term 'tip' was originally an acronym for To Insure Promptness, and it is in this context that tips are often the most useful. At the airport, I always give the skycap a good tip – *before* he checks my bags. Let's say a baggage handler at the kerb figures that he's going to get a dollar for checking some luggage. The executive traveller knows only too well what happens, of course. The skycap is hailed by other passengers, and now there's yet another pile on the kerb. But if you're going to give the skycap a big tip – let's say $5 – hand him the money with the ticket and he'll be very happy. He's really going to pay more attention to your baggage. More often than not, he'll load your bags directly before he takes luggage from anyone else. I always wait until he actually puts the tag on the luggage, and loads it either on the cart or on to something that looks like a conveyor belt. I never enter the terminal if my bags are still piled up at the kerb.

One of the smartest tipping techniques in the world is to tip the telephone operators in hotels when you first get there. Nobody tips them because they are forgotten people – in the background. People tip concierges, bellboys, captains, waiters, etc., but for the business traveller, tipping hotel operators is

seriously effective. They will find you and do things for you if
you want to be found. They won't 'find' you if you don't
want to be found. You can explain special situations to them
and they will kill themselves for you.

One savvy executive I know frequented an 'establishment'
restaurant in New York about twice a month. It was a place
where seating was hierarchical and no one wanted to be in
'Siberia'. He always got a great table, but even though he
was there every two weeks or so, he would tip the *maître d'*
only twice a year. When he did, he'd give him $50. His
theory was that everyone gives the guy $5 or $10, so he
kind of expects it. It doesn't make much of an impression. By
giving the *maître d'* $50, he made himself stand out. He also
created a level of uncertainty that worked to his benefit – the
maître d' never knew when that next $50 was coming.

People Who Can *Really* Help

The Personal Touch taps into a universal human need to be
needed. It even works with small children by making them
want to do what you want them to do. Within the travel
industry, however, some people are in the business of respond-
ing to the Personal Touch, and they can be incredibly helpful
to you when you most need it.

Airline Special Services

The best resource an executive traveller can have at the
airport is a Special Services representative from the airline.
Special Service reps are the Red Adairs of the air travel
business – putting out wildfires and solving problems ordinary
agents fear to tackle. Employees of long standing, they've
earned their stripes with their companies for good reason,
and have the authority to accomplish what most other airline
personnel will tell you simply cannot be done.

They handle celebrities and VIPs, but you don't have to be
rich or famous to use their services. What can they do? They

can rewrite your ticket, break a sold-out flight, or rebook you with another airline if your flight has been delayed or cancelled. They can walk you through Customs and Immigration, or make sure that your missing luggage with all your conference presentation materials is delivered to your hotel in time for the big meeting.

If you're a frequent executive traveller, airline Special Services personnel are available to you, but as with hotels and restaurants, the airline needs to know that you need them. Mike Baverstock, a veteran Special Services agent with British Airways in London, told me, 'There are some people who travel really regularly and never call on our services. Others depend on them. The bottom line is that we would like everybody to understand that we exist. Should they have a problem, they should know that they can ask for our assistance. People prefer airlines where they feel comfortable, where they feel recognized. This recognition and courtesy cost us nothing. The personalization of the travel experience is the important thing. It builds passenger loyalty; it rewards passenger loyalty.'

How do you meet them? If you do a lot of business with an airline, your travel agent or in-house travel department can find out who the Special Services people are. You can also ask at the counter or the gate in the airport if the airline has a Special Services representative. A major carrier such as British Airways will have representatives in every city, but some airlines maintain agents only in larger cities and hubs. (Among US-based carriers, only American, United and Delta have Special Services representatives.) However you learn the name, you will want to make personal contact yourself. Ask to meet him or her. Make it a point to get to know them – before you need them. Introduce yourself and trade business cards. When you return to your office, write a letter confirming the contact. Keep the name handy. You never know when you'll need it. Don't abuse the relationship, however.

When they've worked wonders, it helps, of course, if you can show your appreciation, even in a small way. I'm fortunate in being able sometimes to give out tickets to concerts and sporting events, but remembering people during the holiday season who have helped you all year long is always a good idea. It's something that can pay big dividends not just for you, but for your company as well. If you get some of these Special Services people on your side by doing a lot of nice things for them, they will treat your clients, your employees and your friends very well too.

Your Hotel's In-House Magician

Many hotels have a magician on staff who can do things on short notice, but there's often no limit to what they can do given sufficient warning. This wizard is often the concierge, and getting to know a good one is among the most valuable personal connections you can make at a hotel. For starters, a trained concierge will have the best connections in the city. I've known native Londoners whose out-of-town guests from Chicago got them 'impossible' West End tickets through their hotel concierge.

The concierge concept crossed the Atlantic from fine European hotels. Perhaps for this reason, many executive travellers are intimidated by their concierge. There is also the problem that at some American hotels, the concept lost a little during the voyage. A kid in a hat at an information desk filled with leaflets for local tours and attractions is not a concierge desk, despite a hotel's claim to offer 'concierge service'. A bell captain is not the same as a concierge either, no matter how much gold braid bedecks his epaulettes. Even within a hotel's concierge staff there may be variations in competence. If one concierge in the French Quarter of New Orleans has to look up the phone number for restaurants like Antoine's or the Commander's Palace, wait for the shift to change before you ask for anything else.

The function of a concierge is to do things for you outside the hotel. Don't complain to them about your bill or ask them to arrange a special function in the private dining room. The domain of the concierge begins just outside the hotel walls. Dinner reservations, theatre and concert tickets are the most common requests, but if you need a place to play golf or tennis, a ten-speed bicycle, a behind-the-scenes tour of the local brewery, an expert who specializes in antique watch repair, or a helicopter to get you quickly to a remote construction site, use the Personal Touch with your concierge. The concierge is also trained to solve last-minute emergencies. When you discover while dressing for a black tie dinner that your home-town cleaners returned only the top half of your dinner suit, when you've lost your airline tickets or when you've forgotten your anniversary, get help from the concierge.

A good concierge knows not only his or her own city, but is connected to a concierge network whose branches reach all over the world. They can make things happen for you anywhere. Many hotels encourage their frequent guests to use the services of their concierge – whether they're staying there that night or not. If you're a good client of the Four Seasons Hotel in Washington, DC, and you have a problem, the hotel will encourage you to call them from New York or Paris and take advantage of their concierge services.

How to Complain

What happens when things don't work out? I can envision many of you saying, 'Oh yeah? Well I did all that stuff McCormack told me to do and I still got treated badly.' It helps to know how to complain. When used properly, it's part of the Personal Touch. When something goes awry at the airport, at the hotel, or at a restaurant, and you find yourself dashing off a torrid letter of complaint on the plane home, you've lost the battle. The best and most effective time to complain is at the time and spot of the infraction.

Complain as Soon as You Can

At a hotel, a desk clerk facing a complaint may call for another member of the hotel staff to intercede. Do not deal with him or her until you know what their title is. Is this person the head of public relations – in other words, someone who can make soothing noises but can't really help? Is this the reservations manager, much better, or best of all, the hotel manager himself?

Above all, don't let the problem fester. Michael Gray, general manager of London's Hyatt Carlton Tower, says, 'There's nothing worse than receiving a letter after the guest is gone, because it leaves me powerless to do anything about it. If there's a problem, tell the hotel at the time. Don't hold back. A good hotel and good management will want to hear a problem. I genuinely thank guests who complain to me. I may not like what I'm hearing, but I'm grateful that someone is letting me know. We're human; we make mistakes. But this way we have a chance to put things right during the visit. It will also make us a better hotel for you in the future.'

Air Your Dirty Linen in Public

When you are negotiating a business deal, it is best to do so discreetly and in private. When you are negotiating a solution to an airline or hotel snafu, however, often the best place to do it is in public. The one exception is at a restaurant. There, any disagreement that cannot be resolved with the waiter can usually be settled by a discreet chat with the owner or the *maître d'*.

If you have a hotel reservation but the room you are shown is hopeless, don't stay there even for a minute. Return to the reception desk immediately. Don't call the desk from the undesirable room. Keep your belongings with you. Don't leave your bags in the room when you return to the lobby to complain. Leaving them in the room is an indication to the hotel that they may yet talk you into staying put. Plant yourself, bag and baggage, at the reception desk.

When there is a problem, junior-level airline and hotel personnel may try very hard to shunt you aside into an office or even a quiet corner – anywhere out of the public eye.

Don't go. The business traveller stays put. A public and potentially embarrassing complaint at the reception desk or boarding gate that holds up a lengthening line of other guests or passengers waiting to check in will be resolved a lot faster – and generally more favourably to you – than a dispute behind closed doors.

Find Your Target: Aim High

Sometimes the most difficult part of complaining is aiming your protest where it will do the most good. At the airport, use your connections to the Special Services representatives to deal with your problem. Failing that, the magic words usually are, 'May I speak with your supervisor?'

If I've really been mistreated, it's usually a middle-level employee who is responsible. Because that person reports to a supervisor who's probably going to protect him, I go one step above that to the chief supervisor, since that's where the problem is going to end up anyway.

The first objective is to represent yourself as part of the solution, not part of the problem. I let them know at the earliest point in the conversation my credentials as a frequent flyer and a loyal fan of the airline. From the minute our discussions begin, I'm a cheerleader on the side of the angels. My conversation goes something along these lines: 'This airline has always been great for me, but I wanted to let you know about a problem we have, and I really hope you can help.' I'm not calling to start the battle, but to report the outbreak of a minor skirmish in which I might have been a participant. The situation thus becomes not me v. the airline, but me and the supervisor defending the integrity of the airline v. the intransigent idiot in the middle who's causing all the trouble.

Know What You Want

Decide in advance what you want to have happen. Distil your anger and exasperation into a simple but specific request.

- 'I want to be booked on your flight number 334 leaving in thirty minutes.'
- 'I'm holding a reservation on Another Airlines flight number 123 leaving in half an hour, and I want you to endorse my ticket for your delayed flight over to Another Airlines.'
- 'Here's my confirmation number – I want the room number 679 corner suite I booked three weeks ago.'
- 'You should have told me the place was all torn up with construction. I want you to book me an equivalent suite at Another Hotel at the same rate, and I want you to transfer me and my luggage there immediately.'

Complain Towards the Building of a Better Relationship

Remember the Personal Touch. Once you've found someone with the authority to solve the problem, give them a chance to demonstrate their clout. Most of the time, you'll get the situation resolved in your favour if you remain calm but firm. Don't push someone to the wall. Don't gloat publicly when you 'win'. Winning one battle is not the objective. The war goes on, and will continue as long as you travel. You'll be in the air again next week, and the same faces show up all the time. If you don't push someone to the wall, they are far more likely to work hard on your behalf the next time you need them.

4 A Month on the Road with Mark McCormack

The month of February 1993 was a heavy travel month for me. It was also one in which I was confronted with a number of travel fiascos. How I used the weapons at my disposal to deal with them provides a real-life illustration of the principles put forward in the last chapter. In this chapter you'll spend a month on the road with me and see how I travel. You'll also get a view of how and where I realize time savings, and how I invest them to enhance my travel experience.

Monday, 1 February–Thursday, 4 February: Tokyo

On 1 February I was in Tokyo. I arrived there on 31 January, on a Delta flight from my home in Orlando, Florida. My trip is proof that Orlando International Airport is becoming more and more global. I flew from Orlando to Tokyo direct, staying on the same plane with one stop at Los Angeles. It was a sixteen and a half hour flight – five hours to Los Angeles, one and a half hours on the ground, and ten hours in the air to Tokyo. The flight to Los Angeles was very crowded because it was Super Bowl Sunday, and first class was full of sports celebrities on their way to the game, including Don Shula and Dan Marino of the Miami Dolphins.

I slept much of the time on the plane, which is customary for me. I slept a total of eight hours on the flight. I slept a solid four hours from Orlando to Los Angeles, dozing off shortly after takeoff and waking up somewhere over Arizona. I sleep a great deal on planes. It's a good habit for the frequent flyer to cultivate.

I also slept four of the ten hours on the way to Japan. The rest of the time I was doing paperwork. I didn't have any leisure reading at all with me. I was working on my advance yellow pads, trying to get everything lined up and thought out for the week of meetings ahead.

The service on Delta was good, but the flight did prove the adage about flying the national flag of the home country. When we landed we were left well out on the field and bussed into the terminal. Everything else about the flight, however, was just fine. When I reached my hotel, I went to bed that night around 10 o'clock and woke up at 3 a.m.

On this trip I really dealt successfully with the time change. Every day was very full. The pattern I have developed is simple: I get up very early in the morning, anywhere from 2 to 4 a.m. At that time I make my phone calls, and then do three or four hours of work. Then I have my coffee and begin breakfast meetings at 7.30 or 8 a.m., followed by morning meetings, followed by a business lunch. By the end of the lunch hour I'm usually very tired, and I scheduled no meetings after lunch on any of the days of my trip. I instructed my staff to block off the hours between 1.30 and 4 p.m. for a nap. Of that time I'd end up with about two hours of solid sleep. When I awoke I'd have meetings, mostly business dinners, then sleep about five or six more hours at night. Although it was broken into two segments, I really was getting about seven to eight hours of sleep a day.

That is my pattern in Tokyo. Rise at 2 or 3 a.m. It may have been the wee small hours in Tokyo, but it was like getting up in New York at 1 in the afternoon or Los Angeles at 10 a.m. It was almost like staying on American time.

Friday, 5 February: Tokyo–New York

I was scheduled to leave Tokyo on a nonstop flight on United Airlines to New York that was due to leave at 5 p.m. and land at 3.30 p.m. at JFK. A few months before, IMG had acquired control of the Millrose Games, an indoor track meet held annually at New York's Madison Square Garden and the oldest track meet in the United States. The grand finale and signature event of the Millrose Games is the Wanamaker Mile. I was to present the award to the winner of the Wanamaker Mile Friday night about 10 p.m.

With six and a half hours between my arrival at Kennedy and the presentation of the trophy, I had left myself more than enough time to clear Customs, get home, shower, get dressed, and get myself to Madison Square Garden. I planned to arrive there at about 7 p.m. and have a buffet supper with the executives from Chemical Bank, who were the sponsors of the event. Other dignitaries would be there as well, including the Irish Ambassador to the United States.

At 11 that morning, I routinely asked my office in Tokyo to call up United, make sure everything was under control with the flight, and reconfirm my seat. The news was horrendous. An incoming United flight to Tokyo was delayed and my flight was going to be six hours late. Consequently we didn't have an aeroplane.

That meant that I was going to miss everything at Madison Square Garden, which wasn't very satisfactory. I was the host of the event. This experience demonstrated one rule that many business travellers have learned the hard way: **Don't rely on airlines to let you know when things go wrong** – even though they always ask you for a contact telephone number where they can reach you in case there's a problem. They hardly ever call. In the normal course of events, I'd have just gone to the airport and been told the bad news when I arrived.

When I got the news, I called my secretary in Cleveland, Ohio. We both thought she had done what she normally does, which is double- or triple-book me, and that I might have some alternatives for nonstops. There was one other nonstop flight, but it was full. I hadn't booked myself on it. Normally I will crisscross book, just in case something like this happens. I was moderately depressed and a bit angry with myself because I hadn't followed my own advice.

At least now I had the chance to work on an alternative. I carry the OAG with me at all times, the condensed international and the condensed domestic. The alternative I discovered was a Northwest flight to Chicago, connecting on to a flight to La Guardia on American.

Every time I've flown Northwest in Asia in recent years, I have been immensely impressed with the airline. In the old days Northwest was just awful, and even today you don't hear a lot about them. Singapore Airlines and Japan Airlines get all the raves, but Northwest was super. When we got to Chicago O'Hare, they bussed us into the Customs area and an unusual and impressive thing happened. They had a special bus for the first class passengers. Northwest does this all the time, apparently. They whisked us in and got the first class luggage off first, which is standard procedure on non-American carriers but something very few American carriers do. Because we were an early arrival, the Customs area was a cake-walk. There was no other flight there.

I could have flown either United or American to New York, but I chose American because they have the nearest terminal to Northwest, and I knew that I had to get my luggage from one terminal to another. I went to American, boarded my flight and got into La Guardia at just a little after 6 p.m., compared with my planned arrival time of 3.30 on the delayed United flight.

Mary Wenzel, my New York secretary, met my flight and took me directly to my New York *pied-à-terre*. I worked with her for about half an hour, then freshened up and changed before heading over to Madison Square Garden and my dinner with the Chemical Bank people, the Irish Ambassador, and our client, the Irish runner Eammon Coghlan, who won the Masters' Mile. At the end of the evening I presented the Wanamaker Mile trophy in front of a sellout crowd.

Saturday, 6 February: New York

Coming back I slept seven hours on the flight from Tokyo to Chicago. I had absolutely no time change problem at all coming back, which I attribute to a combination of the naps and getting up at 3 a.m. while in Tokyo. I worked in the morning once again with Mary, starting at about 6 and going over stuff that had accumulated while I'd been in Tokyo. In the evening I worked with my senior personal assistant, Laurie Roggenburk, who had come in from our Cleveland headquarters.

Sunday, 7 February: New York–Orlando

During Saturday night New York was hit by a blizzard. Although the city looked beautiful, it was not very cheerful news for me, since I was due to fly south to Orlando. We started calling the airports. Of course, everything was delayed. La Guardia was snowed in.

I was scheduled on an 11 a.m. Delta flight, but when I got out to the terminal at La Guardia they said it was due to leave at 12.40 p.m. Given the conditions, this was not so terrible. However, I was dubious, since I quickly determined that my aircraft was coming in from Cincinnati and it hadn't left Cincinnati yet. This demonstrates yet another maxim for the executive traveller: **Don't believe the times posted on the Arrivals and Departures boards.**

I consulted my pocket OAG and I saw that there was a 10 a.m. flight on USAir. Even though it was now 10.30, I figured that since everything was delayed, maybe the 10 o'clock flight was still there and was leaving at 11.30 or 12.00. I called USAir from the car while I was sitting out on the kerb in front of Delta. In circumstances like these, **don't dismiss your limousine or car until you are positive you no longer need it.** When weather problems scramble flight schedules, airport phones – whether they are pay phones or phones in VIP lounges – are in short supply. When you're in your limo, you have instant access to a phone of your very own.

Sure enough, the USAir 10 a.m. flight was leaving at 11.30. The best news was that although the plane was not physically at La Guardia, it was already in the air from Buffalo. The driver took me to the USAir terminal, La Guardia's newest and a serenely elegant, state-of-the-art terminal that is very efficient and comfortable. Even though the flight was delayed a little further, it did ultimately leave. I got a bit more work done in the USAir VIP lounge, and arrived in Orlando in time for a meeting I was scheduled to have late that afternoon.

That night I had dinner with Gary Player.

Monday, 8 February: Orlando–Chicago

Monday morning I flew to Chicago from Orlando. I had no baggage, only carry-ons. My wife, Betsy, had left before me on Sunday and had taken my luggage with her. She was there to play in the Virginia Slims tennis tournament.

My flight landed at 11.15. Since I had a lunch date at 12.15 downtown with Bill Smithburg, the chairman of Quaker Oats, I was cutting it a little close. I had a limousine meet me in Chicago, but at the airport they no longer permit limousines to pull up to the kerb and wait. They park in a garage, which is most inconvenient. Nevertheless, the driver met me at the gate and I got to Nick's Fishmarket right on time.

That night I had dinner with my friend Phil Stefani, who owns Tuscany restaurant, which is one of the all-time great Italian restaurants, and with Ivo and Denise Cozzini.

Tuesday, 9 February: Chicago

After making phone calls early in the morning, I had breakfast with Billie Jean King at the Mayfair Regent, followed by a late lunch in Schaumburg, about forty miles outside the city. Betsy was scheduled to play both singles and doubles. Both her matches were on Tuesday. She lost her singles match 7–6 in the second set, but won her doubles that night with her partner, Monica Seles.

The match ended very late, but after the victory Betsy and I went out with Christie Hefner, the CEO of Playboy Enterprises, and her companion, Illinois State Senator Bill Meirovitz. We went to Un Grand Café (the local wags pronounce its name as the Ungrand Cafe), which is one of twenty-eight owned by Chicago restaurateur Rich Melman.

Wednesday, 10 February: Chicago–New York

On Wednesday I had lunch with Rich Melman at a place called Maggiano's. It has a bakery at the front which produces outstanding bread. There is a little café in the bakery, plus a substantial main dining room. It was so good that Betsy and I returned there again that night with my son Todd and Monica Seles. After dinner I flew to New York on the last flight out, which got in at 1 a.m.

Thursday, 11 February: New York–Chicago

In the morning I had a meeting with people from American Express, and lunch with John Mack Carter, the legendary editor-in-chief of *Good Housekeeping*. John used to work with my dad, and he's been a friend for more than 20 years. We had lunch at 21.

That afternoon I met with some businessmen from Argentina to talk about a new tennis tournament in Buenos Aires. Then I flew back to Chicago to watch Betsy and Monica play doubles in the quarter-finals that evening.

Friday, 12 February:
Chicago–Norfolk–Williamsburg, Virginia

The doubles match (which they won) ended very late, about 2 a.m., which made it a short night since I was leaving on a 6.39 a.m. flight to Norfolk, Virginia. It was a sleety, snowy morning. Five or ten years ago the weather would have cancelled everything for 100 miles around, but because of all the new electronics and technology, it was no problem at all. We just took off.

The flight landed at about noon. From the airport I went to Williamsburg, home of the College of William & Mary, one of the oldest institutions of higher learning in the United States, and my alma mater. For the last three years I've been the national co-chairman of a $150 million capital fund-raising campaign.

William & Mary was founded in 1693, and I was there to help the college celebrate its tricentennial Charter Day. I'd also donated some money for the construction of a tennis centre, and had lunch with the tennis coach and the women's athletic director. I was in meetings at the school in the afternoon, followed by a gala evening Charter Day celebration.

Saturday, 13 February: Williamsburg, Virginia

Following breakfast, I arrived for the Charter Day Ceremony at 9.30 a.m. The college had invited HRH Prince Charles to help commemorate the anniversary. The students welcomed him with great acclaim, which was very gratifying for him. He gave a stirring address in honour of the 300th anniversary of William & Mary, after which I joined him (and a hundred or so others) for lunch.

Sunday, 14 February:
Williamsburg–Washington–Paris

The next morning, after brunch with the President of William & Mary, I hired a car from Williamsburg to Washington, DC, where I was to catch an Air France flight to Paris. The three-hour drive allowed me to get in some reading and paperwork. I arrived at Dulles Airport at 4.30 p.m. for a nonstop flight that was due to leave at 6.05. Twenty minutes before we were scheduled to board the plane, Air France announced that the aircraft had '*un petit*' mechanical difficulty. The flight was going to be delayed for seven hours.

This was a catastrophe of the first magnitude. On Monday at noon I was scheduled to have a crucial meeting in Paris with the head of Canal Plus, one of the major private television stations in France. The meeting had been set up for a long time. I had to get to Paris. There was no way I would wait for the flight.

Be there or be square. My staff and I immediately began scrambling. The only alternative seemed to be to catch a United flight to London, and then connect on the Air France hop from London to Paris. This would get me to Charles de Gaulle at around 10.15 in the morning as opposed to 7.30 a.m. Getting to a noon lunch date in the heart of Paris would be tight, but it was doable.

My main concern about the switch to United was that I wanted to make sure my baggage got off the Air France plane. It had to be transferred from an Air France flight to Paris to a United flight to London, then back on to an Air France flight from London to Paris. It was all too easy to envision a baggage handler second-guessing me and leaving the bags on the original flight. After all, either way the luggage was going to end up on Air France in Paris.

I was insistent that Air France retrieve and give me the luggage, which eventually they did. This demonstrates another rule for the smart business traveller: **When you make emergency revisions to your flight plans, never get separated**

from your luggage. Demand that it be physically delivered to you from the delayed or cancelled flight.

I rushed over to United Airlines and personally rechecked my luggage on to the new flight rather than rely on someone who promised to take care of it. Then I called my secretary in London to make sure that someone met me at Heathrow.

On the United flight to London, I was very impressed with the quality of their food, but unimpressed with the length of time it took them to put the meal in front of me. It took them at least an hour and a half from the time we pushed back from the gate until I had the first course in front of me – on a six-hour flight. United inherited this route from Pan Am, and I think it has something to do with the age of the plane and the fact that the galley has to come up on an elevator.

I mentioned it to the flight attendant who was serving me. 'Everyone on a transatlantic flight is trying to get to sleep,' I told her. 'British Airways would have had the meal served by the time you put the first course down.' The flight attendant told me that many of her passengers complained about it, but there was nothing she could do. I made a note to avoid United on this route until the situation improved.

Monday, 15 February: London–Paris

We landed at Heathrow. I knew the United Airlines Special Services people, who used to be Pan Am's Special Services representatives when Pan Am was flying this route. They expedited my way through Customs.

My London personal assistant, Sarah Wooldridge, had come out to the airport in the limo with Peter Herst, our driver. They drove me over to the Air France terminal. Since we had a little time before the short flight to Paris was due to leave, Sarah and I decided to get some work done while we were waiting. In the meantime I sent Peter down to the counter to make sure that the flight was on time. Peter returned with startling news that the baggage handlers at Charles de Gaulle were on strike and that the flight was delayed for an hour.

While we waited in the coffee shop at Heathrow, Sarah and I did get some work accomplished. The flight ultimately landed in Paris at 11.15, and the luggage came out quickly. I had arranged for a driver from the Hôtel de Crillon to meet me. The car took me directly to the hotel. I quickly shaved, washed my hands and face, changed my shirt and drove over to Canal Plus for the meeting. I wasn't there on the dot of twelve, but I was close. In Paris I was reunited with Betsy, who was playing in a tennis tournament, both singles and doubles. She was again paired with Monica Seles. That night we had dinner with Jean-Claude Killy and his partner at La Marée, my favourite restaurant in France.

Tuesday, 16 February: Paris

Betsy played her singles match and lost. Unfortunately, she and Monica played their doubles match very late that night and lost that as well.

Wednesday, 17 February: Paris

Meetings all day. That evening Betsy and I dined at Duquesnoy (another Parisian personal favourite) with Monica Seles, her father, and her coach. We were joined by my daughter Leslie, who works in our Paris office, and her beau.

Thursday, 18 February: Paris–London

Betsy and I flew to London. That night we had dinner with Sir Christopher Lewinton and his wife at the newly-refurbished Ivy restaurant, which was great in the old days and has now made a terrific resurgence.

Friday, 19 February: London

I was in meetings pretty much all day, but had a wonderful lunch in the Rib Room at the Carlton Tower.

Saturday, 20 February:
London–Gleneagles, Scotland

The bulk of the day was devoted to a business meeting with the Chairman of Wimbledon at his home in the suburbs. In the late afternoon I flew to Gleneagles, Scotland, where we would be having two days of internal meetings with executives of our television division. I had sent Sarah up earlier with my luggage. That evening Sarah and I had a dinner in my suite to go over the arrangements for the meetings.

Sunday, 21 February:
Gleneagles–St Andrews–Gleneagles

In the morning, I drove to St Andrews to meet Michael Bonallack, the head of the Royal & Ancient Golf Club. The discussion continued into lunch which was served in a private dining room at the top of the Old Course Hotel. I drove back to Gleneagles late that afternoon where I had a dinner meeting with three senior executives in my suite.

I heartily endorse dinner meetings in your room, particularly if you have serious business to discuss and don't want the distractions and interruptions of a public dining room. But it helps to think it through.

When you dine in your suite at a hotel, particularly a first-class establishment, you are generally assigned a head waiter for the evening. He serves you and stands at your beck and call. If you are discussing confidential matters, you might let the waiter go. But then when you finish the first course, you have to call room service to get him back. It's a needless complication, which I have solved by giving the waiter specific instructions about when and how fast I would like each course served. He knows when he's needed; I don't have to keep calling.

Monday, 22 February–Tuesday, 23 February: Gleneagles

I headed up two days of intensive meetings, lasting from 7 a.m. to 10 p.m.

Wednesday, 24 February: Gleneagles–London

I returned to London for an all-day meeting with Michael Sohlman, the executive director of the Nobel Foundation, who had flown in from Stockholm, for a report on our various activities on behalf of the Nobel Foundation.

Thursday, 25 February: London

I hosted a press conference at the Royal Palace at Hampton Court to announce the inaugural season of a major ten-day festival that our classical music division, IMG Artists, was to present at Hampton Court in June 1993.

That evening I was the guest of Sol Kerzner, the developer of South Africa's famous Lost City resort, for dinner at the marvellous private dining room at Annabel's.

Friday, 26 February: London–Los Angeles–Palm Springs

After an early morning haircut and an interview with a magazine reporter, I flew from London to Los Angeles, then drove to Palm Springs, California, where we were running the Matrix Essentials/Evert Cup tennis tournament and I

would rejoin Betsy, who was playing doubles in the tournament and also providing television commentary on the
matches for ESPN.

Saturday, 27 February: Palm Springs

A leisurely day for me. After internal meetings with our
tennis executives in the morning, I watched the matches
while Betsy attended to her broadcasting duties.

Sunday, 28 February:
Palm Springs–Los Angeles–Vail

After the national telecast was finished, Betsy and I returned
to Los Angeles and flew to Vail, Colorado, for the beginning
of a holiday.

5 Sometimes It's Worth It

Time is money, but money is money, too, and the recent economic climate has forced many firms to cut back on some of the 'frills' of business travel. From either a personal or professional perspective, there's absolutely no point in being a frequent but miserable traveller. It makes you far less able to make the deal or participate in the negotiation, which is why you made the trip in the first place. In the long run, if you travel unhappily often enough, even the most dynamic executive gets used up and worn down. The purpose of this chapter is to illustrate where spending a little more pays off, and where savings can be realized.

There is no denying that comfortable and efficient executive travel is, on the average, about 20 per cent more expensive than the standard business rate. For me, however, the premium pays extra dividends to both the savvy business traveller and his or her corporation. The additional outlay, properly expended, produces a refreshed, invigorated executive who looks forward to travelling on business.

This is not to say that spending more always gets you more. Many executives incur extra charges needlessly, often without being aware of it. By trimming these costs, which frequently do not affect comfort or efficiency, the executive traveller can either allocate those resources towards travel expenditures which make the trip far more enjoyable, or have them accrue on the bottom line.

You Gotta Ask, Part 1

No Charge for Tickets by Overnight Delivery

With a last-minute trip, often one of the big problems to be solved is getting the ticket and boarding pass in hand before departing for the airport. For this reason many executive travellers, even those who have made their own reservations, go to a travel agency to purchase their ticket.

This should not be necessary. If you are a volume traveller, your travel agency should be delivering those tickets to your office, even to your home. (Melhart Travel, our main agency in London, sends tickets by bike to IMG's three London offices every day, sometimes twice a day.) Using a travel agent, however, isn't the only way to get tickets on short notice. Many airlines will send you your ticket by one of the overnight delivery services.

Will you get hit for the cost of delivery? Not necessarily. This is not a service that the airlines advertise. It's not even a service they will offer you over the telephone. However, if you need the ticket right away, all you have to do is ask them to send it overnight. When you consider it, overnight delivery makes great economic sense for them. The airline would pay a 10 per cent commission to a travel agency to write up the ticket. It would cost them $100 on a $1,000 ticket. If they pay $8.75 for a delivery, they can save themselves $91 *and* demonstrate to a frequent passenger that they are providing extraordinary personal service.

It gets to be even more of a bargain when you remember that these people are in the transportation business. It's highly likely that they have special arrangements with one or more overnight express delivery services. It probably costs them virtually nothing to put your ticket in your hands overnight. However, it won't happen unless you ask.

You Gotta Ask, Part 2

You and Your Travel Agent

One of the first opportunities an executive traveller has to save money is with his or her travel agent. Ten per cent is the standard commission travel agents earn on airline tickets. Because times are hard in the travel business, many agents are now rebating – splitting their commission with their best clients. Often this means that they will do little more for you than write up your ticket. However, this is about all the experienced executive traveller armed with an OAG really wants them to do anyway.

Some agencies rebate on any airfare. Others require a minimum ticket price. If you do a significant volume of business, ask your travel agent for a rebate. You'll most likely get the discount if you request it, but most people don't ask. If you are a good volume client but the agency refuses, call around. It shouldn't be too difficult to find an agency willing to give you the break you deserve.

It pays to keep track of the fluctuating relationships between airlines and travel agencies. If your travel agent is suddenly urging you to fly TWA, perhaps it's because that airline has been offering an 18 per cent commission to travel agents for booking business or first class tickets on transcontinental round trips, such as those between New York and Los Angeles.

Does this TWA offer constitute a 'bribe' by the airline that compromises your travel agent's 'independence'? (Remember what I said in Chapter 3 about how a travel agent making a commission from the airlines sometimes forgets who the client really is.) Certainly it does. However, if you find out about it and you are willing to fly TWA, there's no reason why your travel agent shouldn't split the bribe with you and give you a 9 per cent rebate on the cost of your flight.

You Are How You Fly

First Class v. Tourist Class

Nothing clarifies the pecking order in a corporate hierarchy as plainly as who flies what class when travelling on company matters. From an outsider's perspective there are two impressions made by the few firms that let their senior managers fly first class: 1) they treat their executives extravagantly well; and 2) they don't keep a prudent eye on their expenditures.

Image and Status

Within a firm, however, the tug-of-war over first class travel usually boils down to a question of status. Travelling first class validates an executive's perceived sense of personal worth to the company. Noses get out of joint when those who believe themselves 'entitled' to first class travel find themselves in steerage in the back of the plane. At such times someone in my position is likely to hear a great deal about how important it is for the 'image of the company' for an executive to be seen in the front cabin. I've had executives in my own firm ask for permission to fly first class because a client was going to be on the same flight in first class, and they didn't want to be seen with all the tourists at the back. Their reason: they didn't want to be seen flying economy because it put our company in a bad light. You can learn a lot about people's inflated egos by how hard they argue about issues of this sort.

I actually believe it puts our company in a good light because it demonstrates that we are being responsible about costs. I am far less swayed by image problems of this kind than I am by arguments which are rooted in personal physical limitations, practicality and efficiency.

The 'need' to fly first class because a client is flying with you and you have to be perceived as his or her peer is far less persuasive with me than the need to fly first class because

- That time together on the plane is the only opportunity you will have to talk something over with the client.
- You suffer from a bad back.
- You need to sleep on a long intercontinental flight in order to be rested and effective during a full day of appointments and meetings immediately upon arrival.

Integrity

I am assuming a high degree of integrity on the part of my readers. The last thing I would want my book to be used for is to fleece a company for the cost of luxury travel when it is not warranted, or when everyone else in the firm is going through a round of close-to-the-bone budget-cutting.

I applaud the business travellers who use their own upgrade stickers garnered through their frequent flyer programmes to boost themselves out of economy class in order to have a more pleasant travel experience. From a management perspective it demonstrates a team-player attitude towards company travel. At International Management Group, we've had all kinds of policies on the various classes of travel, depending on fares and the deals we've been able to negotiate with the airlines. There have been occasions when we have said to an executive that if he flies first class or business class the company will pay part of the difference, but he's got to pay part of it as well. If someone is truly sincere about the 'need' to fly first class, he should be willing to put up part of the cost out of his own pocket. We might split the cost 50–50, or if the case is truly compelling, we'd pick up two-thirds and the employee would pay one-third.

Doing Business in First Class

I've been able to do a lot of paperwork on the plane, but flying first class has rarely led to new business opportunities for me, perhaps because I try to sleep on my flights. Other travellers, particularly in the entertainment field, however, have sometimes been able to put first class to use. Henry Rogers, founder of the Los Angeles-based Rogers & Cowan public relations firm, tells the story of one of his account executives who violated the company's 'economy class only' policy. On his own authority, without telling anyone about it, the executive had been flying first class between Los Angeles and New York.

It was a major offence, a significant breach of company policy, made without consultation. Rogers called the offender into his office, confronted him with his malfeasance, and was somewhat taken aback by his executive's levity in what he considered a very serious situation.

'I was wondering how long it would take you to catch on,' he told Rogers, laughing. 'In fact, I've kept a record of the results of my first class travel in the past year.' The executive produced a notebook and read Rogers the log of his eight transcontinental flights, including the difference in cost between economy and first class travel, and the names of the people he had met and talked with on each flight.

Then he played his trump card. 'The contacts I made on those flights brought four new high-paying clients to Rogers & Cowan. However, here is my personal cheque for the difference between the two fares.' With that, he placed the cheque on Henry Rogers's desk. Rogers took the cheque and tore it up without looking at it. Although he did not revise the company policy, Rogers did issue a special dispensation for his intrepid account executive, with the proviso that it was only in effect as long as first class travel continued to pay benefits to Rogers & Cowan.

Business Class

Business class on many airlines can be a viable and affordable alternative to first class. It is usually head and shoulders above economy travel – but not always. On lengthy flights, the amenities offered in business class generally approach those of first class, with roomier seats, better cuisine and free entertainment. However, on shorter hops, especially within

Europe, business class can be only a marginal improvement. Business class is surely not worth a premium if the food is better and the alcohol is gratis but the seat is the same cramped size as that in economy.

In general, international business class service is far superior to domestic US business class service. On carriers based in the United States, this is true even on the same airline. I was on one American Airlines flight from Los Angeles to Paris that stopped in Chicago for a change of aircraft. Booked as a first class passenger for the LA–Chicago leg, I was 'just' a business class passenger for the Chicago–Paris portion of the trip.

Domestic first class service was indifferent at best. The flight attendants seemed to be sleepwalking through their duties. However, the business class international service was superior, far better than American's domestic first class service, and indeed better than many international first class flights I'd experienced. I came to the conclusion that the flight attendants closed the privacy curtain between first class and business class not to keep business class passengers from seeing what the first class passengers were getting, but to prevent the first class passengers from realizing that business class service was virtually indistinguishable from their own.

Many airlines have recently upgraded their business class service, including Air France, Cathay Pacific and Japan Airlines. The most innovative business class may well be on Richard Branson's upstart Virgin Airlines, whose 'Upper Class' service is available between New York and London, and Los Angeles and London. Virgin's business class amenities include reclining seats of first class proportions, stand-up bars and lounges (reminiscent of those on the first generation of 747s more than twenty years ago), an inflight entertainment system giving each passenger his or her choice of movies, and free limousine pick-up on departure and delivery on arrival. On some flights a masseuse and manicurist are also on board. What more do Virgin's first class passengers get? Nothing. There is no first class, only Upper Class.

By forcing other carriers to upgrade their own service just

to retain market share, Virgin's amenities have benefited transatlantic business class passengers on other airlines as well. Virgin has certainly spurred British Airways to further refinements in their already generally excellent service. This is by no means uncommon – a rule of thumb to bear in mind is that the more hotly contested a route is, the better business class will be (and for that matter first class and economy as well). You can expect the very best service on heavily-travelled transcontinental and intercontinental business routes, such as LA–Tokyo, LA–New York, New York–London and New York–Paris, where competition among the various carriers is keen.

On travel to more remote or more vacation-orientated destinations, it pays to be cautious. On these kinds of routes, there is a much higher probability that business class may not be worth the money. Consult your OAG or question the reservation agent closely when booking. If you are not familiar with the airline or the aircraft in service on this particular run, make sure you know how big the seat is, how much legroom there is between rows, and whether business class has its own cabin. This last is crucial – on some airlines, business class is like an accordion, stretching if bookings in economy are light, but crumpling down to just a few rows if economy reservations are heavy. I find this unacceptable. Business class service should not be subject to the vagaries of economy class reservations. If an airline is able to turn business into economy at will and vice versa, there isn't enough difference between the two classes of service to justify the added expense. Either find another airline, or save the money and fly economy.

Indeed, if the flight is a short one, let's say two hours or less, the benefits of either business or first class travel may be marginal. I can sleep on a plane under almost any circum-stances, and for two hours anyone can survive the indignities of economy. The business traveller needs to decide whether the money spent by flying business or first class might be better spent by flying economy and allocating the difference to a more desirable hotel room or other amenities which will make your travel more enjoyable. After all, you'll spend a lot more time in your hotel room than you will on the plane for a short flight. Put your money where it will do you and your company the most good.

Some corporations have made this company policy. I know of companies who have started to offer senior executives a personal financial incentive *not* to fly first class. Some authorize a generous hotel room upgrade for the duration of the stay. Others pay half the difference between the economy and first class fares directly to the executive as a bonus.

How Good a Bed Do You Need?

On a long transcontinental or intercontinental flight, what do you do? If you're like most executive travellers, you eat a little, drink a little, and work a little – but mostly you sleep. That means that despite the fact that all airlines try to win you over with their inflight food and service, that is not what the business traveller is really paying for. What you are actually buying is not a seat, but a bed.

How good a bed do you need? It depends on how long your flight is and whether you are a good sleeper on flights. You certainly pay a premium for a seat that allows you a fighting chance at sleep. According to a recent Condé Nast *Traveler* magazine study of service between New York and various destinations in Europe, business class and first class passengers pay a great deal more for a few inches of comfort. The average economy class ticket was $442 round trip, with a seat width of 18 inches and a pitch (distance between your seatback and the upright seatback in front of you) of 31 inches. In business class, the average ticket price jumped to $3,367 with a seat width of 21 inches and a pitch of 40 inches. In first class, the average ticket price was $5,709, with a seat width of 22 inches and a pitch of 60 inches.

In dollar terms, a business class passenger on a transatlantic round-trip flight was paying $325 an inch for extra legroom, and $975 per inch for more rump room. The first class passenger was paying $182 per inch for more legroom than an economy class traveller, and $117 per inch for the space gained over business class. He or she paid $1,316 per inch for more room for his or her posterior than was available in economy. The extra inch of seat width in first class compared with business class cost $2,342.

If you can sleep on a plane and arrive rested, the cost may well be worth it. However, if try as you might you can't sleep on a plane and suffer from terrible jet lag no matter what, you'd be better off surviving the flight as best you can in economy and putting the money into a good hotel suite.

Television host Michael Parkinson suffers no matter how he flies: 'I've never been able to beat jet lag at all. I have a metabolism which requires at least seven days to recuperate if I go to Australia. It's a full seven days before I stop falling asleep with my head in the soup. A man named MacGregor once told me, "There's no such thing as jet lag. All you have to do is don't eat, don't drink, wrap your feet in brown paper and lie on the floor of the aeroplane." I actually tried it once. I didn't eat, didn't drink, wrapped my feet in paper bags and just lay there. It still took me seven days to recover.'

Saturday Night Fever

I recognize that by company policy, many business travellers, especially in difficult economic times, have no choice but to fly economy, no matter whether it's a weekly trip from Sydney to Melbourne or a monthly jaunt from Dallas to Madrid. However, all too often business travellers get nicked for full economy, or 'Y' class fare. Considerable discounts can be achieved by buying tickets a week or two before the date of departure, but most of these seven- or fourteen-day advanced purchase tickets have an irritating proviso appended to them: to qualify, you must stay over a Saturday night. Economy class business travellers, the vast majority of whom want to be in their own home on a Saturday night, are the intended victims of this stipulation.

For a trip between London and New York, the difference is

not insignificant. As I write this, a round-trip economy ticket from London to New York, including a Saturday night stay-over, can be yours on Air India for £160, on Virgin Atlantic for £199, or on British Airways for £240. The fully flexible (and fully priced) economy fare is £720. (You'll find the same daft pricing on domestic US flights. Depending on what airline you fly, the round-trip unrestricted economy fare between New York and Los Angeles is approximately $1,300, versus less than $350 for a ticket purchased a week or two in advance with a Saturday night stay.) It's irritating, to say the least. There are few inflight experiences more galling than spending several hours wedged into a middle seat in economy, squeezed between two fellow passengers who paid less for their two tickets combined than you paid for yours.

Unless you stay over a Saturday, it may seem that there's no way around the problem. Let's say a business traveller wants to fly from Los Angeles to New York and back again next week. He wants to leave on a Monday and return on Wednesday. He's not staying over a Saturday so he's out of luck, right?

Wrong.

It may sound counter-intuitive, but the answer for the clever business commuter who is a repeat traveller between the same two cities is to book two flights rather than one. In our Los Angeles–New York example, the first flight would be a round trip LAX–JFK–LAX, leaving Los Angeles on Monday and returning, well, let's say seven weeks from now. The second flight is a round trip originating in your destination city, in this example New York. The JFK–LAX–JFK round trip would leave New York on Wednesday and return, again, seven weeks from now. (The exact dates of the return flight segments on both tickets are relatively unimportant. It could be two weeks from now, or six weeks from now. However, if you can pinpoint the date and schedule of your second trip, you're that much further ahead.)

The important thing is that both round trips are long enough to include a Saturday night stay. For the first trip, use the LAX–JFK flight coupon from the first ticket, and the

JFK–LAX flight coupon from the second ticket. The remaining flight coupons are used for the second trip.

What have you done? You've booked two trips for less than the price of one, and in the process saved over $1,800, without giving up anything. By my evaluation, someone clever enough to have pulled this off is entitled to a limo and a couple of very nice meals on the expense report.

Cabs, Limos, and the Bottom Line

When you travel on business, unless you are an individual entrepreneur, never lose sight of the fact that you are spending someone else's money. I own my own company. When I travel, I can measure for myself whether to spend an extra $200 on a limousine because it makes me happier, or whether I want the extra $200 in the profit line of the company. I hold myself accountable for my expenditures. I'm not trying to impress anyone; it has nothing to do with my 'image'.

Although I can make a decision to get a limo or not on my own authority, the questions I ask myself are the same as the ones any business traveller should be able to answer, even if they come from the chief financial officer of General Motors or an auditor from the Inland Revenue: 'Can I get $200 worth of work done in the car? Is the added convenience worth $200 in time saved versus the hassle of getting a series of cabs or the struggle and expense of parking a rental car?'

A limousine to me is almost always worth it. I work in cars a great deal, dictating in them or going over paperwork. In cities where we have offices, I will often ask one of my secretaries to accompany the driver in the limo coming to the airport to pick me up, so I can work with her on the way back into town. I also use the phone in the car a great deal. If my home office hasn't already done so, I can determine the latest on-time status of the flight, confirm hotel reservations in my destination city, and verify meeting dates, times, and agendas.

A limousine doesn't have to be 35 feet long and seat seven

people to be functional. Many limousine services offer sedans with car phones. If you are travelling alone, there's plenty of room to spread out. In fact, I prefer cars that are not ostentatious. There's no point in having everyone point at your limo wondering which rock star or politician you might be. In London I have a car and driver. The car is an estate car, or station wagon. It holds a lot of luggage, and is great if I'm having a business meeting on the way to or from the airport. I can eliminate clutter and put my briefcase behind the seat, but I have access to papers and documents if I need them.

You and Your Expense Account

Guard Your Image

It's a good idea to be sensitive to how your travel expenditures will be perceived by others within your firm. The ill will you engender by flamboyant high-end travel, even if ultimately it is financially beneficial to the company, may poison your in-house relationships. From this perspective, it is far preferable for an executive traveller to select a hotel with those useful but conspicuous 'frills' included in the basic cost of the room. This is especially true if the company is facing a round of budget or personnel cuts. Itemized costs for health clubs and limousines may look a bit too much like 'let them eat cake'. The executive at Rogers & Cowan who always flew first class to New York may have brought in a bundle of new contracts, but I'll bet he didn't endear himself to his colleagues who were still stuck in economy class.

Flag Your Eyebrow-Raisers

He probably wouldn't have endeared himself to me, either. Although I would, of course, have been delighted that he had brought in so much new business through his new contacts in first class, I would not have been pleased by his catch-me-if-you-can attitude. Henry Rogers tore up his cheque, but I'm not so sure I would have. I may well have permitted him to fly first class in the future, but I also might have accepted the cheque to teach him to clear that stuff ahead of time. If you have an eyebrow-raiser like that – an egregious expense that's way out of line but justifiable – I believe it is far better to call attention to it upon submittal than to wait for it to be challenged.

If you have the perfect answer to 'Why did you fly first class?', short-circuit the interrogation process and save everyone (including your superior) a lot of time. It doesn't take much to annotate your expense account, saying, 'Joe Smith was on my flight. I upgraded myself and concluded a $50,000 sale.'

It happens in our company as well. There is a very successful restaurant in Miami called Joe's Stone Crab, which doesn't take reservations. One of my executives submitted a $150 expense account for a meal there – $110 for the dinner, plus a $40 tip. Because of the outlandish size of the tip, it got bounced up to me. The executive explained that a leading tennis player was with him. Although the player in question is now a superstar in the tennis world, his face was not at that time necessarily one a *maître d'* would recognize. The line at Joe's Stone Crab was huge, so my employee tipped the *maître d'* $20 to get a table. The other $20 was the waiter's tip on a $110 meal, which was acceptable. I thought he handled it very expeditiously, and the extra $20 was money very well spent in service to a valuable client. However, if he had annotated his request for reimbursement when he handed it in, he would have showed a whole lot more responsibility than he did by submitting it and waiting for someone to catch it and refer it to me.

If you don't call attention to the discrepancy, it may appear as if you were trying to put a fast one over on your company. Once you have been challenged even on a justifiable outlay, your subsequent expense submittals are likely to receive far more scrutiny. If you're supposed to stay at a hotel for $150 a night and you spent $200, then rather than trying to slip it by, hoping nobody catches it, highlight it yourself. Call attention to it, but explain why you did it.

The Little Hotel Bill and How It Grew

On the other hand, $150 hotel rooms turn into $200 hotel rooms every night, all over the world. As a business traveller staying at a hotel, you are an easy mark for surcharges and hidden fees imposed by hoteliers who all too often seem to have their hand buried in your back pocket. Any business traveller who has ever awakened thirsty in the middle of the night has confronted the $10 bottle of mineral water and the $8 bottle of orange juice in the mini-refrigerator.

Sometimes you succumb. Sometimes you don't. One wise and wily associate of mine, who always brings her own water on planes (see Chapter 3), packs some extra bottles of Perrier for her hotel room for just such occasions. She only runs into difficulty when she has to remove some bottles from the refrigerator to make room for her own water. Often the bottles removed turn up as charges on her statement, even though they were not consumed and were placed prominently on the dresser.

Then there is the long arm of government. Room occupancy taxes levied by governments large and small cannot be avoided. Nevertheless, they can be shocking. Most British hotels quote room rates that include the 17.5 per cent VAT, but you have to add your own 10–15 per cent service charge when the bill is presented to you. Other hotels tack on a 15 per cent service charge but add the VAT later on. In New York City, there are no service charges but hotel guests pay a whopping 19.25 per cent in taxes over and above the cost of their room. That makes the $150 hotel room a $179 hotel room, even before you pick up the phone.

Hotel Phone Charges

The most maddening charges are associated with costs which I believe ought to be part of the service, such as toll-free phone calls and receipt of faxes. It is quite understandable to charge guests for sending faxes, but to charge them anywhere from 50 cents to $2.50 per page for incoming faxes strikes me as nothing but gougery.

At the otherwise wonderful Stanhope Hotel in New York, an associate made only local calls, credit-card calls, and toll-free calls to the airlines to firm up his outbound flight plans. For a three-day stay, there were over $60 in phone charges on his bill. He was not only charged $1 for each toll-free call and an 'access fee' for each credit-card call, he was also charged for each local call. Some calls were 80 cents; others were $2. What was the difference? It wasn't the time of day. When he examined the bill carefully, he found that the 'cheap' calls were calls which did not even go through – when he had run into a busy signal or someone was not in. The expensive ones were those when he had actually talked to someone. The only times when it didn't cost money to pick up the receiver were when someone called in or when he asked for a wake-up call.

Compared with the other costs of doing business on the road, hotel phone charges are not a lot of money. Nevertheless, I like to ask for a full statement of them when I check in, especially if I'm registering at a hotel where I've never stayed before. Hotel telephone surcharges are often between 15 and 30 per cent above what the phone company charges. You may also find that many hotels have a minimum three-minute charge for an operator-assisted call (i.e., any call that is not local), even if you only talk for thirty seconds.

When I check in, I also like to ask how calls will be shown on my statement. I like to be assured that when my bill arrives, all the calls are logged as to time, duration, and phone number called. Although most newer hotel billing systems in the United States do itemize calls in this manner, this is not always the case in Europe and Asia. It's not very enlightening to receive a bill with a long list of telephone charges, with no more description than 'local call' or 'long distance'.

To be fair, hotels spend a great deal of money updating their telephone equipment. The fax and modem revolutions have placed increased demands on phone service. Maintenance and staffing add further to costs. However, in my judgement these expenses don't justify the premium that is exacted from the business traveller. Hotels spend a lot of money installing toilets and showers, too, but I don't have to pay extra every time I use one. The same is true for health facilities. In most hotels, use of the health club is included in the cost of the room.

I'd much prefer to pay more for the room itself and have all local phone charges included. As it is, I often get hotel bills that are fifteen pages long because I use the phones a lot and each call is listed separately. It's wise to keep a log of phone calls you make while in your hotel room, so that you are prepared to dispute any questionable charges. Many executives do this as a matter of course, just for their own records.

Beating the High Cost of
International Hotel Phone Charges

Many foreign hotels (especially in Europe) are shameless about extorting a pound of flesh from the business traveller to make an overseas call. Hotel surcharges of up to 300 per cent on the cost of an international call are unfortunately not uncommon – nor are they prominently displayed or announced. All too often, travellers get the highly unpleasant bad news only when they are checking out. By that time, of course, it's too late. When you're rushing for the airport, you're in a very weak position to dispute a $80 charge for a ten-minute call from Frankfurt to New York.

I always ask for a statement of telephone charges when I check in, particularly in a new hotel or one where I have not recently been a guest. I also ask how the calls will be shown on my bill. If the calls are not itemized, I make a point of keeping a very careful record of my outgoing calls.

Travellers unwilling to pay hotel surcharges know they can make overseas calls from international telephone booths, or from government post offices with international telecommunications facilities. If your objective is to contact your family to let them know you've arrived safely, this arrangement is inconvenient but workable. However, for important business phone calls in which you need to sound professional and have access to documents or statistics spread out around you, it is entirely unacceptable. Only Superman should do business in a phone booth.

When you call international long distance from your hotel room, the point at which you incur the charge is right at the switchboard, when the hotel operator places your call. Therefore the way to beat the system is to go around it and place the call yourself. In doing so you have an unlikely ally – the telephone companies. A number of them now offer charge cards which give you access to special services. With some, it is possible to dial a local number from your hotel room in a foreign city and be connected to an operator who places your call, or to a recorded voice that leads you through the international calling process. A charge for a local call appears on your hotel bill abroad; the charge for the international call appears on your phone bill at home.

Hotel Phone Charges That Are Worth It

For a hotel with a state-of-the-art phone system, however, I don't mind paying a premium. The Hilton in Lake Buena Vista, Florida, has a telecommunications system that controls far more than your incoming and outgoing calls. Buttons on the phone can turn on the heat or the air conditioning. Other buttons control the TV. The room phone also serves a security function – it lights up if the room door is not locked and bolted.

Each phone unit provides access to two separate phone lines, a hold button, and word- and data-processing capabilities. If you don't want to be disturbed, you can press a button which will block your line and forward your calls to the front desk where the staff will take messages. The system even works when you're not there. Housekeeping staff use the phone to key in a code when they enter your room, and another code when they leave. As an energy saver, the system also adjusts the temperature when guests leave their rooms, and then readjusts it to 'occupied' status when guests key back in.

The Rihga Royal in New York will give you a cellular phone to use during your stay. The cellular phone is tied into your room phone. If you don't pick up the phone in your room within four rings, it automatically forwards the call to your cellular phone – anywhere in the city. If you don't pick up on the cellular within three rings, it bounces back to the hotel and takes a message on your voice mail. How much for this super service? $15 per day in a standard room, no charge if you are staying in a suite. (Rihga suites are also equipped with fax machines.)

This is a bargain. Isn't it inconsistent to complain about being nicked for a few bucks for local calls but happily spend $15 a day for a cellular? Nope. I live by the phone. Our business is dependent on maintaining communication with cities from Tokyo to Cleveland to London to Paris. For me, this kind of telephone service is a bargain. Unlike the hotel charges for garden variety phone service that I grumble about, I'll happily spend the extra money for extraordinary service like this because it makes my trip so much smoother. And that's a very different thing from spending it when I get the feeling that I have no choice and I'm being ripped off.

Pay More if It's Worth It

In other words, pay more if it's worth it. Let me give you an example of the mental gyrations I go through to decide when something is actually 'worth it'.

In November 1992 I locked myself into a difficult week at the end of the month. I had to be in Frankfurt on Sunday, 22 November. That night I would fly to Milan to deliver a speech on Monday to Italian sports executives. On Tuesday morning,

I would fly from Milan to London on my way to Edmonton, Alberta, where, on Wednesday afternoon, I was scheduled to give the first of two speeches. I also planned to attend a hockey game on Wednesday night. On Thursday morning I would fly to Calgary to give the second speech, after which I was planning to fly on to Maui, Hawaii, where my wife was hosting the tenth annual Betsy Nagelsen Kapalua Pro-Am Invitational tennis tournament.

My wife's tournament is a holiday for me and the sort of bonus that makes the five intense days preceding it seem worthy of my best effort. After my speech in Calgary, my fondest wish was to arrive in Maui as early as possible. My OAG revealed that I could get there at 8.30 on Thursday night if I flew Canadian Pacific from Calgary to Honolulu and then changed planes to Maui. The only kicker: the Canadian Pacific flight didn't have first class service and the people who were sponsoring my speech were going to reimburse me for a first class ticket. If I wanted first class service from Calgary to Hawaii, my alternative would be to fly through Denver and then on to Hawaii. However, I wouldn't get in until midnight.

In the end I decided that arriving early was more important than flying first class. But I didn't intend to fly in misery. Instead, I booked two business class seats side-by-side (which cost $250 more than the single first class seat I was contractually entitled to). The $250 would come out of my pocket, but it would be worth it if I could put my briefcase next to me and work or really stretch out and recuperate.

The thought process is simple: once I make up my mind that a trip is a worthwhile exercise, I want to make that worthwhile exercise as comfortable as possible for myself.

As it turned out, when I showed up at the Canadian Pacific counter at Calgary airport to claim my two business class seats, the ticketing agent informed me, 'The flight is only half full, Mr McCormack. You won't really need this second seat, since no one will be seated next to you anyway. Why don't you save the extra ticket for another time?'

It is this sort of little thrill that makes business travel such an interesting adventure. Despite all the efforts to make sure that everything goes my way, sometimes things work out even better!

6 The Travelling Office

When you mention 'travelling office' today, most people think of laptop computers, mobile telephones, beepers, fax machines, and other technology. These electronic marvels can offer valuable assistance, but they are not my primary definition.

For me, the travelling office is both a state of mind and a system of organization for continuing to do business effectively while on the road. Since I am on the road many more days of the year than I am in any one office building, I am constantly 'in' my travelling office – whether I am in a hotel room, sitting on an aeroplane, or in one of my actual offices at a branch of International Management Group.

Yes, I have several rooms in different cities with walnut panelling, impressive plaques on the walls, bookcases full of important-looking volumes, large desks, filing cabinets, and so forth. But that is not where the work gets done. The work gets done in my head. That is also the truth for people who operate primarily in an office environment. For all of us, the best 'office' is one in which we have immediate access to necessary decision-making information, comfortable surroundings in which to think, and communications facilities to discuss our thoughts with associates.

Do You Need to Bring That Plaque on the Wall?

Earlier on, I discussed the need for 'attitude adjustment' in order to be more efficient and positive about business travel.

Part of that adjustment is rethinking what an 'office' means to you and how you bring it on the road. For example, be honest with yourself: are the architectural surroundings and decorations of your physical office important to you and – more important – to your clients? If your answer is Yes, that tells you that you may need to spend money on fairly luxurious accommodations when you travel. If the answer is No, then let's discuss what aspects of your office you do need to bring with you when you travel.

In my experience, there are real advantages to conducting business while travelling. You can cut down on your paperwork, make better use of your secretary, focus on the most essential aspects of your work, and see your job and your company in a new perspective. Your travelling office can truly be a more efficient version of that room in your office building if you plan to make it that way.

Being 'Out of Town' Has Its Advantages

No doubt you have read the management studies about the high percentage of telephone calls, memos and letters dealing with various problems received in an office on Monday which – if unanswered – resolve themselves by Friday. You can get the same effect by being 'out of town'. Callers who insist on the urgent need to speak to you in the office in London suddenly lose their urgency when they have to reach you in Singapore or Sydney. Employees who would have involved you in a decision-making meeting find that they can summarize their recommendations in a memo for your approval when you are not in the office. Almost everyone tends to cut down on the conversational chit-chat when they are talking to you on a long-distance line from the other side of the world.

In other words, when you are travelling, your business associates will extend to you a level of courtesy and thoughtfulness about your time that they should be giving you every day. When you are not easily accessible, your associates will do a little bit more of the work themselves. But – and this is a major BUT – be sure that they are reporting to you on what they are doing. The best part of a travelling office is that you can be selectively inaccessible while staying in close touch with your business. How close depends on the lines of communication you establish, and we will discuss that in a moment.

The Time Zone Advantage

In an international business such as mine, travelling through time zones can offer you opportunities to extend your business day that many travellers do not consider. For example, I always get the jump on my business day by rising early. If I am on the east coast of the United States, at 5 or 6 o'clock in the morning I talk to associates in Europe (five or six hours ahead), and if I am on the west coast I catch New York business people in their offices at 7 a.m. my time (10 a.m. theirs) before I have an 8 o'clock breakfast meeting in my hotel. After a business day in Los Angeles or San Francisco is over, I make calls to Asia before dinner and have the advantage of reaching people there at the beginning of the next day. I always schedule my telephone call list with one of those convenient little world time-zone maps in mind in order to calculate the most efficient times.

This is another simple area in which too many business people feel 'victimized'. They complain to me that wherever they are in the world, they are never near a telephone when they need to talk to their home offices. With a little planning, their 'problem' can be an opportunity. If time changes make communications with your office difficult during normal business hours, arrange telephone appointments with your secretaries or associates at home. Most of them will be impressed that you are making the effort to talk to them after their dinner time – when, in fact, this may be a convenient early morning hour for you.

Just as your associates will be more considerate of your time when they call you long distance, they will also be more likely to take your calls when you call long distance. I am a strong believer in setting up specific times for telephone appointments and placing the calls myself when I am on the road, so generally my calls are expected. But, when I have to call someone unexpectedly, the news that 'Mr McCormack is calling from Bangkok' will often inspire a secretary to put someone else on hold who is calling locally.

What to Bring – and What *Not* to Bring

I do not presume to know the diverse business requirements of my readers nor the specific materials each of you may need to carry on a trip. But I do know that most business people head towards the airport woefully disorganized, usually without many time-saving and useful tools, and often carrying materials that they don't need on the road. To know how to pack your 'travelling office', you need to plan three ways of bringing materials:

- Materials and equipment you will need *en route* to the airport, at the airport, on the aeroplane, and *en route* to the hotel. This will usually be in your carry-on bags.
- Materials and equipment you will need to take in your checked luggage to work efficiently in your hotel room.
- Materials and equipment that can be shipped to the hotel or rented in the city you are visiting.

Mark McCormack's Travel Itinerary Checklist

Let's start with your travel itinerary. Most busy executives are satisfied with the computer printout provided by a travel agency, which contains the bare bones of airline, hotel, and sometimes rental car arrangements. This is not adequate. Here is a check list for the information a thorough business traveller's itinerary should incorporate:

1. The name and telephone number of the car service picking you up.

2. The car number, licence plate number and name of driver for your pick-up.

3. The name of the person who confirmed your pick-up and the time of the last reconfirmation by your office.

4. The names and telephone numbers for two or three other car services (especially necessary if you are not leaving from your office).

5. Your flight number, departure time, gate number, seat number, and the most exclusive telephone number for flight information from that airline. (That is, if you are a Gold Card Frequent Flyer, make sure you have the Gold Card information number instead of the general number. Be certain your itinerary also includes your Gold Card number.)

6. Directions to your departure area and the airline club lounge (especially important if you are departing from an unfamiliar airport).

7. The times and flight numbers of alternative flights that you have booked, with telephone numbers for those airlines.

8. The names and telephone numbers of Special Services personnel at the airline. (Or, if you have particular contacts at the airline club lounge, include those names.)

9. The name and telephone number of the car service picking you up in your arrival city.

10. The car number, licence plate number and name of driver for your pick-up in the arrival city.

11. The name of the person who confirmed your pick-up and the time of the last reconfirmation by your office.

12. Specific information about best transportation alternatives at the airport if your car does not arrive on schedule.

13. Name, address, telephone number, and confirmation code number for your hotel.

14. Specifics of your arrangements with the hotel, including rates, room location, special requests. The name of the person with whom these arrangements were confirmed – or, better still, a copy of the confirmation fax from the hotel.

15. The names of the hotel manager and concierge.

16. The names, addresses and telephone numbers of two alternative hotels.

17. The name and telephone number of your travel agent. Get the home telephone number, too (just requesting this will guarantee you a more careful quality of service).

18. A home telephone number for your secretary. (She is an important lifeline – more about that below.)

19. The address of one or more banks or other locations where you can use your ATM card (automatic teller machine or 'cash' card), and their hours of operation.

This checklist sounds as though it might be a lot of work. But, in fact, it simply requires you or your secretary to ask just a few more questions while you are setting up an itinerary. Much of the information can be recycled trip after trip. And the first time you need that information, the extra effort will have been repaid.

The next group of travel documents that you should carry with you is quite valuable in an emergency. **Always carry them in a place separate from the originals**. These are photocopies of your most essential documents:

- Passport.
- Visas.
- Other relevant ID.
- Medical prescriptions.
- Insurance and credit cards.
- Traveller's cheque details.
- Airline tickets.
- Driving licence.

At home or with your secretary, you should also have photocopies of your credit cards. When you are going to a foreign country, you should have the address and telephone number of your embassy, as well as the name of a contact at the embassy. If you purchase traveller's cheques, here is the place to note down the serial numbers, in the event of theft. Again, this procedure may sound too cautious, but you will be very happy to have the information in the unpleasant event that you need it.

Don't Leave Home Without the Pocket OAG

No business traveller should leave home without a copy of the **OAG Pocket Flight Guide**. This Official Airline Guide comes in separate editions for North America, Europe/Africa/ Middle East, Pacific/Asia, and Latin America/Caribbean – each of which is updated monthly. This puts information about all scheduled flights at your fingertips. Back at your office, a frequent business traveller should also have the OAG Desktop edition, which contains fuller information, including fares. This is your most essential tool in dealing with airlines and travel agencies.

In addition to those fundamental travel documents mentioned above, I always bring my most valuable business documents in two large briefcases that I carry on. From the time that I depart on a trip to the time that I set them down in a secure hotel room, they never leave my sight. They are under the airline seat in front of me, next to me in the limo, and in my hands during most transfers. Normally, I take only the materials I need for two weeks, although sometimes I have to carry a month's worth of documents.

The contracts and memos I need for my business undoubtedly will be different from the papers you carry for your business. But if you need them for your business, put them together in one carry-on bag (or, in my case, two), and treat that bag almost as though you were a bank courier who has it handcuffed to you.

In those briefcases, I carry a number of yellow pads, which

are what my computer-literate friends might call my data bases. For example, for a city such as London, I have a pad with lists of restaurants and notes on their qualities. Some restaurants I have tried and some are recommendations from associates – or suggestions from newspapers, magazines or travel newsletters which I may have clipped. After I have gone to a new place, I will usually add some notations on my yellow pad to remind me of the particular strengths of a restaurant or a *maître d*'s name or a dish that I liked. On another pad, I have the names of shops, art galleries, plays, concerts, or other experiences to which I can look forward. On another London pad, I have lists of friends, with addresses and telephone numbers. These personalized guidebooks – they could be notebooks or computer files, too – can be part of adding the Personal Touch to your travel experiences.

Regarding business documents, I avoid grabbing the entire file for a project unless I need to read it. I prepare a folder for each appointment that I have made, and in that folder I include copies – not originals – of the relevant papers. (The only time I carry original documents on a trip is when they need to be presented to a client or are contracts for signing.) My secretary keeps a duplicate of each folder so that she knows which documents I have and can refer to them quickly. I keep the folders in the chronological order of my appointments.

What *Not* to Bring on a Business Trip

Too Many Clothes

Most travellers, business people or not, overpack on the theory that they 'might' need that cardigan sweater (that they haven't worn at home in three years) for an early-morning golf game – or whatever. Part of the problem for many men (and I am not being sexist about this) is that they ask their wives to pack for them. Unless your wife has made business trips to Stockholm – dressed as a man, presumably! – how would she know what to pack for that trip? For fear of not preparing you for every contingency, she overpacks. The savvy business traveller takes responsibility for his or her own packing.

When I pack, I have my itineraries at hand, and I envision how I will be dressed and what materials I will need for each phase of the day. If I have planned to use the health club at a hotel, I will bring exercise clothes. But I don't just throw my sweats in a bag because I might need them. If you are going to be seeing the same business associates several times on a trip, you will need more changes of clothes. If you like to change shirts for the evening, as I do, calculate the need for laundering some of them with the overnight valet service at the hotel. With a few contingency exceptions – a raincoat or a folding umbrella – there should be a place on the schedule for every item in your bags.

The next time you waver between packing a 'nice to have' item on a business trip – say, a fourth business suit for a four-day trip – consult the following packing list of the *Daily Mail*'s intrepid sports columnist Ian Wooldridge. This remarkably lean but adequate list enumerates the entire contents of Mr Wooldridge's suitcase on a round-the-world tour of international sports events during which he was away from home for fifty-five days, travelled 32,400 miles, made twenty-three takeoffs and landings, and was subjected to temperatures that varied from sub-zero in St Moritz and Aspen to 109 °F in Melbourne.

    1 Navy lightweight suit
    1 Navy blazer
    1 Pair white cotton trousers
    1 Pair beige chino trousers
    1 Pair grey wool trousers
    1 Pair of salopettes (quilted skiing trousers)
    1 All-purpose quilted car jacket
    1 V-neck lambswool sweater
    1 Woollen ski hat
    1 Sun hat for fishing
    1 Pair black formal shoes

1 Pair brown leather docksiders
3 Dress shirts
3 Silk ties
4 Golf shirts
4 Boxer shorts
4 Pairs of socks
4 White handkerchiefs

Medicine bag (none of which was ever needed!):
anti-diarrhoea pills, painkillers, cold relievers,
multiple vitamins, plasters, block suntan cream,
anti-mosquito spray and antiseptic cream.

Standard wash kit, with lots of shampoo.

Too Much Paper

Not unlike throwing the entire closet into a bag, some business people throw the entire filing cabinet into their briefcases
on the 'just in case' theory. The smart business traveller
plans more carefully. If you sincerely intend to sort through
your mail and browse all those trade magazines on the plane,
then by all means put them in your carry-on bags. But
there is no point hauling pounds of paper on to the aeroplane
if it could be in your checked luggage or – even better –
overnighted to your hotel. Decide what you will have time to
do on your trip and plan when to do it. Schedule the packing
or shipping of materials accordingly.

Readers of my previous books on business know that I do
not believe in elaborate presentations for clients. (I think
these dog-and-pony shows tend to divert discussion from the
deal to the *show*.) But I recognize that demonstration equipment is essential in some businesses. It is *not* essential to
require each sales person or speaker to bring inordinate
amounts of equipment, boxes of catalogues, or company
supplies as excess baggage. When I see men and women in
the baggage claim areas struggling with large containers, I

wonder if their companies ever heard of air freight. This is poor planning in the extreme. Piano movers are not generally the most exhilarating speakers, and no one can be expected to give an energetic after-dinner presentation if he or she has been wrestling with heavy packages all day. Businesses that need demonstration equipment should plan to ship ahead.

The Magic Bag of Travel Tricks that Turns into a Life Raft

In addition to the valuable papers that must stay with you and the materials you intend to read or work with in transit, every smart business traveller should **pack a survival kit** – enough bare-bones essentials for a day or two – in your carry-on luggage. This small bag of 'travel insurance' might include:

- A fresh shirt.
- Prescription medicines.
- Personal toiletries, including a toothbrush, deodorant, make-up, razor, comb, hairbrush, shampoo, and compact hairdryer.
- Tissues.
- Aspirin.
- Spare contact lenses or eyeglasses.
- A change of socks (or pantihose).
- A change of underwear.

Of course, you may wish to add or substitute other indispensable items to your personal survival kit. On long flights, this kit is a pleasant convenience. However, when (not if) you are separated from your luggage – as a frequent flyer, this will happen to you eventually – this little bag is a joyous security. Far more baggage is misplaced than is permanently lost or stolen. Having interim clothing and supplies minimizes potential inconvenience if your luggage arrives after you do. If you are on a short trip, it can make the difference between being able to continue your trip and accomplish what you set out to do, and having either to extend your stay or turn around and come home. Moreover, if you are stranded at an airport or at an any-port-in-a-storm hotel by weather, labour problems or other travel difficulties, that bag will look a lot like your personal life raft.

What Can You Accomplish *en route* to the Airport?

One of the most foolishly wasted opportunities for business travellers is the trip to the airport. If you ask most travellers what they do while they are being driven for half an hour or an hour across familiar terrain, they will usually reply that they look out of the window or talk to the driver. Here's a chance to make time that the smart traveller doesn't miss. Frequently, I ask my assistant to make the trip with me so that I can go through mail or dictate some memos. Sometimes I will schedule a business meeting with an associate. He or she rides with me to the airport and occasionally we will continue our discussion in the airline lounge until my flight is called. Some executives regularly schedule business meetings in these lounges to save themselves the trip into town when they are visiting a branch office for the day.

There are many other ways you can use your time going to the airport, even if you don't have a limo and a secretary. One economical variation might be to drive your secretary to the airport – you can dictate *en route* – and let her drive the car back to your office. (Repeat the procedure when she picks you up from your return flight.) Or make a similar arrangement with an office colleague: if he or she wants a lengthy meeting with your full attention, here's the chance.

I have a friend who prefers to drive to the airport and enjoys listening to audiotapes of books on the way. As he was leaving for a recent trip, one of his junior executives handed him a tape.

'What's this?' he asked, hoping for a new bestseller.

'It's the report I've been trying to get you to read for two weeks,' answered the ambitious associate. He was rewarded with a phone call from the airport to congratulate him for a good report and for his innovative presentation.

Sometimes, depending upon the time of day, I will schedule a series of telephone calls from the car. If so, I try to alert the car service of my intentions to ensure that there's a phone in the car and to have my assistant set up telephone appointments. You can accomplish the same good use of time with a cellular telephone. At the very least, I'll use car travel time to sort through mail, although the movement of a car sometimes makes that less efficient than doing it on the aeroplane.

My Secretary Works *Harder* When I Am Out of Town

Periodically, I will visit the offices of a contact and notice a secretary reading a book or magazine in the mid-afternoon. Invariably, when I ask why she is not busy, she answers: 'Oh, my boss is out of town and I have nothing to do.' I shake my head in amazement. My secretaries work harder when I am out of town – and I am *always* out of town. I am blessed with some exceptionally dedicated and hard-working personal assistants. And I have trained them to give me maximum support as I travel. They keep my home office running and they keep my travelling office connected to events that occur while I am away. How does my secretary function as the prime connection to my travelling office? Let me count the ways:

1. **Pre-Trip Planning**
She assists in all of the pre-trip planning, so that she is aware of my travel logistics, the documents I am carrying, the places I will be visiting, the people I will be seeing, and the hour-by-hour specifics of my itinerary.

2. **Communications**
She talks with me several times a day at prearranged times to

keep me informed of phone calls, memos, minor or major crises, and general office functioning. She knows where to reach me at any time of the day if there is an emergency. She also knows not to bother me with anything less than an emergency when I am having important business conferences, in transit, or relaxing. Usually, I call her at the appointed times and I try to stick to a fairly rigid schedule. But when I make an unscheduled call, I expect that either she will be there or she will have left detailed instructions about where she can be reached. Nothing can be more frustrating than to call your assistant or one of your business associates for a piece of vital information and be sitting there listening to a bland recorded message or having someone say they have no idea where X or Y is. There is no time for 'telephone tag' when you are on the road, and the efficient business person plans his or her telephone appointments with the same care given to personal appointments. Your secretary must be available for your calls at all times. Depending upon my time zone, I call her at her home when necessary.

3. Confirmations and Revisions

My secretary reconfirms all travel arrangements, and she confirms both my personal and telephone appointments. As the schedule shifts (as inevitably it does), she prepares a new itinerary with detailed instructions for me each day, including lists of phone calls which must be returned.

4. Keeping in Touch with the Office

At the end of each day, in addition to the revised daily itinerary, my secretary provides me with what I call a 'Headline Fax'. This is simply an overnight report on the highlights of the previous business day. Results of meetings, important phone calls, reports from branch offices, significant pieces of mail, personal reminders – almost anything I should know about or that might need my attention is noted briefly on this fax. Ideally, it is the first piece of paper waiting for me in the morning, having been slipped quietly under the door in the middle of the night without setting off the blinking red light on my nightstand telephone. If I need more information about any item on the Headline Fax, my secretary can send it to me.

5. Crisis Management

When things go wrong, your secretary must be Crisis Central – because you are in no position to handle crisis details at a distance, even in the most efficient hotel room. She should be well-versed in how to get information to you, how to offer brief (usually non-committal) assurance to your clients, and how to convey your thoughts or instructions to associates if you are not able to give them directly. Sometimes, you are the cause of the crisis. If you are sick, stuck in a holding pattern over Heathrow, or diverted by a snafu – guess who must tactfully handle the apologies and the postponements?

The Telephone: Your Most Important Travel Tool

By now, it must be obvious that I regard the telephone as the most important tool that the business traveller uses. Airlines and hotels feel this way, too, which is why they are trying to outdo each other with telephone services – and charge exorbitantly for them. In order to maximize your travelling efficiency, you need access to the best telephone service almost continuously. The specific telephone services are changing rapidly, but you should know about a few of the most useful currently available.

In the United States, AT & T recently introduced an Easy-reach 700 service which allows you to carry one telephone number with you wherever you go in the USA. By dialling your personal 700 number, clients and associates can reach you through hotel phones, car phones, portable cellular phones, pay phones, or just about anywhere there is a telephone with a number. This is the ultimate forwarding service. You are not tied down to any particular phone, and people who need to reach you have one number where you can always be reached. Special, designated callers can even call you for no charge. The catch, of course, is that there are times when anyone would rather be out of touch. This is a useful service to supplement or substitute for your secretary.

At the most rudimentary level, every traveller – business or otherwise – should have a telephone charge card. These are free of charge and will save you money calling from most hotels. There is also a list of tie-line numbers for use in different countries, which help you to beat the escalating cost of long-distance calls. New companies are entering the long-distance telephone competition every day, so it may pay to shop around.

The business pages of every newspaper are inundated with advertisements for mobile telephones, car telephones, and cellular phones. If you don't own one, you will want to consider hiring a car service or a taxicab with a mobile telephone when you are *en route* to the airport. Perhaps there is no need to use it on most of your trips to the airport, but when there is a need, you will be glad to have it, and the additional cost, if any, is modest. The major car rental organizations have cars with mobile telephones that can be activated by credit cards, the cost and availability depending on the country you're in.

US cellular telephone owners will have little or no trouble using their phones anywhere in the United States and Canada. Beyond those borders many variables apply. The AMPS (Advanced Mobile Phone Service) system that is stand-ard in the US is technically usable in fifty other countries with compatible systems, but billing arrangements may be difficult. All of Europe works on the GSM standard, so renting a phone is your best option. Although the charges for cellular telephone use are still high, some travellers have found to their astonishment that those charges are less than the tele-phone surcharges some hotels are adding to your bill.

Think of Your Hotel Phone as a Pay Toilet

Because hotels know that the telephone is the second most important piece of equipment they provide (after a bed), some of them have decided to gouge business travellers with outrageous rates and surcharges on calls that cost the hotel little or nothing. I have heard hotel managers explain to me that they justify these charges because hotels have to spend millions to provide up-to-date telephone equipment. OK. Hotels spend millions on plumbing, too. Why don't they charge you every time you flush?

Most travellers do not find out about these unconscionable telephone rates until the end of their stay when they are handed a bill that is two or three times what they anticipated for the entire cost of their visit. Save yourself an unpleasant surprise by asking the hotels in your destination cities to provide their telephone policies and surcharge structures *before* you arrive. (While you're at it, request their charges for sending *and receiving* faxes.) Some of the flagrant abusers in this area may make you consider staying at another hotel. Enquire, also, whether your hotel blocks calls to telephone charge-card access lines. This practice has become common in several cities. If you plan to stay in a hotel that heaps draconian surcharges on your telephone use, you may want to consider borrowing a desk at a colleague's office for some phone time each day or investigating the availability of nearby pay telephone facilities. (Frankly, both choices would so negate any other pleasures of a hotel for me that I would go elsewhere.)

Assuming that you can endure the telephone rates, find hotels that provide the sort of telephone service a good business traveller requires. Personally, I need a room with at least two lines and at least three phones – one by the bedside, one in the bathroom, and one on the desk. In a larger suite, I need more phones. I don't use computer modems or fax equipment, but if you do, be sure that your hotel is updated to provide the necessary connections. Despite all of my best efforts, occasionally I still end up in a room with the phone on the wrong side of the bed or, worse, on the desk with a four-foot cord. One solution for the resourceful traveler is to **carry your own 25-foot telephone extension cord.** Most hotels use universal jacks. Just plug in and put the phone where you want to use it.

Making the Executive Club a Swank Office

A relatively new innovation in hotel service that is making the travelling office concept a reality is the 'club', 'concierge', or 'executive' floor. These can make the larger hotels where they are normally found far more pleasant for the business traveller. The idea is that a large lounge area, usually on one of the top floors of the hotel, provides privacy and luxury for small business meetings that would be awkward in a room. In addition to amenities such as computer terminals, photocopy machines, fax, phone and VCR, some of the clubs incorporate libraries with local information. Depending upon the style of business entertaining you need or the number of meetings you will be hosting, the club floor can be a useful asset.

Free hors-d'oeuvre, coffee and drinks in a prestigious atmosphere can make your business clients feel more comfortable than in a restaurant. Most of these clubs are also staffed with hotel employees prepared to do anything from changing your airline reservations to taking dictation. The most elaborate hotel clubs right now are found in Asia, places such as the Regency Club on top of the Grand Hyatt in Hong Kong which has a spectacular view of Victoria Harbour and a staff of eleven women and two men to tend to your every need. The Shangri-La chain throughout Asia features Horizon Floors with 24-hour business services. At the Hotel Seiyo Ginza in Tokyo, you are assigned a personal 'secretary' and 'room assistant' when you arrive.

For business travellers on a tight budget, these club floors can be a particular bargain. Often your membership of a frequent flyer or hotel frequent-traveller programme is enough to get you an upgrade on to these floors. But a serious business person who offers the potential of return business can usually negotiate an upgrade to the club floor if the hotel is not full – and few are full in these recessionary times. Even if you are not able to obtain a free upgrade, the additional cost for most of the clubs may be worth it to you in comfort and convenience.

Your Choice: Pads and Pencils or Laptops

In order to have a true travelling office, some business people need to bring along equipment. The fast pace of new technology, together with modern telecommunications linkage, is providing us with more efficient and economical equipment every month. Although I am still perfectly happy writing my notes and memos on a yellow pad with a pencil, I have been impressed by colleagues who can crunch numbers on a laptop with Lotus 1–2–3 spreadsheets or zap the latest version of a colour advertising campaign to a client via a modem. These electronic 'toys' can be expensive and cumbersome, but they make work more efficient for some travellers.

Today, you can purchase 486 laptop computers with large hard disks which will give you the computing power of the desktop models back in your office. You can transfer files and programs between desktops and laptops easily, and travelling representatives of data-intensive companies will benefit from these powerful units. One modest investment that I recommend to laptop owners is a password entry program that does not permit access to unauthorized persons. These protection programs are fairly standard now in offices, but business travellers often forget to put one on their portable unit.

If you decide to carry a laptop computer, inevitably you will need a modem, which allows you to communicate to other computers anywhere there is a telephone line. For large quantities of data – words, numbers, even pictures – a computer is a faster and more accurate tool than a fax. A modem can also connect your laptop computer to electronic networks all around the world which allow you to access databanks of current stock and bond information, medical or legal data, news wire services, and library services. One way to avoid the excessive telephone charges in hotel rooms is to **take advantage of E-mail or electronic data delivery systems** which will hold letters, messages or reports for you from anywhere in the world, and allow you to download them into the laptop in your hotel room.

The most annoying problem still facing electronic road warriors is battery life. Despite the manufacturers' promises, most laptop batteries will only hold up for two to three hours of normal use, which is far too short a time to make use of a flight from New York to Los Angeles. The serious road warrior simply carries extra batteries (make sure that they are easily replaced in your brand of laptop), and a charger if need be, and forgets it.

I Have Seen the Future, and It Computes

Despite my own preference for working with old-fashioned paper and pencil when I am on the road, I certainly take advantage of many technological advances, such as fax and cellular telephones. I am also convinced that the travelling business person of the future will use more and more electronics. The alert executive should be aware of the technology that is on the horizon.

In a few years, the next step in personal communications services (PCS) will be the satellite cellular. Instead of being chained to the local radio broadcast for your calls and counting on the development of international 'roaming' agreements, cellular telephone owners will be able to bounce their calls directly to and from communications satellites which will provide rapid access and better (lower noise) sound quality. Obviously, satellite fax and satellite computer modem connections will be available at about the same time. As we solve the problems of data compression, eventually individuals will have the same wireless PCS as television stations enjoy right now. Marshall McLuhan's notion of the global village looks set to be a reality early in the twenty-first century.

7 Insider Techniques
in the Trenches

Travel as Murphy's Law

More so now than ever before, it's a jungle out there in the world of business travel. Because so many more people are on the road and in the air, congestion and delays have become far more common – and more difficult to deal with. The biggest and most important insider technique of all is to **expect the unexpected, and plan for it in advance**. Always have a back-up plan. Always line up your alternatives in the event that your plane is late or cancelled, your luggage is lost or damaged, or if you discover that your hotel is under new management.

In general, the travel industry has done a mediocre job of planning for the travel explosion, and airline deregulation has surely not helped. From airlines to hotels to rental cars, the age of computerized reservations, which was to have simplified everything, appears to have succeeded only in making everything more complicated. Computers have above all facilitated a far more complex pricing structure than was ever possible in the good old days. And if you sometimes get the feeling that they're making up prices on the spot, you're not far wrong.

Although some part of successfully dealing with these situations is attitude adjustment – treating these difficulties not as débâcles to be endured but rather as interesting challenges to your ingenuity – there are techniques which help level the playing field between you and your hotel and airline. This chapter deals with how to cope with the lumps and bumps of airline and hotel pricing structures and airport snafus, the maddening delays and disasters large and small that rob so many executives of any joy whatsoever in the travel experience.

When Your Flight is Delayed or Cancelled

Knowing what to do when your flight is delayed or cancelled is one of the things that distinguishes veteran executive travellers from novices on the road. The first thing to understand is what rights you have when negotiating with your airline.

These rights vary with the situation. If your flight is cancelled because of weather, air traffic delays, a labour dispute, or a mechanical malfunction of the aircraft, the airline staff will generally try their best to assist you in making other arrangements, but you are not 'entitled' to a free meal, immediate booking on the next flight out, or a free hotel room if you're going to be stuck overnight. Airline schedules are not considered guarantees, and your recourse in commonplace difficulties like these, which are entirely beyond the control of the airline, is very limited.

What the Airlines Are Supposed to Offer You

In the United States, the airline doesn't owe you anything – except a refund in the event that you don't make the trip at all. Airline policies in the event of delay or cancellation are wildly disparate. It also appears that there may be little internal consistency within a particular airline on what passenger inducements and mollifications are offered when a flight is late. It was formerly commonplace for the pilot to announce complimentary alcoholic beverages on an inbound flight that was stacked up for over an hour in a holding pattern waiting for landing clearance at JFK – the airborne equivalent of 'breaking out the grog' on a rough sea voyage in days of yore. As the New York skies have become more congested, however, delays have multiplied and free drinks have gone by the board.

On one recent United Airlines flight that was delayed for an hour due to a minor mechanical malfunction, flight attendants distributed vouchers good for a $25 discount on a future United trip. I've often received far less remuneration for far greater inconvenience. There are airlines that make little more than an apology, even for a flight delayed for several days. It is worth noting that United's generosity occurred on the Chicago–Los Angeles route, where competition among airlines is intense.

In Europe, passenger logistics problems due to delayed and cancelled flights tend to get solved in a distinctly hierarchical manner. First and business (or club) class passengers almost always have priority with airlines in getting staff assistance with making alternative travel arrangements or with getting a hotel for the night. Holders of discount economy class tickets generally get far less support. The stranded travellers you see holed up at Gatwick, sleeping amid their piles of luggage while waiting for the weather to clear, are not first or business class travellers. When things go wrong at the airport in Europe, you truly get the service you've paid for.

Keep Cool and Negotiate

No matter what kind of ticket you are holding, however, if you choose to try for a different flight rather than wait it out, you are at the mercy of the gate agent or supervisor. Your job as an executive traveller is to **become your own best negotiator** with airline personnel. Getting angry is not only unproductive but counterproductive. There is no sense alienating the only people who can remedy your problem.

If a last-minute delay is announced or you are seated on a plane which pushes back from the gate but then does not take off and instead returns to the airport, your first move should be to grab your pocket OAG. If you have planned ahead, you should already be aware of some alternative flight arrangements that are open to you. If you've *really* planned ahead, you may still be holding reservations on a later flight. Even if you have not done those things, however, if you have the OAG with you, half your battle is won.

Information is Power

Information is power in this situation. Even if you are still stuck on the tarmac on an aircraft with a mechanical failure, at least you can find out who else has a flight going that you can make. Once you find the alternative flight and get off the plane, it is at this stage that your skills as a negotiator *and* your good relationship with an airline's Special Services representatives may come into play.

You're Still Your Own Best Travel Agent

No matter how helpful the airline staff may be, remember that **you are still your own best travel agent**. This not only helps you, it helps the airline as well. Mike Baverstock, the British Airways Special Services representative, once explained to me exactly what it's like to deal with the madhouse that ensues due to delayed and cancelled flights from his side of the counter. 'Keep in mind that we at Special Services or at the gate might be surrounded by as many as forty or fifty people whose lives and schedules, to them, are as important as yours is to you.

'You can save me about five minutes by telling me specifically the airline name and number of the flight that you want to get on – that five minutes could be your saving grace. It takes no time at all for me to verify that the flight you have chosen does exist; it's certainly a lot faster than having me start from scratch and hunt through the entire schedule for you. If an executive traveller is able to present me with a concrete option, he or she is 50 per cent ahead of everyone else. From an efficiency perspective, I'll probably deal with them first, since their situations can be resolved rather quickly. I can get them on their way and concentrate on the rest of the problems that require more attention. The faster we can deal with the cases that are easy to solve, the faster everyone is going to get where they're going.'

Consider the Indirect Route

As was the case with my delayed flight from Washington, DC, to Paris that I talked about in Chapter 4, it helps a great deal to be flexible and inventive about your alternative arrangements.

Peter Kuhn, an executive in my London office, has studied my methods well. 'If you are stuck in a city, don't necessarily insist on another flight going straight to your destination. It may be more important to get a flight going somewhere – anywhere,' he says. 'I got stuck in Milan one evening when my London flight was cancelled. I didn't want to spend another night there, since hotels are expensive and the airline was not offering to put us up. I found an Air France flight heading for Paris rather than London. I flew into Paris, hopped a shuttle within half an hour, and was back home rather efficiently. You've got to keep thinking about where you can go that might get you to where you need to be.'

Losing Ground Is Not Necessarily Losing Time

Kuhn's advice is even more valid if you are faced with being stranded in a small city, where flight options are limited. **Maximize your alternatives**. When you are trying to work round a delay or cancellation, the more choices you have, the better shape you're in. For example, there are considerably more ways to fly to London from Frankfurt than from Marseilles. If it looks like you might get stuck in Marseilles and a flight to Frankfurt opens up, grab it. Going to Frankfurt is technically going 'backwards', since it takes you geographically further away from London. However, in situations like that, head for the hub that gives you the widest range of alternative flights. Remember that your objective is not to fly the fewest possible miles, but to get where you're going in the shortest possible time. Of course, if you can catch a flight to a hub that's closer to your destination, that is by far the best option.

Above All, Get Your Flight Coupon

If you do change flights *and* airlines, you must **retrieve the value portion of your ticket coupon and get the gate agent to endorse the ticket over to another carrier**. This may be more difficult in some cases than in others. Special Services representative Mike Baverstock, who has a relatively enlightened view of the problem, says, 'It's important to be honest and keep people informed. However bad the flight situation may be, it's better to be honest and up front about it. If you have a delay, the worst thing you can do is hang on to a passenger if there's an option by which he or she can get to their destination quickly. I always send them off to another airline with my blessing. I believe that sooner or later the loyalty factor will come into play because you were genuinely interested in helping them.'

Not every agent at every airline is so broad-minded. There will be times when gate agents will be reluctant to surrender your flight coupon and see you 'defect' to a competitor. If you are holding a restricted ticket, the airline is not required to hand you over to another carrier; worse, the second airline is not required to accept the ticket if its value is less than their own fare for a ticket without advance purchase. Nevertheless, these switches are often made, but money still talks. If you hold a first class, business class or full fare economy ticket, you are in a much better bargaining position.

If your ticket is one of a block of tickets bought under a special arrangement between your company and the airline, your Personal Touch getting the ticket endorsed over to another carrier will be exercised to the fullest. There's no harm in taking your best shot with the gate agent, but it's quite possible that your choices will be limited to other flights within the route system of the deal-making carrier. If you *really* have to get to your destination and your airline can't provide a viable alternative, **get the value portion of your flight coupon back in any event.** It's unused and is available for use by you or another member of your company on a future trip. Make your own reservations with another airline, with the understanding that it's going to be more expensive and you may have some explaining to do when you file your expense report.

Use the Agents at the Lounges

When flights are cancelled or delayed, if a Special Services agent is not available (or your airline does not maintain them at this particular city), chances are that the gate agent will be swamped. If you still have the value portion of your ticket, you may be better off returning to the airline's executive lounge to complete your alternative travel arrangements. The agents who staff these lounges have been given this elevated status because of their competence and ability to deal with the needs of business travellers. When a particular flight has a problem, they are also going to be far less busy than the gate agent. They will be able to solve your problem much faster.

Know When to Hold 'Em or Fold 'Em

How do you know when to stick with your original carrier and when to bolt? It's not easy. A lot of the time it depends on your experience of the airline, what you know of their reputation for honesty when there is a delay, *and* whether you've checked in your luggage.

Sir Christopher Lewinton, Chairman and CEO of TI Group Plc, says, 'I try not to fly with marginal airlines because they haven't got the back-up. I fly with mainstream airlines. You have greater flexibility within the airline's own route system if things go awry. There is a much better likelihood that they will be able to fix a minor problem quickly or produce a second aircraft if something is really wrong.'

Bob Anderson, former CEO of Rockwell International, feels

that it helps to set a limit for yourself and to know when you have reached a crossroads. 'If I find when I get to the airport that the flight is delayed forty-five minutes, I usually figure that's the point I really have to make a decision. You ought to make up your mind. Either decide to sit there and ride it out, because of some feeling you have about the situation, or decide to jump ship.

'If you put off making the decision, you might be there three hours or you might be there all night, waiting to see what happens next. Airlines don't always level with you, or else they give you a definite time for departure when the truth is that they really don't know. They think they have to say something – I suppose they can't just put a big question mark up there on the departures board – but forty-five minutes usually doesn't mean forty-five minutes. It's almost always more.

'For me, forty-five minutes or an hour is the limit. If I get that kind of delay before I've even boarded the aeroplane, I will do anything I can to get to the destination I want to go to by some other route that I know is going to move. If I'm booked on American and next door is Delta going to the same place within half an hour, I jump. To maintain my option to be able to do that, I normally take all my baggage as carry-ons. If you have given them your luggage, you're trapped. The chances of getting that back and catching another flight are damned near impossible.'

The Fictional Departures Board

Unfortunately, Anderson's scepticism is well-placed. In many situations there is a tendency to string the passenger along. Delays are often tacked on in increments just small enough to make it appear not worth the trouble to find another flight. Your plane will be leaving in another twenty minutes, then another, then another. Whether airlines do this on purpose or just out of faulty information is immaterial. My own rule of thumb is **never believe the departures board**.

If there is a delay, always talk directly to the agent at the gate. Don't just accept that the flight is late, find out why. Sometimes this will give you a clue which will inform your decision on whether to bolt or wait it out. If the agent tells you that a flight is late due to 'late inbound equipment' it means, in plain English, that your plane is not in the airport. At this point the right question to ask is whether the plane has left its prior destination. It is also important to be able to use a little maths and a lot of common sense.

A flight listed as sixty minutes behind schedule is going to be much more than an hour late if the aircraft is inbound from another city an hour away but hasn't taken off yet. Not only does the flight have to take off that very minute and make the one-hour trip, it also has to discharge passengers, load luggage and supplies, and reboard. Under these circumstances your flight is going to be at least an hour and a half late, and more likely closer to two hours behind schedule. This is an all-too-common situation on shuttle flights, where a problem early in the day will ripple through the entire schedule. For an airline that flies closely-scheduled turnaround flights, there is often no way to make up the time.

A Sure-Fire Warning Sign

Although the airport departures board can provide false reassurance about how soon a delayed flight is leaving, it does provide the executive traveller with the first indication of potential trouble on what you might otherwise believe will be a prompt departure. **Beware the flight departing 'on time' without a gate number.** If you arrive at the airport at 7.20 a.m. for an 8 a.m. flight and no departure gate has been posted, your warning antennae should be twitching. Begin reviewing your OAG for flight options – a flight with no gate that close to departure time is a flight that does not have an aircraft.

Despite what the gate agent may say, even if the carrier can roll out another plane, a delay is all but inevitable. Meanwhile, as the airline is trying to maintain the fiction that your flight is on time, your best flight alternatives are fast disappearing. This is especially true on popular long-distance routes, where competing airlines tend to bunch departure times together, vying head-to-head for your business. Providing you're not tied down by checked-in luggage, now is the time to figure out a substitute flight, head for the phones (or get out your cellular phone), call another airline's reservation number, and book yourself a seat. Tell the second airline that you are already ticketed, then ask for the value portion of your flight coupon back (if you have surrendered it), have it endorsed by the gate agent to the second carrier before a huge backlog of disgruntled passengers piles up, and make your alternative flight.

Gone but Not Departed

The tendency of many airlines to fib about delays can sometimes work in your favour. It's not necessarily true that a flight which the departures board lists as having taken off is really gone. The folks tracking departures don't monitor radio contact with the tower or wait to see the wheels lift off the runway before listing a flight as having departed. They are dependent on information they receive from the gate agents. If the gate has not reported the flight as delayed, the centre that programmes what you see on the board assumes an on-time departure and posts it as such.

Since minor delays in boarding generally are not mentioned, even if the departures board says your flight has left, don't give up. If it's a matter of a couple of minutes, say eight or less, the odds are that your flight is still at the gate. I've made more than one tight connection on a flight that had theoretically already departed, but in fact was still boarding the last passengers.

Not All Stand-bys Are Created Equal

If you choose to stand by for a fully-booked flight for which you have no reservation, is it worthwhile to check in as soon as possible and secure an early place in line? Maybe yes. Maybe no. If space does become available, assignment of seats to stand-by passengers is not necessarily accomplished on a democratic first-come, first-served basis. With stand-by flights, as with delayed flights, paying full fare for your ticket does entitle you to some privileges. Many airlines board stand-by first class and business class passengers first, followed by full-fare economy passengers, and then on down the financial pecking order from the most expensive (least discounted) tickets to the cheapest. Some airlines also consider whether you are a member of their frequent flyer programme in determining where you are in the stand-by hierarchy.

Being Bumped is Different

Your passenger rights when you have been bumped from a flight are very different from your rights if the flight has been delayed or cancelled. You have consumer advocate Ralph Nader to thank for that. In the late 1970s, Nader was holding a confirmed reservation and a ticket and was bumped from an Allegheny Airlines flight. He sued, claiming breach of contract. His experience eventually resulted in new Federal protection for passengers.

In the United States, if you have a confirmed reservation (with your ticket marked 'OK' in the status column) and your airline cannot offer you the seat you paid for on your flight, *and* you check in the prescribed number of minutes before flight time (usually twenty minutes before departure), you have been 'denied boarding' and you are entitled to compensation as determined by the Federal Department of Transportation. If you are late checking in, your right to compensation evaporates.

As the economic climate has deteriorated, the incidence of bumping has declined, simply because fewer flights are over-booked. However, it still occurs, particularly at peak hours (early morning and late afternoon flights from cities like

London, Frankfurt, Chicago and New York) and peak seasons (late November through New Year's Day in New York City can be hellishly crowded). You also increase the risk of getting bumped when major events are going on in major cities (e.g., in October in Frankfurt during the Book Fair, in June in London when Wimbledon and Ascot are in full swing). You might expect major cities to be able to handle the crush of visitors, but the real hazard occurs in smaller cities when the whole world wants to be in town (I'm thinking here, for example, of Edinburgh after the British Open golf championship, where there can be an overload of departing travellers for the normal handful of flights).

Your Rights If You Are Denied Boarding

In the United States, if you have been denied boarding, met the ticketing and check-in criteria, and your airline does not find another way to get you to your final destination within an hour of the original schedule (and most of the time this is impossible), your airline owes you money. Specifically, it must pay you the amount of your one-way fare (or half the cost of your round-trip ticket) up to a maximum of $200. If you arrive at your destination more than two hours late (a real likelihood), compensation is doubled. International flights inbound to the United States (even on a US carrier) are exempted. So are charter flights and any flight using an aircraft seating fewer than sixty people. Other rules – or no rules – apply in other countries. Check before you leave.

Let's Make a Deal

Rather than pay out actual cash to those who have been denied boarding, many airlines prefer to offer free tickets to travellers who have already made the flight if they volunteer to be bumped to a later flight. When a flight is oversold, the airline asks passengers whether they might be willing to take a later flight. As a further incentive (some might call it a bribe), they are offered cash and/or another free ticket in addition to passage on a later flight. If an insufficient number of volunteers come forward at the first offer, the airline will keep sweetening the deal until the situation is resolved.

I have to assume that the executive traveller is not interested in cash or free tickets used as rewards to tempt passengers to surrender their seats on an overbooked flight. Tourists and students (some of whom have made a cottage industry out of being bumped from what they know will be oversold flights in exchange for future tickets) are the passengers most likely to accept the airlines' offers. For the executive traveller, the goal is to avoid finding yourself on the wrong side of the jetway when your flight leaves the airport.

How Not to Be a Bumpee

The first rule to follow is **be early**. Arrive at the airport early. Check in early. Board early. It's preferable to get your boarding pass when you get your ticket, before you arrive at the airport. There are some people who like to wait until the last minute to get on the plane. I'm not one of them. (My wife is, however.) To me it is far preferable to board the aircraft early, stow my carry-on baggage and settle into my seat. I get to hang my garment bag before everyone else jams theirs into the closet; I get to ask the flight attendant what the choice of meals is and register my preference. Sometimes I do work before take-off; other times I just fall asleep.

In Europe this technique sometimes doesn't work. On the continent many carriers board economy first, business second, and first class passengers last. Having a boarding pass with an assigned seat reduces *but does not eliminate* the possibility that two passengers will be assigned to the same seat. When this occurs, the bottom line is that on an overbooked flight, possession of a seat is nine-tenths of the law. No matter what I'm planning to do on the aircraft, if the flight is overbooked and I've boarded early, I'm the one who is sitting in the seat and it's the late arrival with the identical boarding pass who has the problem.

A Thorny Issue

Bumping of ticket-holding passengers is a direct consequence of flight overbooking by airlines, which in turn is a direct consequence of multiple reservations by executive travellers – in short, people like you and me. Because we business travellers want – generally with good reason – to keep our travel options open, we make a lot of reservations that we don't keep. Generally speaking, we don't cancel them either, either because we don't have time or because we want to have an option in case the worst happens at the airport. This leaves airlines with a significant number of no-shows for each flight.

To offset the no-shows, airlines deliberately overbook their flights, generally by 10–20 per cent, sometimes by a lot more. At peak times airlines can overbook by as much as 70 per cent (which goes a long way towards explaining how two passengers can have boarding passes with the same seat number). 'An MD-87 holds 133 people,' says one top airline executive. 'We will often book it to 180 people, but even so, more often than not it will push out of the gate carrying 110 passengers. Every so often we guess wrong, or one of our competitors has a mechanical difficulty or a cancellation.'

Yield Management

The executive's description of deliberate overbooking is a thumbnail sketch of 'yield management'. In the airline business, yield management is the way air carriers deal with the evanescent value of an airline seat. Once the plane leaves the ground, the revenue that the carrier might derive from that seat is gone forever. From the airline's point of view, every empty seat is money out of pocket. In an industry wracked by deregulation and economic recession, where profits have recently dissolved into a sea of red ink, overbooking is an economic necessity.

Yield Management Horror Stories

In addition to deliberate overbooking, the other component of yield management is the intricate Rube Goldberg fare structure that gives passengers and travel agents both incredible bargains and financial nightmares – sometimes on the same trip. Yield management is the reason why you can fly the 3,000 miles between Los Angeles and New York on an advance purchase round-trip ticket for about the same price as the 450 miles between Los Angeles and San Francisco on a last-minute round-trip ticket.

Not only are fares illogical on a cost-per-mile basis, they always seem to be in constant flux. If you think that airline fares change by the minute, you're not far wrong. Actually they may change by the second. Under the yield management system, airlines have the capacity to reprogram their computer reservations systems to accept as many as *200,000 fare changes a day*.

This process surely has its flaws, and the airlines are not always the beneficiaries.

'It's a dark science,' says Sandy Gardiner of British Airways, 'and certainly not a perfect science.'

Gardiner told me that the blemishes in the yield management system were all too apparent at a conference of British Airways executives. 'At one point in the conference our general manager for pricing walked up to the podium and asked how many fares we thought there were between London and New York. We all thought about it for a moment and concluded that there must be about fifty. He then took out a large roll of paper and threw it out. It unravelled itself clear across the room. He told us that the number was in the thousands.'

The Revenge of the Travel Agents

Travel agents are among the victims of this lunatic pricing system. Their clients are always coming back at them after a trip with reports of a fellow passenger who paid less –

sometimes a lot less – for a seat on the same flight. Until recently it was a hopeless battle. Not even the most conscientious travel agent could keep track of the myriad fare changes. In self-defence, some larger travel agents have resorted to guerrilla warfare against the airlines to try to beat them at their own game. They have purchased 24-hour fare-checking programs which continually monitor airline price structures.

If the travel agency's computer program spots a change in the airlines' computer fare listings and that change benefits a client, it automatically alters his or her reservation and grabs the reduction. These watchdog systems also check for changes in seat options. Maybe that bulkhead seat on the aisle between Seattle and Miami was not available when you booked your flight, but if it opens up after you've purchased your ticket, it will snatch it on your behalf, even if the seat clears at 3.48 a.m., your agent is on maternity leave, and you are in Budapest.

Individual Commando Action

You don't always need a travel agent to outfox the yield management system. I tip my hat to one California business traveller who had been booked on a 12.30 p.m. Southwest Airlines flight from Burbank to Oakland with a bargain fare of $59 round trip. When a morning meeting ran late, he realized that he would not make his plane. The next flight out was a United flight at 2.15 p.m. He knew he wouldn't be able to match the $59 fare, but as a last-minute passenger he was unwilling to get stuck paying $168, more than five times what one leg of his original round-trip ticket cost. The next best choice was a 6.30 p.m. United flight at $79, one way. The price was acceptable, but it meant he would be unable to keep his dinner appointment.

Undaunted, the intrepid businessman arrived at the United counter at Burbank at 1.15 p.m., purchased his ticket for the 6.30 plane, and asked whether there were any seats on the 2.15 flight. He was hoping that under yield management, some previously reserved discounted seats for the 2.15 flight had been released to the agents at the airport. However, the agent at the counter informed him that the 2.15 flight was now not only sold out but overbooked – even his $168 seat was no longer available. Worse, the stand-by list was twenty passengers long.

The valiant businessman tried yet another approach. At 1.35 he called United's reservations number and asked whether there were open seats on the 2.15 flight. To his astonishment, he was told that there were seats available. He booked not only a reservation in his own name, but one for an imaginary travelling companion as well, and got seat assignments. As it turned out, he had the entire row to himself. How much did he pay? $79.

What happened? Within twenty minutes the flight with no space available at $168 and a twenty-person waiting list had turned into a flight with empty seats at $79. Because an empty seat is lost revenue, United made a yield management decision that it was better to sell last-minute seats at $79 than not to sell them at $168.

Keep Checking

What is the moral of this story? **Never assume anything.** Keep checking fares, even after you have your ticket. Don't take no for an answer, no matter how long they say the wait list is. The truth is that no airline really knows whether a flight is overbooked until boarding has begun. You can all but count on the fact that airlines will hold a block of a certain number of seats for high volume travel agents, frequent flyer celebrities and bigwigs, airline executives, staff and other users. As long as these seats remain on hold, they will show up in the computer system as occupied – sold, in other words. If these potential passengers can't use the space that has been reserved for them, the seats are released back to the airline at a certain point before the flight leaves. The time and date when these seats are released varies. If an airline tells you a seat is unavailable (or unavailable at a discount price), don't give up. Keep calling back. The discount ticket that was out of the question yesterday (or an hour ago) might be available today.

Surviving Baggage Claim
Have Bag, Will Travel

Every business traveller strives mightily to avoid checking in his or her luggage. Sometimes the efforts to circumvent the limits on cabin baggage appear comical. From the way Sarah Wooldridge, my London assistant, describes my appearance at the check-in, I'm sure that to some observers she and I look like two overloaded Bulgarian spies. She claims that when I go into the terminal, I always have too much hand luggage and that I check in with my two briefcases. Meanwhile she is hiding behind a pillar with my garment bag.

Airlines, particularly US carriers, have become increasingly bureaucratic about the number of pieces of carry-on luggage that are permitted. It's a limitation which I think has the potential to work in favour of women. I've seen women passengers board the aircraft with two carry-on items plus a huge bag, which on most airlines should put them over the limit. They get away with it because that huge bag is technically a 'handbag'. Since I'd been harassed about my garment bag and two briefcases, I asked the airline for the definition of a handbag and was told that a 'handbag' has a strap and a zipper. If one wanted to be contentious about it, I suppose a male executive traveller could carry a small flight bag and call it his handbag.

Don't Surrender Your Valuables

Never pack anything in your checked-in baggage that can't be easily replaced. This includes your house keys, car keys, tickets for the next leg of the trip, driver's licence, passport and any other identification. It also includes obvious valuables like jewellery, cameras, furs and electronic equipment, as well as valuable papers and documents. By valuable papers and documents, I mean not only negotiable stock and bond certificates, *but also*

- The floppy disk containing the final manuscript of your novel.
- The pictures of your newborn child.
- The original receipts and other documentation you are carrying to your tax audit.
- The approved contract with your best client – the one existing copy bearing the pencilled-in changes initialled by the CEO.

Pictures, contracts, receipts, manuscripts and computer files, although they are priceless to you, have no inherent value so far as the airlines are concerned. If they go missing, you will have a very difficult (if not impossible) time getting compensation for them.

What the Airline Owes You If Your Bag Is Lost or Damaged

Not much.

Within the United States, an airline will provide lost or damaged baggage compensation up to a maximum of $1,250 per person – not per bag, per person. The airline is liable only for the *depreciated* value of your belongings, not for their replacement value – you won't get enough compensation to replace a four-year-old designer suit with anything more than a nice jacket off the sale rack at Macy's. Before they compensate you, it is likely that you will be asked to furnish purchase receipts for items you claim were in the bags in order to document their value.

On US-sourced international flights, you get even less protection for lost or damaged luggage. Baggage is insured by the kilogram – $20 per kilo, or roughly $9 per pound – about what you pay for a good fillet of salmon, but hardly sufficient to replace your business wardrobe. Rather than weighing each bag at check-in and recording that weight on your ticket, many carriers assume that each bag weighed the maximum they will accept – generally 32 kilos, or about 70 pounds. This makes the international liability limit just $640 per bag.

Outside the United States, the compensation you can expect to receive for lost luggage varies from airline to airline. Under the international Warsaw Convention, which governs these things, airlines are obliged to pay pretty trifling amounts per bag. Whenever you travel, therefore, make sure that you have taken out adequate private insurance.

Excess Valuation Insurance

Depending on what business you are in, there may be occasions when checking in luggage containing valuables cannot be avoided. Within the United States, if you are at your maximum carry-on limit and you are concerned about the safety of the items in your checked-in luggage, you can purchase excess valuation insurance from the airline. Most airlines don't publicize the service but it is available – you just need to be sure to check in a little earlier to complete the paperwork.

Although there are variations among airlines, the excess valuation premium costs approximately 1–2 per cent of the value of what you are insuring, over and above the $1,250 liability limit imposed by the US Department of Transportation. For between $20 and $40, you can insure an additional $2,000 worth of your belongings. By taking out excess valuation insurance, you also give your baggage a very high profile with the baggage handlers and other airline staff. Your bags are specially tagged with an identification which indicates that your luggage is to get the kid gloves treatment. It also puts any potentially larcenous baggage handlers on notice that your belongings are all but radioactive. Behind-the-scenes thieves know that if they tamper with 'excess valuation' baggage they will incur the wrath of not just the passenger but the airline itself. On one occasion when I took out excess baggage insurance, as I was waiting at the carousel for my bags to come down the chute, an agent walked up to me and physically handed me my luggage.

If Your Baggage Goes Astray

We've all seen the forlorn individuals desperately searching various nooks and crannies of the baggage claim area for their luggage. We've also seen the same lonely suitcase making repeat laps of the baggage carousel with no one to claim it.

How do you deal with the airline if your luggage is lost? Very carefully. What you do, when you do it, and what you sign at the airport affects your ability to collect from the airline in the event that your bags are permanently lost.

Bureaucracy at Its Worst

If your baggage doesn't show up, it is once again time to call upon your relationship with the Special Services representatives, if they are present and available. If not, you will be forced to deal with the staff of the baggage claim office, who are considerably down the corporate hierarchy from the Special Services agents.

Invariably, you will be given a form to complete. Resist the temptation to carry on business as usual and complete the form in your office or at the hotel. Read it carefully. On some airlines these forms are merely reports of lost or damaged luggage. Others also include a claim for damages against the airline. Insist on the latter, even if it means completing two separate documents. **Complete the form(s), even if the airline representative assures you that your baggage will be along on the next flight.** Describe your luggage and its contents as fully and completely as possible. Some battle-hardened travel veterans (who probably learned from bitter experience) even carry a snapshot of their luggage for just such occasions.

Make sure you get a copy of anything you sign, that the date and time of filing the form are noted in writing, and that you have the name, title, and telephone number of any airline employee you deal with. **Do not surrender your baggage claim tag** unless you get signed proof from the airline representative that custody of the tag has been transferred to the airline. If you must give them the tag, record all numbers on it – that tag is the only evidence you have that you ever checked in your baggage at all. If possible, have a copy made for the airline and keep the original yourself.

A few carriers will not accept the claim form until they have declared your bags irretrievably lost. However, the act of completing the form will help acquaint you with what you will need to furnish as documentation in case the worst happens. It will also offer an opportunity to build a bit of a personal connection with the baggage claim supervisor, who probably has all too many of these kinds of problems to deal with.

Damaged Goods

Almost as disheartening as missing luggage is the sight of a cardboard box or plastic tub coming down the chute, housing the mangled remains of what was formerly a suitcase – your suitcase. Here again, what you do and sign at the airport may affect your ability to collect from the carrier. If your bag has been damaged (incidental scuffs or smudges aside), the airline will pay for repairs or make the repairs itself. Repairs are utilitarian, not cosmetic – if the new green handle or bright orange zipper makes the bag functional, whether or not it matches the original leopard-skin print is not a factor in determining compensation. If the suitcase can't be fixed, then as is the case with missing baggage, the airline will pay for its depreciated value, not for the cost of a replacement.

Airline responsibility for damaged luggage is spelled out in the Conditions of Carriage, and varies from one carrier to another. Most impose a strict time limit on a passenger's right to claim compensation for damaged baggage or missing items from claimed baggage. This may well be one reason why baggage thieves are all too common – airlines have established a very limited liability and the passenger has very little recourse. The time limit for filing a claim can be as long as twenty-four hours, or as short as no time at all.

American Airlines signs off on your bags the moment you claim them and step out on to the kerb. 'Acceptance of baggage by the bearer of a claim check without filing a written complaint shall constitute evidence of delivery by American of your baggage, with all original contents, in good condition.'

Clearing Customs

For the great majority of business travellers, the main aggravation of going through Customs and Immigration is the time it takes. Most of us will gladly pay whatever import duties we owe, provided that we can pay them quickly and get on with our journey. Unless you have been on an overseas shopping spree, most business travellers have nothing to declare. Nevertheless, some people in the 'nothing to declare line' are going to get stopped. How can you avoid being one of those people? **Dress the part**. Go through Customs – in any country – looking like what you are: an executive business traveller. The odds of your being stopped as a well-groomed, respectable-looking person wearing a suit (and tie, if you're a gentleman) going through the 'nothing to declare' lanes with a porter are tiny. If you're under thirty, or look under thirty, the odds increase a little. If you don't have a porter and are on your own, the odds of being stopped increase a bit more. If you are a man and aren't wearing a tie, the odds go up again. If you're wearing torn or grungy jeans and a two-day stubble, the odds are almost 50–50 that you're going to get stopped. Add a surly expression, a pony tail and an earring and it's almost a sure thing.

The Trojan Horse in the Three-Piece Suit

How well does dressing the part work? I've heard many stories of prosperous families returning to the United States from European vacations with purchases that should have been declared and getting through without challenge. What's the strategy? The family sent three-piece-suited button-down Dad ahead through the 'nothing to declare' line, carrying just his distinguished business traveller sang-froid, his briefcase, and a small suitcase. Ten or fifteen minutes later, Mom and the kids straggled through, carrying all the rest of the myriad suitcases with nothing in them but a few souvenirs and dirty laundry.

Owned Up or Locked Up?

I suppose these families think they are clever enough, but I can't recommend their approach. **If you're over the limit, declare it**. The duty isn't that great on most items. Customs officials have seen most of the scams. Sewing 'J C Penney Made in the USA' labels into a bespoke pinstripe suit from Gieves & Hawkes on Savile Row doesn't work. Neither does scuffing up a new Hermes handbag to make it look 'old'. The downside of being caught in terms of hassle and embarrassment is far worse that the duty you have to pay.

Don't Get a Record

Suppose you *did* go on an overseas shopping spree? What if your clients or suppliers gave you a valuable gift? In most countries, you are permitted to return from a foreign trip with a fixed monetary total of items for personal or household use. If the value of these items exceeds that total, you must declare the price you paid for them, or estimate their worth at the time of purchase.

If you don't know whether you are over the limit, one technique is to **declare something**. First of all, it's not worth getting caught. Once you've been apprehended trying to clear Customs without paying duty, your name goes into a computerized record as someone to be checked out next time around. Pay the duty on your excess, which won't be very much. Provided that you are dressed in your executive traveller 'uniform', as soon as you've made your declaration and paid your excess duty, it's been my experience that Customs inspectors move you on quickly.

Barter and Volume Discounts
with Airlines and Hotels

With the deterioration in the economy, not just in the United States but in Europe as well, the canny traveller has many more opportunities to obtain discounts and barter deals from airlines, hotels, and rental car agencies. All are based on repeat volume travel, often to the same destination or group of destinations.

Sometimes the arrangement is a volume discount. At IMG we work on this approach a lot. Because we send people regularly between Cleveland and New York, we are in a great position to deal with Continental Airlines for a bulk purchase of tickets at a prenegotiated price, usable by any member of our firm. Buying tickets in this fashion may not always beat the rock-bottom special discount fare, but it does take the financial sting out of the emergency last-minute trip. The downside is a certain loss of flexibility. In case of a delay or cancellation, negotiated tickets such as these are generally not transferable from one airline to another.

At other times we make barter arrangements with airlines and hotels. If we're running a German tennis tournament where Lufthansa is one of the official sponsors, part of our compensation from the airline may be several hundred thousand dollars' worth of airfares for IMG. When American Airlines sponsors a gymnastics meet that we created they may give us vouchers for $50,000 of air travel.

If you take this approach, **make sure you can take full advantage of what you are being offered.** You can most assuredly make use of $50,000 worth of airfares on American Airlines. We call that Class A barter. On the other hand, $50,000 worth of hotel rooms in Pakistan may or may not be a good deal, depending on how much business you have in Pakistan.

Sometimes a Bargain Isn't a Bargain

Sometimes these corporate policies are not too well thought out. At one time we had a company policy which dictated that if there was barter available, you had to use it. At first blush, it made a great deal of sense. However, strict application of the policy resulted in a situation where five executives from our London office flew to Orlando, Florida, on American Airlines because we had a barter arrangement with that carrier. They went through $22,000 worth of barter when they could have purchased five London–Orlando tickets on British Airways for about $3,000 ($600 apiece) because of a special promotion that BA was offering at the time.

Little Fried Onions and Patty Melts, Medium Rare

You have to apply a certain amount of creativity and ingenuity to your barter arrangements. For example, if your law firm has offices in Century City in Los Angeles, you may be able to strike up a deal with one of the local restaurants. There's a Hamburger Hamlet right there on the Avenue of the Stars; it's a quality chain with restaurants in many major business cities. Why not approach them and say, 'Look, you probably do $200,000 worth of legal work a year. If you give us $200,000 worth of lunches and dinners, we'll give you the legal work for nothing.' Everybody wins – that $200,000 worth of legal time probably costs your firm a third as much, which is probably about what $200,000 worth of ground beef, lettuce, tomato, and sesame seed buns costs the restaurant.

Lettuce, Toilet Paper and Widgets

At IMG we have a relatively easy time making barter arrangements directly with airlines and hotels because we can offer them useful business and promotional opportunities – sponsorship or a hospitality tent at a sporting event, good seats at concerts and tennis matches – which they in turn can use to entertain their favourite customers. However, even if your business can't offer 'glamorous' barter possibilities such as these, you still may be able to strike up a deal through a 'second-hand' barter arrangement.

Many airlines with excess capacity have reduced their overheads by making barter arrangements for travel credits with their suppliers – the firms who furnish their fuel, their spare parts, their lettuce and their toilet paper. If your firm does business with these suppliers, perhaps you can negotiate those air credits into your working relationship.

You and Your Hotel

When you call a hotel chain's toll-free reservations number and ask the price of a room in a city you're planning to visit, do you take the first price they quote you?

If so, you're a travel chump.

Since the late 1980s, the world has been awash in vacant hotel rooms. Average occupancy rates in the United States for hotels and motels is currently less than 60 per cent, and the rates are way off 100 per unit in almost all Western countries. In other words, on any night there's an almost 50–50 chance that a room will be empty. So what?

So, welcome to your second seminar in yield management.

Yield Management, Part 2

To an airline, every vacant seat in a departing aircraft represents money flying away. To a hotel, every bed that goes unfilled on a given night is money out of the window. Indeed, for hotels it's worse, since they lose not only the cost of the room, but the prospective revenue from meals, room service and, of course, their beloved telephone charges.

To cope, hotels have started copying the airlines in dealing with their excess capacity. This means that unless you want to be in Monaco over the Grand Prix or New Orleans at Mardi Gras, or anywhere there's a major event attracting large numbers of high rollers, you're in a strong position to negotiate.

Marxist Economics

Sometimes the yield management game produces Marxist consequences (Groucho, not Karl). At a prominent Manhattan business hotel, an associate of mine observed a gentleman approach the front desk and enquire whether there was a room available for the evening. The clerk checked through his computer inventory and informed the prospective guest that he had a room available at $185. The man shook his head, saying the rate was too expensive, and turned to leave. Despite his behind-the-counter handicap, the younger and faster desk clerk caught up with the gentleman before he went through the revolving door and into the night.

'Sir?' he asked. 'How much *would* you be willing to pay?' By the time the two had strolled back to the front desk, an agreement had been reached for a charge of $119 for the night.

How Do You Rate?

At most hotels, each room has a number of different possible rates. At the Loews Anatole (a gargantuan conventioneer hotel) in Dallas, there are as many as nine different rates for each room. At other hotels, there may be as many as thirty different tariffs (not including eleventh hour *ad hoc* negotiations like the scenario above). Many hotel chains are empowering their reservationists and desk clerks to be flexible when it comes to rates and discounts. Rates vary by day of week, season, number of advance bookings, and recent occupancy trends. What you pay also depends on how you made your reservation. Did you use a toll-free number? Chances are you'll pay more. Did you go through a travel agent? Unless your agent has a special deal with the hotel or its chain, you'll pay more that way, too.

This happens all over the world. Hotel rates are negotiable. You will get your best rate as an individual frequent guest or as one of a group of frequent stayers under a prenegotiated arrangement.

A New Relationship with Businesses

Michael Gray, manager of the Hyatt Carlton Tower in London, told me how his hotel negotiates with executive travellers. 'The corporate market is demanding lower rates,' he says. 'In return for that discount, corporations are narrowing down their lists of approved hotels. Instead of authorizing use of one of ten hotels in London, now they are listing only six. If my hotel is going to be one of the six, I'm going to get some positive spin-off from the four that are not chosen. We can afford to give a discount; we are at least going to see our occupancy go up.

'For a really major volume user who would book several hundred room-nights a year, we're talking about discounts of 30–40 per cent, which is very good for both of us. If we're going to give a reasonable rate to that company, then the company must do its best to increase our volume. The companies must guarantee a minimum volume so we know that the discounted price doesn't affect our ability to continue to provide service. The Carlton Tower is prepared to work with companies on this basis, but there has to be a lot of respect and integrity between the corporation and the hotel in carrying out the agreement.'

In other words, if you deliberately overstate the number of room-nights to strike the best possible deal with the hotel, you will have considerable difficulty renewing your arrangement.

You Are Still Your Own Best Travel Agent

How do you get a good rate if you're dealing on your own? **You are *still* your own best travel agent**. Whenever you book a hotel room, remain focused on what you are buying. Remember that you are not just reserving a place to sleep, you are *negotiating a room rate*. Unless you have reason to suspect that rooms are scarce where you're headed, you're holding all the aces when you call.

Toll-Free, but Very Costly

Beware of a hotel chain's toll-free number. Toll-free hotel numbers and toll-free airline numbers are two very different things. There is no financial penalty for calling toll-free airline numbers – airfares don't cost more when you deal over the phone. However, there may be a considerable extra cost attached to calling a hotel's toll-free number. This is because airline yield management decisions are made at corporate headquarters, not at the departure gate, and hotel yield management decisions are generally made not by corporate overseers but by individual hotel managers.

'We like to promote our toll-free numbers as a convenience to our guests in making their reservations with us anywhere in the US or around the world,' explains a Hyatt representative. 'We quote the latest published rates but each hotel manages its room inventory differently, and the national reservations folks don't always know as fast as we do when certain rooms and rates become available.'

It's fine to use toll-free numbers for basic comparison shopping for the lowest 'official' room rates offered among the major chains. Remember, however, that many telephone reservationists are paid on a salary plus commission basis. In short, they make more money when you pay more for a room. They may also have far less flexibility and authority to negotiate with you.

In addition to comparing 'standard' rates, the toll-free number is the easiest way to get the direct number of the particular hotel you are interested in. By calling the hotel itself, you can **deal directly with your hotel of choice.** Desk clerks don't work on commission, and they are closest to the general manager, who is responsible for decision-making about room rates.

Special Today, or How to Grill a Reservations Agent

How do you get the best possible rate? **Keep asking questions.** Every hotel has a corporate rate. To get it all you have to do is ask, even if you're a corporation of one. Is there a weekend rate? At business hotels, this is often very inexpensive. If you're arriving on Thursday, could you get the weekend rate with an early check-in? Is there anything else less expensive? Always ask for the best rate available.

Sometimes you can do better just stepping up to the desk and asking for the best rate when you check in, even if you already have a reservation at a price you believe is reasonable. One canny traveller, who had reserved a room at a super special rate of $65 for a one-night weekend stay, noticed as he was waiting to check in that a departing guest was paying just $49 a night for his room. Choosing not to reveal that he had a reservation, he enquired whether there were rooms available, and asked for the cheapest room. He was quoted a rate of $39, $10 less than the departing guest, and $26 less than the rate he had been quoted on the toll-free reservation number. (In fairness, however, it should be noted that his original $65 rate had included a 'complimentary' breakfast!)

Although this particular incident occurred at a Hilton hotel, it could easily have happened at any one of the other major chains as well. During times of economic slowdown, and especially during slow seasons, with every question you ask your quoted rate could go down, often far below what you might expect. A $175 room at the Hyatt Regency in Washington, DC, has been known to go for as little as $69 a night.

Ah, but while a flight is just a flight, rooms come in many shapes and sizes. How do you get the best room in the best hotel, and how do you use it to your best advantage? We'll talk about that in Chapter 10.

8 Creative Variations on Executive Travel

Had I but world enough and time I should travel everywhere by train, but another condition is that the year would have to be no later than 1938.
Keith Waterhouse, *The Theory and Practice of Travel*

All of my earliest travel memories involve trains – in exactly the golden age of train travel before World War II that Waterhouse yearns for. My dad took me a number of times on the Twentieth Century Limited and the Commodore Vanderbilt. Most exciting of all, however, was our annual winter trip to the Gulf Coast of Mississippi. My parents took me out of school for a week on one end or the other of a vacation and we travelled to Mississippi on the exotically-named (to me at least) Panama Limited.

I was a true train freak. I counted down the days and hours till we were to leave. I looked forward to this trip so much that I memorized the names of all the stations – in order – from Chicago to Champaign, Illinois. I took special pride in calling them out before the conductor did. There were a lot of them, even before we had got half-way through Illinois. After we left Chicago there was: Kensington, Harvey, Homewood, Madison, Monee, Peotone, Manteno, Bradley, Kankakee, Chebanse, Clifton, Ashkum, Danforth, Gilman, Onarga, Delray, Buckley, Ludlow, Paxton, Rantoul, Thomasboro, and finally Champaign – all in a space of 126 miles.

I've been a train lover ever since, and assiduously seek out those remaining trains that evoke the bygone era, not necessarily in ambiance but in service and comfort. Although I find the Orient Express a bit overdone, I always take the sleeper to St Andrews from London when I travel to the Dunhill Cup in Scotland. I always use the Bullet Train from Osaka or Nagoya to Tokyo. Right now my favourite is the Blue Train, which runs between Johannesburg and Cape Town. The food is first rate, as is the wine cellar. What makes it even more special is that many of the compartments have not only bathrooms but bathtubs as well. The train travels over the Karoo Desert and stops in Kimberley, the diamond-mining town. When you awaken the next morning, you are in the wine country of the Paarl River Valley north of Cape Town.

To be sure, as an executive traveller you may have to differentiate between taking a train just to experience the train and taking a train to get where you're going, but trains are just one example of the many ways in which the routine aspects of business travel can be altered to make the experience more enjoyable. Some are actually more efficient and more cost-effective than the conventional way of doing things. For example, the opportunity to stay at a historic or out-of-town hotel often compensates for additional transportation time with its charm and lower cost. Moreover, as greater numbers of businesses leave urban centres for suburban locations, some of these hotels can actually have a proximity advantage.

Also increasingly common in the realm of business entertaining is the use of resort hotels for client or staff meetings. By providing a pleasant atmosphere – a retreat from the usual office surroundings – these hotels offer executives a positive environment for deal-making and problem-solving. The classic example of this is the annual sales meeting, which is designed both to reward the sales representatives of a company and to make more pleasant a tough dialogue about projections and sales expectations.

In this chapter I will discuss innovative ways to travel, out-of-the-ordinary places to stay, and novel ways to hold meetings, all of which demonstrate how mixing business with pleasure rewards the travelling executive, not just personally but professionally as well.

Innovative Ways of Getting There

The Grand Gesture

Kerry Packer is the wealthiest man in Australia, the owner of the Channel Nine television network and a good friend of mine. While I was in Melbourne doing television commentary on the Australian Masters golf tournament, he called and asked me to join him for dinner. Kerry was in Sydney. I said, 'Well, I'd be delighted, but it's going to have to be a late supper. I won't be finished on the air till 4 p.m. It's an hour and a half to the airport. The earliest flight I can catch is the 6.30, which gets into Sydney at 8. After waiting for my luggage, I won't be able to get to dinner much before 9 p.m.'

This was not what Kerry wanted to hear. 'Nine?' he sniffed. 'That's too bloody late. I'll send the chopper and the jet for you.'

I finished my commentary at 4 p.m. as scheduled. After that, things moved with military precision. I jumped into a golf cart and headed for the fifth hole, where the Channel Nine helicopter had landed. The chopper took me to the private terminal at Melbourne Airport, where Kerry's personal jet was waiting for me. We took off immediately and landed in Sydney at 6.30. A limousine waiting at the steps of the jet delivered me to Packer's flat at 7.40. I expected to sit down promptly and tuck into dinner with my friend. Ludicrously enough, however, Kerry himself did not arrive until 9 – the same time I would have arrived on his doorstep by less extraordinary means!

That story is quite a spectacular example of a creative variation on traditional business travel, but very few of us can travel the way Kerry Packer does. Even if you don't own your own helicopter and private jet, however, sometimes you can still find a creative and stimulating way to get there.

Exotic Car Rentals

There are some people who love cars as much as I love trains. If you have to arrive somewhere in style, consider renting something other than a run-of-the-parking-lot four-door saloon. Agencies that specialize in exotic car rentals are located primarily in parts of the world where the car is still king, such as Los Angeles. Zipping around Manhattan in a large Mercedes that you yourself are driving brands you not as a moneyed sophisticate but as:

- An out-of-towner with a profound sense of masochism,
- A chauffeur with the night off, and/or
- A prime carjacking prospect.

Although they are most assuredly more expensive than your basic Ford, fancy wheels like Mercedes, Lexus or BMW, or even an off-roader like a Range Rover, may be worth the extra cost to make a distinctive impression on a client.

Depending on your timing, you may also be able to negotiate a special deal with the rental car agency. Even if you can come up with a relatively reasonable cost, I'd recommend clearing this sort of rental ahead of time with the powers that be in your office – this is not an expenditure that you want to spring on your company as a little surprise when you return. Know in advance how much a conventional rental car would cost – if having the hot rod will really make your trip, offer to pay the difference. You should be aware, however, that some insurance policies and credit card back-up coverage exempt exotic or otherwise unusual rental cars. Make very certain you are covered before you decline the collision damage waiver.

Letting the Train Take the Strain

We have with us at IMG an executive named Bev Norwood. At one point he was doing work in Europe, and needed to spend three days in Paris and two in Barcelona. The conventional business traveller would have set up his schedule to work first in one city, then fly to the other.

Not Bev. He bought a Eurailpass and began his work schedule in Paris. He worked in Paris all day Monday, got on the overnight train to Barcelona, had a good meal and a good night's sleep on the way, did a day's work in Barcelona on Tuesday, got on the overnight train to Paris, spent the day in Paris on Wednesday, got back on the train to Barcelona, worked in Barcelona on Thursday, got on the train for the last time and returned to Paris to finish up the week on Friday.

Did he spend a lot of money on travel? It's true that his Eurailpass was more expensive than one round-trip airfare between Paris and Barcelona. *However*, he saved the cost of four nights of hotel rooms in two of the most expensive cities in Europe, so IMG came out way ahead. Bev Norwood came out way ahead, too. It goes without saying that he had a dandy travel experience, but because train stations are more centrally located than airports, he also saved a lot of time and was much nearer to where he was going to be doing business during the day. In addition, he spared himself all the hassle involved in getting between the city and the airport. And he assuredly impressed his boss with his attitude about cost cutting!

Pablo Casals and Me

After a late meeting with members of the International Olympic Committee in Lausanne, I had to be in Barcelona the next day for a morning appointment. There was no flight that could get me out of Geneva, the nearest airport to Lausanne, or into Barcelona at the desired time, so getting there posed a problem. To solve it I took a sleeper train from Geneva called the Pablo Casals.

I didn't expect much, but it was the only way I could fit the trip to Barcelona into my schedule. It was a wonderful journey, just two or three stops along the way, with terrific service. I had a comfortable room complete with shower and internal telephone. I gave the porter my passport, so I was not awakened at the border crossings in the middle of the night. He even provided a very timely, gentle and genteel telephonic wake-up call in my compartment. After a hearty breakfast, I arrived in Barcelona at 9 a.m. in fabulous shape.

Trains: Slow, Inconvenient and Expensive?

Everyone 'knows' that modern trains are slow, inconvenient and expensive, especially in the United States.

Not so. Indeed, the time and trouble inherent in fighting your way to and from the airport sometimes makes the train a much better deal. My friend Marvin Bush, who lives in Washington, DC, but often visits New York City on business, agrees: 'My image of going from Washington to New York is rushing to National Airport, placing your bag carefully above your seat and having twenty other people cramming theirs on top of yours. When you land, everybody is in a hurry to get out of the aeroplane. There's a great deal of pushing and shoving.

'I take the Metroliner. I can make phone calls from the train. I can spread out my work or my reading. I've got elbow room. I can write letters. I don't know anyone who can sit on that shuttle and get any real work done. It's a three-hour trip – that's door-to-door.'

Time Is Money

That's fine for a guy like Marvin who can spend the extra time, right?

Maybe if you're in a peculiar sort of business in which you go from an airport conference at La Guardia to an airport conference at Washington National, taking the shuttle is preferable. But if you're going from midtown Manhattan to inside the Washington Beltway, my money's on Marvin.

Marvin v. The Shuttle

Let me describe a hypothetical race between you and Marvin leaving from midtown Manhattan and ending on the Capitol steps in Washington. We'll assume you both leave Rockefeller Center at the same time.

Marvin takes a five-minute, $6 cab ride to Penn Station. He gets on the train. It leaves.

You get into a cab headed for La Guardia, crawl across the Triborough Bridge and get stuck in a traffic tie-up on the Grand Central Parkway. The trip costs you $30. You make the plane, barely. It sits on the ground for at least twenty minutes waiting for clearance before taking off.

Marvin sits in comfort in the train's club car, with complimentary meals and wine, hot towels, and real service. He makes phone calls and does some paperwork. He's been on the train for over an hour before you've even left the ground.

You are sitting in a flying bus. After being delayed on departure, you are also delayed in a holding pattern on approach. Eventually you land at Washington National, where you wait an extra fifteen minutes for your luggage. You finally get a cab into the city.

Marvin and the Metroliner pull into resplendent Union Station, in the heart of Washington. He and his luggage get off the train at the same time. He hops a waiting cab.

You show up at the Capitol, frazzled and desperately in need of resuscitation, about five minutes *after* **Marvin**, who magnanimously offers to buy you some gin-enriched therapy at the Old Ebbitt Grill. 'And by the way,' he says, putting a comforting arm around your shoulder, 'I was able to hold a teleconference with our attorneys in the office while I was on the train. We've reviewed all the changes to our contract that you asked for. You and I can discuss them over cocktails...'

To add insult to injury, **Marvin** paid about half as much for his travel experience as **You** did. To be sure, at off-peak travel hours when the airports are not congested, you might beat Marvin timewise into Washington. But not for long. Amtrak is planning to introduce high-speed trains on the New York–Washington corridor, which will tip the scales even further in favour of train travel.

Sometimes the best alternative airport is the railway station.

Remember the Tortoise and the Hare

There's also a follow-up lesson to be learned from this example. The corollary is that **it's not always how fast you get there, but what shape you're in when you arrive.** Not that Marvin Bush would take advantage of you, but if you are foolish enough to negotiate with Marvin after he's scraped you off the ceiling of the Old Ebbitt Grill, you may find yourself agreeing to more than you might have otherwise.

The Changing Face of the Business Trip

The changing face of the business trip goes hand in hand with the changing face of what used to be the typical vacation. The classic two-week American vacation, generally in summer when the kids are out of school, is as extinct as the stegosaurus. Instead, executives are taking mini-vacations, often by adding a weekend or a few days to a business trip. A recent survey commissioned by the Omni hotel chain found that 80 per cent of frequent travellers took a family member on an extended business trip within the past two years.

I find this an altogether positive trend. **It's OK to combine business with pleasure.** Before the chorus of harrumphs from the ascetics in Accounting about 'frivolous travel', 'paid holidays' and 'vacation business trips' swells to a crescendo, I should quickly point out that this process pays dividends not just for the business traveller but for his or her company as well.

Saturday Night Fever, Part 2

Although the refreshed and invigorated executive is a corporate asset that cannot be quantified, it is much easier to put a cash value on the ticket price reduction that results from a Saturday night stay.

For example, if you are going to New Orleans from Chicago for a three-day business trip, the regular economy airfare departing on Monday and returning on Thursday is about $785. With a Saturday night stay, the fare drops to as little as $258. Who would you rather see in the office on Monday morning – the guy who had to come back on Thursday night, or the guy who spent the weekend in New Orleans with his wife and saved the company $527?

Weekend Hotel Bargains

I'm not suggesting that the organization pick up the tab for the executive's weekend getaway, but even the hotel portion of the extended stay may offer cost-saving possibilities for the business traveller and for the parent company. As we discussed in Chapter 7, hotel prices in recessionary times are anything but firm. This is especially true at business-orientated hotels, many of which are likely to be virtually empty over the weekend.

Over and above whatever special corporate or frequent-stay rate the business traveller can negotiate, if you extend your trip to depart on Sunday rather than Thursday, those extra couple of weekend nights are likely to be a bargain. As an inducement, many hotels will even give the executive traveller the super-low weekend rate for the entire length of his or her stay. To sweeten the deal further, they may throw in other amenities like free parking and/or free breakfasts. (Find something wrong with that, Accounting!) As with most other hotel discounts, however, **you gotta ask**, sometimes more than once.

Out-of-the-Ordinary Places to Stay

Of Hotels, Inns and Dormitories

Most executive travellers have seen enough sterile modern hotels to last a lifetime. Far too many business hotels are merely 'in' their cities, not 'of' them. From the architecture to the amenities, there is a sameness about them that was probably intended to be comforting but turns out to be monotonous instead.

Don't stay where you get the feeling that you could be anywhere. If it seems that you might be able to relocate the hotel to another city in the next time zone without any noticeable difference in what goes on inside the building, you are far less likely to enjoy your trip.

Don't stay where you get the feeling that you could be anyone. All other things being equal, I much prefer staying in an older, smaller hotel with interesting architecture, a unique sense of place, and personal service, to staying in a newer, larger hotel where I'm just a name and a room number. By 'all other things', I mean primarily plumbing and telecommunications. However, small interesting hotels where the staff call you by name, with good plumbing and phones that work, are not hard to find. Almost every major international city offers charming alternatives to the standard-issue business hotel, generally at about the same price, sometimes for substantially less.

You can also find these havens in less cosmopolitan centres as well. In Stockholm, for example, which I visit regularly for the Nobel Awards ceremonies in December, I tend to stay at the 320-room Grand Hotel, not only because it is a first-rate business hotel but also because a lot of the Nobel activities revolve around it. The convenience is irresistible. But visiting at another time of year, I could easily switch my allegiance to the more intimate confines of the Victory Hotel, just five minutes from the Grand, in a 500-year-old building in the Old Town. With a treasure trove of nautical antiques filling each of its forty-eight rooms, plus a Michelin-starred restaurant and world-class wine cellar, the Victory makes a trip to Stockholm special.

I have the same experience visiting Toronto. It's hard to argue with the overall excellence of the Four Seasons Toronto; with 600 rooms, it's amazing how attentive and alert the staff are. But I have a soft spot for the Sutton Place Hotel, where the staff are equally attentive but the size (180 rooms) is much more accommodating for a travelling executive who wants to feel at home.

I don't have compelling business reasons to visit Kuala Lumpur regularly, but like all business centres in the Far East, it has a spate of five-star hotels. Yet when I visited there two years ago, I made a point of staying at the Carcosa Sera Negara, which came highly recommended by friends and which I jotted down in my 'Take to Malaysia' file. (That's also a key to taking advantage of out-of-the-way special places: When people tell you about them, don't rely on memory. Write it down. As the Chinese proverb says, 'The palest ink is better than the best memory.') Housed in two turn-of-the-century mansions on forty acres of tropical gardens overlooking the city, the Carcosa Sera Negara made me rethink the rest of the world's standards for luxury and efficiency. Two butlers are assigned to each of the thirteen suites and are at your disposal from the time they pick you up at the airport to the time you depart (when they will take you to the airport or go in advance to take care of check-in formalities).

In an American city such as Seattle you can stay in one of the 865 rooms of the twin towers of the Westin (often likened to a pair of corncobs by the locals), wait forever for your luggage (and for the elevators), and get lost amid the weddings and high-school graduation parties if you stay over the weekend. Or you can be coddled at the Alexis in Seattle's lively historic district, where fifty-four rooms surround a sheltered courtyard and the ambiance resembles a private home. The Alexis offers complimentary continental breakfast, shoeshines and morning paper, a steam room that you can reserve just for your own use, and a restaurant that attracts not only business travellers but local epicures as well.

In St Louis, the traditional business hotel is Adam's Mark, all 910 rooms of it. It's a fine, first-class business hotel that provides everything an executive traveller could need. However, you don't give up much if you stay at the half-timbered Seven Gables Inn twenty minutes from downtown St Louis, in Clayton, which is a business and financial centre in its own right. Affiliated with the Relais et Chateaux group of hotels, the Tudoresque, turn-of-the-century Seven Gables has all of thirty-two rooms, an award-winning restaurant with a marvellous wine list, a real concierge, plus fax facilities and audio-visual equipment.

Not Just the Fax, Ma'am

Hotels like this are not exceptions. They exist all over the world. You can **recharge yourself by selecting a hotel with more to offer than just business facilities.** Finding hotels like these takes a little more work, but that's where planning comes in, as I discussed in Chapter 2.

The Last Resort

Many conferences and conventions are held at resorts; however, these hotels can sometimes function as excellent places to do business. A good example is the Claremont Resort Hotel in Oakland, California. The Claremont is a splendid old Victorian dowager of a building, fully restored, situated on a beautifully landscaped twenty-acre site, with a pool, comprehensive health club, ten tennis courts and large, well-appointed rooms.

If you are meeting with representatives from the University of California or from a Berkeley- or Oakland-based business, the geographic advantages of the Claremont are clear. But is it the most convenient hotel to stay in if the majority of your appointments are going to be in the Transamerica Pyramid or the Embarcadero in the heart of San Francisco?

Hardly. It takes about 35–40 minutes to get into downtown San Francisco from the Claremont. Does this knock it out of the running as a place to stay? Perhaps, but think about it. If you do have to do business in the city, you're not going to be spending very much more time getting there than locally-based executives who commute in daily from Berkeley, the Oakland hills, Walnut Creek, or any of the other prosperous Alameda County suburbs.

Do any of the people you will be dealing with live nearby? If so, it won't be inconvenient for them to stop by and have a drink on the way home from the office. Offer them a little tour of the historic old hotel. (The Claremont has a bit in common with local landmarks in many cities, in that most residents have seen it as they drive by, but very few of them have actually been inside the building.) Or invite them to come and play a few games of tennis – if your spouse will be joining you for all or part of the trip, make it a game of mixed doubles.

What's happened here? By staying out of town, you've given yourself an opportunity to strengthen and personalize your business relationship with the people you came to see. Your own trip has also become far more enjoyable. All of a sudden that off-the-beaten-track hotel has become an asset rather than a liability, and that 40-minute trip into San Francisco is getting shorter and more worthwhile all the time.

Novel Ways to Hold Meetings

If you think this sounds far-fetched, it's not. More and more business is being done in non-traditional ways and non-traditional locations. People doing everyday business are always posturing. They put on their 'game face' or their 'negotiating face' in the office. Even at a conventional business lunch they are likely to be on guard and maintain their façade. However, if you put people in unfamiliar territory, especially unfamiliar territory which is also fun or interesting, they are far more likely to drop their game faces and relax. When people are comfortable, they will be more receptive to whatever you're trying to talk to them about.

One of my favourite techniques is to **shake people up** – nicely, of course. Introduce them to places they've

- Never heard of;
- Would never go to on their own;
- Would never consider in a business context; or
- Would never associate with you.

This goes not just for hotels but for restaurants as well. Most business meals are held at places known to be safe and predictable by those organizing the event. Alas, they are usually known to be safe and predictable, and hence not very interesting, to others attending as well.

Neutralizing the Environment

When you do business in non-traditional ways, it serves to **neutralize the environment**. By neutralizing the environment, you have given yourself the edge and 'disarmed' your counter-part. Not that all business relationships are adversarial, but almost inevitably one of you will be more comfortable on a given turf than the other.

Better it should be you. In his struggle to adapt to that new environment – which he is actually going to like – your counterpart or potential business client comes to like you in the process because you are approaching a business relation-ship in a different, unexpected and refreshing way.

The Lube 'n' Tune Lunch

How do you neutralize the environment? You have to be ingenious about it, and unafraid to consider possibilities that are a little offbeat – or maybe even very offbeat. Find a venue for lunch or dinner that's not necessarily a restaurant. Find a venue for a meeting that's not necessarily an office. In New York you might take a walk in Central Park and have lunch at the Zoo. Former racing driver turned immensely successful transportation entrepreneur Roger Penske once invited his bankers to his Pennsylvania headquarters for lunch. Where did he serve the flawlessly prepared gourmet meal? In his immaculate garage.

How About Dinner at Gump's?

Other examples of this kind of creativity abound. Gump's is a renowned gift and housewares shop in San Francisco. Like the cable cars, columnist Herb Caen and Irish coffee at the Buena Vista Café, it's a venerable and very San Francisco institution. Gump's is famous for its china and crystal departments and for its elaborate room displays. A few of the better hotels in San Francisco have developed a relationship with Gump's whereby business executives can host meetings and dinner parties catered by the hotel, but held in the display rooms of the store after hours. I don't know a San Franciscan who wouldn't jump at the prospect of having a private dinner at Gump's. Could the same arrangement be made with Harrods or Fortnum & Mason in London, or Fauchon in Paris? You'll never know unless you ask. This is the kind of assignment that a good concierge loves to undertake.

One-on-One in a Rowboat

There's a wonderful place in Seattle called the Wooden Boat Museum on Lake Union. It's not a hot museum frequented by tourists, but it's not a dusty, static display either – there are about forty boats there that you can rent and take out on the lake. One enterprising business acquaintance of mine asked a potential client to meet him at the Wooden Boat Museum for lunch. He picked up a couple of great sandwiches and some terrific microbrewery beer from a nearby deli, ushered his quarry into a boat and rowed around the lake for a while.

Although I believe in unorthodox venues for business lunches, I found this to be somewhat beyond the pale. A rowboat? My friend explained his reasoning. 'I didn't do this out of the blue,' he said. 'I knew the guy liked boats – he keeps a sailboat at his weekend place in the San Juans.

'I also knew that by the time we got to a restaurant, got a table, talked about the weather, his wife, my wife, his kids, my kids, what the specials are for the day, the Mariners and the Seahawks and the Supersonics, the mess at Boeing and the rest of the small talk, that I'd have about eight minutes to get my point across. The deal I was proposing was a bit complicated. Eight minutes just wasn't going to do it.

'I knew he was comfortable on a boat. I needed his undivided attention. On the boat I had an unbelievably captive audience. It was perfectly private. There were no interruptions. We relaxed and had lunch. On the boat I had as much time as I needed.'

He made the deal.

The Eight-Minute Man

My friend came up with a delightfully ingenious solution. If you read 'The Rules of Lunch' in Chapter 10 you will find that he actually followed them to the letter, but on his own terms. In the process, however, he highlighted a real problem with the business lunch. It's very true that **the real time you will have to make your pitch is often ten minutes or less.**

Save the charts and the overhead projections for a breakfast meeting or for a separate presentation in a conference room. **Don't turn lunch into a lecture. You defeat the purpose of lunch by overburdening it with exhibits and paperwork.**

Beating an Unhasty Retreat

With impeccable meteorological logic, January sales conferences are held in Majorca, not Manchester, and July corporate strategy and budget meetings convene in Scotland, not Scottsdale, Arizona. It's a foregone conclusion that company retreats and business conventions will be held in vacation-like resorts during times of fair weather – sunny, not rainy, warm but not hot.

If it is your responsibility to plan one of these conferences, I urge you to use the same kind of creativity that you would in planning a smaller business lunch. You will find that a bit of ingenuity deepens the experience for the participants and often pays financial dividends as well.

Scout for Package Deals

Belt-tightening has cut sharply into conference and convention travel, giving you even more clout for negotiating discounted airfare and hotel rates. Some airlines and hotels have joined forces (including Hyatt and United Airlines) to offer discounted fares and nightly rates at excellent hotels.

Watch for Last-Minute Possibilities

Booking in advance is not necessarily a guarantee of a bargain. Sometimes even a popular destination will end up with a hole in its schedule, either because the economy is lethargic or because of a cancellation. If the group you are planning for is small, you may find yourself with an eleventh-hour windfall.

Playing the 'High Season' Game – and Winning

Many if not most resorts have rates that fluctuate by the season. Off-season rates can be as little as half (or less) the going rate at the height of the 'fashionable' period. In tropical and subtropical locations, summer is *outré*, winter is fashionable, and you will pay through the nose to be there during the holidays. In cooler or mountainous retreats, the seasons are reversed. However, it takes nothing but a little common sense (and perhaps a bit of personal experience) to realize two important but somehow not quite obvious facts:

- Weather doesn't turn from good to bad overnight.
- Even 'high season' is no guarantee of good weather.

For the conference planner, seasonal weather fluctuations and seasonal hotel rates are an opportunity, not a problem. If you study hotel rates and weather trends carefully, you are likely to discover windows of opportunity (generally just before or just after the peak season) when the weather is terrific and the prices are reasonable.

Even Off-Season Has Its Charms

I'm not recommending Florida during October (prime hurricane season) or Cannes in the heat of August, but don't overlook the attraction of some locations in their least popular seasons. During the summer, many skiing destinations are covered with wildflowers and offer terrific hiking, fishing and/or boating, as well as a plethora of empty hotel rooms. By the same token, the area around Santa Fe, New Mexico, believed to be at its most fashionable in summer during the opera and chamber music festivals, is fascinating as well as beautiful under a dusting of snow in the winter with a piñon pine fire in the grate.

Give Good Lunch

The common thread running through all these examples is to be inventive and play against the hackneyed approach to executive travel. Positioning yourself as an executive who 'gives good lunch' – a person who can share more than speeches and memos with business associates, and who comes up with original venues for meals and meetings – has always been good business.

9 Pace Yourself, Reward Yourself, Invigorate Yourself

An important part of the Hit the Ground Running attitude is finding ways to keep your energy level at a maximum. As I have already discussed in previous chapters, the smart business traveller is not afraid to take a nap in the afternoon in preparation for an evening of meetings, and he or she often will find time for a game of golf or a few sets of tennis. If you are working at 110 per cent, you need to relax. You have to renew your energy and you need to set goals with self-motivating rewards. For some travellers, a short jog or a brisk swim in the morning is part of a regular domestic regime that helps them keep their equilibrium. If you include it in your schedule, you can do it without endangering business appointments.

Simply staying healthy on a trip is an aspect of business travel that is too often neglected. Depending upon the distance travelled, many people give their biological systems some abrupt shifts and shake-ups. In this chapter, I will give you my common-sense tips on how to maintain health and energy levels; how to adjust to time and climate changes; and how to beat the toughest physical problem that long-distance travellers face: jet lag. Diet, vitamins, water intake, sleep patterns, and meal schedules can be important factors in maintaining focus and stamina.

There are many avenues of tension relief and relaxation. Smart business travellers should explore all of them – from stretching exercises on the aeroplane to utilizing exercise facilities in various hotels around the world – until they find the ones that work for them. Depending upon age level, not every traveller needs intense aerobic activity – a good brisk walk through a scenic park or historic part of town can serve double duty as exercise both for the body and for the psyche of the Hit the Ground Running traveller.

Find Your Own Rhythm – and Dance to It

I cannot emphasize too often that effective business travel is really an extension of an effective business life. If you establish a routine for yourself that works at home, try to maintain it on the road. Eliminating exercise or moments of relaxation from your schedule ultimately does not contribute to your effectiveness.

I set a fast pace for myself and enjoy it. Staying busy means staying vital and engaged with life. I freely admit that there are mornings when the alarm clock goes off at 4.30 a.m. and it is not an inspiring sound. But as soon as I am caught up in the action of the day, I feel energized. When I hit my stride, I anticipate the meetings on my schedule, enjoy my accomplishments hour by hour, and look forward to moments of reward that I always include.

Whatever your customary pace is, stick to it. There are people who will work from 7 a.m. through dinner with no time off, to get something done in three days. The same agenda might take me six days, if I only worked in the mornings and made phone calls and took a nap in the afternoons and had social dinners. Some people will fly into Japan and get it all done in three days and get out. Others would like to see a little of the town and work a little less frenetically, either because they are more effective that way or because they prefer it.

Keep Your Eye on the Ball

If you do try to have an intensely programmed business trip, make sure you aren't losing your effectiveness in the process. As Sir Christopher Lewinton puts it, 'There can be a tendency to confuse effort with results when you travel. I look at my effectiveness and the quality of the decisions I make – which is the thing that really matters. We all have different mechanisms, different body rhythms. I don't find that hopping the redeye does any good for me at all. I work better after having gotten a good night's sleep in a bed. It's no use hopping an overnight flight and pretending that I've gained those hours. I haven't really.'

Whatever the pace you prefer, set it deliberately and plan it out. Too many people just allow life to happen to them. An astonishing number of executives allow their business – and by extension, their business travel – to 'happen' in a similar way. I have already discussed the importance of participating in the details of your business travel and organizing your daily schedule. But there is a subtle aspect of your daily planning that only you can determine, and this is your own sense of rhythm or pacing.

In sports, the concept of pacing is well established. No marathon runner will survive long by sprinting from the starting line. Jockeys will plan different strategies for races of different lengths. Boxers vary greatly in how they approach a fight. And many coaches will tell you that pacing is the secret to winning the game.

As I hope you have understood by this point in the book, the concept of Hit the Ground Running means to arrive at your business destination in motion – with your schedule planned efficiently, your business tools at hand, and yourself in command of this valuable time out of the office. It certainly does *not* mean to dash off the aeroplane and keep running madly through an overbooked series of appointments. What I do, and what I advocate that the smart traveller should do, is to determine a series of goals for a trip, make a schedule that will fulfil those goals, and carefully plan the details that will enable you to move through that schedule efficiently and energetically. To achieve your goals on any given trip, you must pace yourself.

To keep your adrenalin flowing and keep your energy focused, you must find the rhythm that works for you. If that rhythm requires some 'down time' for rest and relaxation in mid-afternoon, or a pre-dinner jog, then plan for these activities. Write them into your schedule. If you don't feel good unless you have started your day with a workout, then include a workout among the priorities on your daily travel itinerary. Don't just hope you will 'find' an hour. Recognize your needs – both physical and psychological – and include them in your plans. You will be healthier and happier for doing so.

Finding the Health Club that Meets Your Needs

Michael Gray, general manager of London's Hyatt Carlton Tower, told me that he has been amazed at how important health clubs have become to a hotel from a marketing standpoint. 'Quite a few people said to me that their travelling executives will choose a hotel simply on whether it's got a health club. It's really up there as the number one criterion.

'The interesting factor from the hotelier's point of view is that very few of those people are actually using the fitness facilities. The majority of our Carlton Tower health club users are outside members. We average just twenty people a day from our hotel guests, which is very small. People pack their swimming gear and running shoes, and rarely find the time to use them. The use of the club at our hotel is included as one of our general services. There is no extra charge, yet usage is still surprisingly low.'

In recent years, many hotels have added fitness centres or health clubs. But they vary widely in size, sophistication, and cost to guests. What some hotels call a 'fitness centre' is nothing more than a converted closet with an inexpensive stationary exercise bicycle and a few weights. For example, the Sheraton Boston Hotel and Towers advertises a 'health/ fitness centre'. In reality, the 'centre' consists of three Lifecycle machines, a set of Universal weights, a Jacuzzi and a large indoor/outdoor pool.

At the Four Seasons hotel chain, however, well-equipped and staffed fitness centres are a priority. 'If you don't have a good fitness centre, your guests will know right away,' claims Charles Ferraro, vice-president of operations for Four Seasons. 'A good health club has become an expected amenity.' A few years ago, they spent $3 million on the health club at the Four Seasons in Washington, DC. In Los Angeles, the Four Seasons facility has four Stairmaster machines, six stationary bicycles and three treadmills. In addition, if you prefer to sweat in private, they have a Stairmaster that can be put in your room upon request.

An aspect of health clubs that hotels are beginning to appreciate is qualified staff. 'You need good supervision at a hotel,' says Tom Pheil, health spa manager at Loews Santa Monica Beach Hotel. 'The biggest problem at a hotel health club is guest ego. That's the most important reason why a hotel fitness centre needs certified trainers to be there. We've had guys come in who have never rowed before on a rowing machine and they set it for the Olympic level. Or people who have never exercised hard lose their balance and fall off the treadmill. It can be dangerous.' Good trainers can be helpful for more experienced exercise enthusiasts, too. At the Plus One Fitness Clinic in New York's Waldorf-Astoria, personal trainers are even available to go running in Central Park with visitors who are apprehensive about running alone.

If your workout requires more specialized high-tech equipment than most hotels provide, you will want to plan ahead and stay in a hotel that has a fully-equipped gymnasium nearby. If you already belong to a club that is part of one of the large chains, such as Bally's, which owns more than 400 health clubs in the US, you can usually arrange to use facilities in other cities for free or a nominal charge. If you are a member of a club affiliated with the International Racquet Sports Association, you will find clubs with tennis, racquetball and squash courts in several countries.

I am always interested in new golf courses or good tennis courts near my hotel. I have found that golf, tennis and other sports associations will help you locate facilities in cities where you are travelling. There are frequently specialized guides for hiking, jogging or bicycling available in different areas. To accommodate your exercise needs you have to make a few telephone calls, but it will be well worthwhile for the health of your next trip.

My friend Robert Anderson, former CEO of Rockwell International, sums up the argument for exercise pretty well: 'I think exercise helps most executives on a trip if they make time for it. Most business trips are usually pretty pressured, but one thing you can always find time to do is your exercise – all you need is an hour. Most hotels have made great improvements in this area in the last few years – it used to be that to get any exercise you had to run around the halls. People are beginning to recognize that they really need their exercise, just to feel better, to do the job well.'

Other Forms of Relaxation

Although I am an advocate of exercise for relaxation, I recognize that many people prefer less strenuous ways of taking their minds off business and shedding their stress. My wife and I both enjoy bringing new books with us when we travel. Reading books is usually a late evening pleasure for me, because there is just no time during the rest of the day. (I also like to enquire if the hotel television system receives ESPN or CNN.)

A number of my executive friends have become enthusiasts for books on audiotape and will carry boxes of cassettes or CDs and a Walkman on their trips. Lots of people in an aeroplane are wearing headsets for the movie or the programmed music, so no one pays any attention to another passenger who is happily 'reading' *War and Peace* with his or her eyes closed. (Some even arrange to have reports or information from their offices put on to cassettes so that they can absorb the material without reading.)

The idea of meditation conjures up mysticism and New Age religions for some people, but I know many business travellers who find that meditation exercises are an effective way to deal with tensions, focus energies, and just relax. If you close your eyes and meditate in your office, there is always the lurking concern that someone will think you are 'sleeping on the job'. In the privacy of your hotel room, you have an opportunity for refreshment that many people claim is more revitalizing for them than a nap. Of course, half the people on aeroplanes are sitting there with their eyes closed. Maybe more of them are meditating than we know!

The Global Traveller's Greatest Health Threat: Jet Lag

The bad news is that there is no cure for jet lag. The good news is that there are lots of things you can do to mitigate the effects of zipping your body through time zones too quickly.

There are entire books on the subject of jet lag, yet no one has been able to pin it down. Some researchers say that, for every time zone you cross, it takes one day to adjust your body clock. Unfortunately, business travellers can't wait around for their circadian rhythms to catch up. They suffer the familiar agonies of insomnia, fatigue, aching muscles and headache. If they are lucky, their jet lag will not induce more extreme symptoms, such as disorientation, memory loss, gastric distress, heart-rate problems, reduced reflexes, or lowered immune response (which can lead to many other medical complications).

A curious aspect of the jet-lag problem which none of the scientific studies address is that most people suffer jet lag more severely travelling in an easterly direction than they do heading west. For example, business people travelling from New York find that they are hit with more symptoms of jet lag going to Europe than upon returning. Same number of time zones, same distance – but there is no explanation for the difference in experiences.

Many Japanese corporations and a few American companies have corporate policies requiring employees to wait one full day after a transcontinental trip before entering into business negotiations on behalf of the company. Sir Christopher

Lewinton agrees. 'In the decision-making process, I try to build a gap between travelling and making a decision. When you travel a lot, your gyroscope flips a little and you need to ground yourself again and stabilize. Providing the decision can wait a day or so, I'll tend to wait to make a commitment.

'There's an element of being persuaded that you're a real man – that you can come off a plane and make a decision straightaway. I think that's nonsense. When I'm pressed, I'll say, "Wait a minute! Tell me what the penalty is for deciding this tomorrow rather than today."'

This makes sense if you have the time. All too often, however, I don't. Frequently I am moving through time zones so many times a week that if I stopped to adjust at each destination, I would never have time for business. I am not immune to jet lag. But I have developed ways to reduce the initial symptoms to a manageable level and to recover my body clock quickly. Needless to say, I make no claims to medical authority, but here is what works for me:

Mark McCormack's Rules for Taking the Lag Out of Jet Lag

1.   Hit the Ground Running
The smart traveller will plan every step of the departure, the flight, the arrival at the airport, the trip to the hotel, and the schedule after arriving, so that he or she is already caught up psychologically in the destination's time zone before departing. Set your watch to your destination's time. Think about your activities upon arrival. Give your mind every chance to tell your body what will be expected.

2.   Drink Large Quantities of Water
If you don't want to bother with bringing your own bottled water, try to persuade a flight attendant to give you a bottle right after take-off. Dehydration is often responsible for many symptoms described as 'jet lag'. Most of the medical experts will tell you not to drink alcohol or caffeine on the flight because it will exacerbate the effects of dehydration. I don't follow this advice strictly. I enjoy having a few glasses of

wine in the evening or with dinner, and I find that maintaining this simple ritual makes me more comfortable. But I drinks lots of water, too.

3. Exercise

I suppose this rule could be a subsection of rule 1, Hit the Ground Running, because I believe in taking a vigorous walk (not necessarily a 'run') as quickly as possible after arrival – unless you are arriving at an hour which dictates immediate sleep. I exercise a bit in the aeroplane whenever I am not sleeping. Get up, walk around the cabins, touch your toes, suck in your gut, and generate some circulation in your body. Some flight attendants are downright hostile about passengers being out of their seats for any reason. Ignore them. Claim you need to use the rest room and take your stroll.

4. Eat Lightly – On Your Own Schedule

Order special meals of fruit or salads and try to eat them approximately when you would normally be eating in your destination time zone. This, of course, can be difficult because airline service is often organized around the timing of in-flight movies and will allow no individual flexibility. To circumvent this problem, you can carry your own food and eat it on your own schedule or simply skip most of what is being served on the aeroplane. (This is not difficult to do if you are sleeping through the food service anyway.)

5. Give Your Body Time Zone Signals

Patterns of illumination and social behaviour tell your body what time it is, too, according to scientists at the Argonne National Laboratory. This translates into emphasizing the obvious. If you are arriving at your destination in the daytime, get out and be active in sunlight as much as possible. When you sleep, be sure your room is quiet and has good blackout drapes or you use a sleep mask. Do not stay up later than you normally would simply because you know that you are ahead a few time zones.

Gary Player offers an insight that combines several of these rules: 'I'm very averse to coffee, to caffeine, but coffee has been one of my great saviours. I don't drink coffee ever while playing in golf tournaments or in general. But when travelling, when I arrive at my destination in the morning, obviously my time sense is screwed up. I have a cup of coffee to jolt me up and keep me awake. One of the secrets of good travelling is to get off the plane and get on the local clock as though there is no time change. You've almost got to brainwash yourself. It's like golf. Never think about the putt you missed. Think about the one you're going to make. Never think back to what the time was where you were coming from. Think about what the time is where you are now.' (Researchers confirm Gary's intuitive idea about having a cup of coffee upon arrival. The methylated xanthines in caffeine help to reset the body clock.)

All of my suggestions about jet lag may be irrelevant soon, however. Scientists at the Oregon Health Sciences University in Portland are well on their way to developing a jet-lag pill. They have discovered that the body's circadian rhythms are controlled by a hormone called melatonin produced by the pineal gland. Melatonin (playfully dubbed 'the Dracula hormone') is stimulated by darkness and acts directly on the brain's timing centre. A tiny dose of this hormone will fool the body into believing that it is time for bed. So, in the near future, we may just have to pop a pill to reset the body clock.

Fear of Flying is Not Just Erica Jong's Problem

Novelist Erica Jong wrote a sexy book called *Fear of Flying* several years ago, and 'FOF' has been the subject of jokes ever since. But, according to surveys, one out of every six people harbours a serious, deep-seated fear of getting in aeroplanes. Often, this fear manifests itself in excessive drinking and eating or other nervous behaviours. Sometimes it is mistaken for jet lag. If you secretly suffer from fear of flying and are worried that this will affect your business opportunities, get help. Several airlines and private clinics run modestly priced weekend and evening programmes to deal with fear of flying. They claim a high rate of cures, and any travel agent should know where to contact one of them in your area.

Dr McCormack's All-Purpose Travelling Medicine Chest

Travellers heading to the major business centres will generally find pharmacies available with the usual array of over-the-counter remedies. But if you wake up in a hotel room at 3 a.m. feeling lousy, you will wish you had brought along a few items. Here are my suggestions for a compact, all-purpose travelling medicine chest:

- All prescription medicines you are taking (bring prescriptions to satisfy Customs agents)
- Aspirin or mild painkiller
- Antacids of some sort
- Pepto-Bismol
- Cold/flu remedies
- Eye drops
- Laxative
- Diarrhoea remedy
- Bandaids of various sizes
- Small scissors
- Antiseptic ointment
- Bug repellent
- Anti-fungal foot powder
- Sleeping pills or sedative
- Sleep mask
- Earplugs
- Small packs of tissues for emergency toilet paper and that head cold that's just leaving or just coming on
- The name and phone number of your physician at home
- The name and phone number of someone in the city where you are staying who can speak for you if you are incapacitated
- Your international vaccine record
- Your blood type and allergies

Sometimes You Feel Like You Are What You Eat

I advocate adventurous eating, but because travellers are particularly susceptible to nervous stomach troubles, jet lag and exhaustion, they should use some good sense when dining out. Too many travellers find that the expense account is an invitation to gluttony. This is bad economics and bad dietary sense. My friend Bill Fugazy, chairman of the board of Fugazy International, observes: 'Most people find business travel very tiring. The reason is that they drink too much, eat too much, probably don't get enough sleep, and never exercise on the road. The excess liquor and food is very bad for your constitution.' Worse than overeating can be eating foods prepared in ways your stomach is not equipped to handle. For example, the classic French *haute cuisine* can be loaded with buttery, egg-enriched, creamy sauces. Many a self-diagnosed case of 'Montezuma's Revenge' turns out to be hot Mexican peppers and spices wreaking havoc in a gringo stomach. Be cautious of the same zingy problem with certain dishes of Chinese, Indian or Thai food.

Worth a warning of its own is MSG or monosodium glutamate, which many Chinese restaurants sprinkle all too generously into soups, rice, and dishes of all sorts. MSG (like soy sauce) is high in sodium and may affect blood pressure. This substance can have even more unpleasant side effects for many diners, including headaches and nausea. Most waiters in Chinese restaurants are familiar with the problem and will respond to a request that the chef leave out the MSG.

Try to **be moderate in your consumption of alcohol**, even if your clients are not. Many Americans who travel in Europe are surprised to discover that wine – and the pleasures of the table in general – are much more a part of life there than they are at home. This does not necessarily mean that you should completely abstain. It means that you should maintain the same reasonable drinking habits that you have at home.

Whenever I hear cautions about drinking on business trips, I am reminded of the first time I met the great Olympic skier Jean-Claude Killy in the summer of 1967. (The next year in Grenoble, he swept away three gold medals.) We had lunch at a good restaurant in Geneva with my friend Hank Ketcham, who draws the Dennis the Menace cartoon strip. After we sat down, Killy ordered a glass of red wine. Somewhat naively I expressed surprise that he would be drinking wine while in training for the Olympics. In response, he smiled warmly and asked me, 'Would you rather I drink milk – and ski like the Americans?'

Bloom Where You're Planted

Several years ago the tennis press reported 'Andre Agassi hates Paris'. Richard Evans, formerly of the London *Sunday Times*, reported that Agassi absolutely detested the City of Light, one of his very favourite places on earth. Evans went on to explain that he had a trainer with him all the time, and every night he sent him out for burgers and french fries from McDonald's, and the two of them would sit in front of the TV in the room eating burgers and fries with his brother and coach. Evans wrote, 'How can he hate Paris when he's never really been there?'

The simplest and most gratifying way to enjoy your trip to another city is to discover the pleasures of the city you are visiting. Although some cities are more pleasurable than others, virtually no major business centre is completely devoid of charm. To reward yourself for being on the road, **you must get out and see some of the city you are visiting.**

For the executive traveller, the keys to finding health, pleasure and relaxation while travelling are moderation, exercise and a willing spirit. **Be adventurous.** No matter how many times you've been to a city, **find ways to make your travel experience fresh for yourself each time.**

10 Successful Travel is an Accumulation of Details

God is in the details.
Ludwig Mies van der Rohe

Mies van der Rohe, one of the masters of modern architecture, knew that command of the details was what separated interesting yet simple structures from monotonous grey boxes. A smooth and comfortable journey is no different. This chapter covers an assortment of details about various aspects of business travel. Taking care of these details greatly enhances your odds of having an agreeable and fruitful trip. If neglected, however, they can easily come back to haunt you, making your time away from home unproductive, uneasy and unpleasant.

At the Hotel

Check-In Tips

There are few sights more disheartening to an arriving business traveller than a lone beleaguered clerk at the registration desk and a line that's thirty people long. Some business hotels are beginning to offer accelerated check-in for their frequent guests. It's still a very uneven process, however.

With or without accelerated check-in, you shouldn't have to stand in that line. You can speed the process yourself by doing a great deal of the check-in work over the phone before you ever arrive at the hotel. Start by giving the hotel your credit card number and making sure that the hotel knows what time you are due to arrive. Tell them that you need accelerated check-in and ask for help in avoiding the lines. It also helps, of course, to plan your arrival time off peak, away from the crush of other arrivals.

Which credit card you give the hotel when you check-in matters a great deal. **Use a no-limit card to check in** (American Express, Diners Club), even if that's not the card you will eventually use to pay your bill. If you check in with a Visa, Mastercard, Access or any card that has a credit line, the hotel blocks or reserves a healthy chunk of credit for your bill to protect themselves against absconding guests. This chunk will be far greater than your actual bill. You won't even know that they did it – until you get a nasty and potentially embarrassing surprise when your credit card is refused after you try to pay for a client dinner at Michael's or Aquavit or Le Recamier. It's a very simple matter at check-out time to alter the method of payment. The hotel just destroys one charge slip and prepares another.

Easy Come/Easy Go? Maybe Yes/Maybe No

Although many hotels have found ways to speed up the check-out process, expediting check-in has been slower in coming. Marriott and Hilton are now offering members of their frequent-stay programmes a chance to bypass the front desk entirely and check in at a special counter. All they need to do is present a credit card to receive a room key and check-in packet.

Does this speedy check-in pay dividends to the business traveller? It depends. Instant check-in is fine if you are staying at a hotel you know well and the staff is familiar with your preferences. It's also fine if all rooms in the hotel are more or less the same.

But do you *really* want to stay in a hotel where all the rooms are plain vanilla? In larger cities, not just in Europe but in the US as well, the older hotels are the most interesting places to stay. In better old hotels, all rooms, even at the same price level, are most assuredly *not* the same. Within a given hotel chain, the same level of accommodation changes markedly from one property and one city to another. There is a big difference between a suite at the meticulously-restored nineteenth-century Willard InterContinental in Washington, DC, a suite at the rather stolid, glass and concrete-block InterContinental in Frankfurt, and a suite at the up-to-the-minute InterContinental in Seoul, with wet bars in the room and a shopping arcade below.

Old Wine in New Bottles

Despite the potential benefits of frequent-stay programmes, I can't recommend loyalty to a particular hotel chain the way I can recommend loyalty to an individual hotel where you are well treated. More often than not, hotel chains manage rather than own the buildings with their names emblazoned on the canopy. In some cases, when the property changes hands or the hotel becomes otherwise troubled, what was formerly a Sheraton last week reopens with a great deal of fanfare as a Marriott after the soaps and stationery have been changed.

In very few cases is the hotel revitalized from top to bottom, so that major building flaws, like slow elevators and bad water pressure, will remain. If the phone cords were short before, chances are they're still going to be short under new management. This happens not just with small run-of-the-mill properties but with large business hotels as well. The Pan Pacific in San Francisco was the Portman just a few years ago. Even New York's venerable Plaza, which for many years has been operated by the Westin chain, was once a Hilton property.

Hotel names can also be confusing to the executive traveller. The Ritz in Paris has no corporate affiliation with the Ritz in London or the Ritz in Madrid. The Ritz-Carlton chain operates none of these European Ritz hotels, nor the Carlton Tower in London.

Personal Service

What's the point? Cultivating a relationship with a particular hotel where the service is good and where the staff knows you and your preferences is a great way to get the most out of your business travel. Herbert Striessnig, general manager of the Savoy in London, said it best of all: **'The best hotel in the world is the hotel you're best known in.'**

British television personality Michael Parkinson, our long-time client, finds Mr Striessnig's hostelry to be among his favourites because of its personal service. 'When I was working at TV-am,' he recalls, 'a condition of the deal was that I spend a weekend at the Savoy, because I had to get up very early in the morning to do the programme. The first night I stayed at the Savoy, I told the fellow at the desk that I wanted a wake-up call at 3.30 a.m. He was astonished – he'd never had a request like that before. At 3.30 I was awakened not by the telephone but by a man shaking my shoulder. I opened my eyes and there was this immaculate man in tails and a white stiff collar who said, "Mr Parkinson, I have regretfully to inform you that it's 3.30 in the morning." That's a great hotel.'

Play the Field

Because of changing ownership and management of hotels and the fact that most chains own many types of hostelries, **no single hotel chain has 'the best hotel' or 'the best hotel for you' in every city you visit**. Therefore cultivating an exclusive or semi-exclusive relationship with a particular hotel chain based on its 'frequent stay' programme is not nearly as rewarding as developing a rapport with staff at a particular hotel. Play the field and stay in the hotel that best meets your needs. If that turns out to be the Four Seasons Clift in San Francisco, the Westin Plaza in New York and the Hyatt Carlton Tower in London, I think the gains in service and comfort far outweigh any frequent-stay benefits that have been forgone.

Room-by-Room Through the Crillon

I sleep in hotel rooms at least as often as I sleep in my own bed at home, so I'm choosy about my hotel accommodations, even at the Crillon. The first time my wife accompanied me to Paris for the French Open tennis tournament, we were shown to what had become my customary suite at the Crillon. It had always been fine on previous trips, so I moved in without hesitation.

The suite was on the top floor and had a very big bedroom and a huge balcony overlooking all of Paris. However, it had just a tiny sitting room. It didn't take long to discover that the accommodation that was quite wonderful for one solitary traveller was impractical for two busy individuals. Once I had established my office beachhead, there was no real personal space for Betsy to call her own. We were constantly falling over one other, something which was not a problem when I was travelling alone.

The Crillon was full and moving was impossible so we muddled through, but I asked my London assistant, Sarah Wooldridge, to find out what my options would be for the next visit. With typical thoroughness, she looked at every suite in the hotel. She checked for detail and weighed the pluses and minuses of each room – this one's got a bath; that one has a large bed; this other is not near the lift. The suite we settled on is very nice, but not nearly so impressive as the grand suite on the top floor with the balcony. It has more space in the sitting area and is very practical. Betsy has a place for all her tennis gear and a staging area of her own. So what? **The best room in the hotel is the one where you are most comfortable and productive, not the one which is most 'prestigious'.**

A Hotel Room Punch List

Am I suggesting that you go through all 3,000 + rooms of the Las Vegas Hilton before you settle in? Of course not. Some room requirements you can establish when you make your reservation. Noted travel writer Ian Keown came up with the business traveller's dream checklist for a hotel room – however, he was quick to add that he's never stayed in a room that's even come close to having all his desired attributes.

The Keown Test: the Perfect Hotel Room

Down to Basics

- Double bed (or larger) with a firm mattress and a choice of pillows.
- Swivelling reading lamps with 75-watt bulbs for the bed-side.
- Bedside table with 3-way lamps and a control console for lights, TV, radio, and drapes.
- Real desk with swivelling, high-intensity desk lamp and a proper desk chair.
- Armchair, ottoman or sofa.
- Coffee table that converts to a dining table.
- Coffee maker with a selection of coffees and teas.
- Well-stocked minibar with two-way loading cubicle.
- Lighted closet with removable coat hangers for trousers, dresses and skirts; a full-length mirror, and a luggage rack.
- Individual heating/cooling controls.
- Double-glazed windows that open and close.
- Do Not Disturb signs – and hotel help that heeds them.
- Doorknob cards for ordering breakfast.

Keeping in Touch

- Two-line telephones with message light.
- Three telephone extensions, one each for the bedside, desk and bath.
- Notepad and pen beside each extension.
- Voice mail or video message retrieval.
- Teleconferencing capability.
- Fax and computer modem capability.
- Incoming calls that revert to the operator after five – not fifty – rings when the guest is out.

- Telephone messages placed in the concierge slot and under the door.
- Service for in-room rental of fax machines, personal computers, dictating equipment, cellular telephone and beepers.
- Accessible electrical outlets.

That's Entertainment
- Clock/radio with alarm and readable operating instructions.
- Colour television with remote control.
- Cable television, including CNN.
- Video player with in-house movies available.
- *TV Guide* or equivalent opened to the correct date.
- Stereo system with compact disc-player – and CDs available.
- Other essential – though less entertaining – information on your television screen, including airline flight information, the weather, and your ongoing bill.

Cleaning Up Your Act
- Bathroom with separate shower stall and separate toilet.
- Twin vanities, preferably in separate dressing area.
- Bathrobes, and hooks on which to hang them!
- Hairdryers.
- Make-up mirror.
- Adequate shelves for toiletries.
- Taps that are easy to operate, overhead showers with variable speed, and shower curtains that cover the entire shower.
- Large bath towels.
- Trash can that can be opened without stooping.
- Toiletries, including shampoo and conditioner, bath gel, toothpaste, razor, toothbrush, and cotton balls or swabs.

Safe and Sound
- Electronic card locks.
- Double-locking doors.

- In-room private safe (preferably electronic).
- Adequate soundproofing – between rooms and between the room and the corridor.
- Double connecting doors.
- Drapes and curtains that shut out all the light.
- Smoke detector and emergency evacuation directions.

Hotel Services

- Evening turndown service, with fresh towels and a bottle of mineral water rather than candy or brandy on the pillow.
- 24-hour room service that offers omelettes any time.
- Room service order-takers who are not located among the pots and pans in the noisiest part of the kitchen.
- 24-hour business centre.
- Health spa or gymnasium, sauna and pool, which are open after normal business hours.
- Concierge floor with private keys, complimentary breakfast and cocktails, local and international newspapers, and a lounge with telephones and quiet corners for mini-meetings.
- All-day dining room – with no music.
- Same-day laundry, dry cleaning and pressing service available seven days a week.
- Complimentary shoeshine.
- Daily newspaper delivery to your room.

I'm in agreement with Keown except on a few minor points:

1. I hate the minibars and try to avoid using them.
2. I've never seen a hotel hairdryer that any woman with hair longer than mine thought was any good at all.
3. I've learned *never* to trust hotel alarm clocks *or* wake-up calls.
4. There should be a master switch by the door *and* by the bed.
5. Beware of shoeshines if you don't have an alternative pair of shoes.

Some explanations:

Minibars

It always seems that a hotel staff member is trying to inventory and replenish the minibar at the very moment you are on an important phone call. Some newer hotels have now been engineered to permit restocking from the hallway, but I still find minibars to be a second cousin to pickpocketing or petty larceny.

Hairdryers

I don't know any woman with hair longer than mine who thinks that built-in hairdryers are any good at all. They usually generate too little air, too much noise and not enough heat. 'They're a disaster,' agrees Raymond Bickson, general manager of The Mark Hotel in New York. 'You can never control their speed, and they always seem to be placed in the most awkward positions, so you have to be Houdini to dry your hair.'

Alarm Clocks and Wake-Up Calls

On a business trip, the downside of not getting up is too serious to contemplate. 'Never, ever trust wake-up calls or the clock radio or alarm clock the hotel provides,' counsels Graham K.L. Jeffrey, general manager of the Willard InterContinental in Washington, DC, making no exception for his own establishment.

It's very sound advice. Far too many things can go wrong. If you have trouble programming your VCR, you will have trouble programming the clock radio, especially overseas, especially if you're trying to do it when you're tired and jet-lagged. Assuming that you do figure out how to set it, you may find out that the alarm is broken – the hard way. The clock radio is routinely placed next to the bed. Even if it does go off at the right time, it's all too easy to reach out and turn it off without really waking up. As for wake-up calls, they're just too unreliable. Every experienced business traveller can tell a story or two (at least) of the wake-up call that arrived half an hour late – or not at all.

How do I get up when I travel? I have systems and back-up systems. **Bring your own battery-powered alarm clock, set it yourself, and place it across the room**, not next to the bed. I also ask for a wake-up call, but Graham Jeffrey provided me with the best strategy of all: 'Always place a room-service order the night before, even if it's just for coffee,' he recommends. 'It's a great back-up, and besides, you have to get up to answer the door.'

Master Switches

Many hotels will put a master switch right by the front door, which is great when you're coming or going. One switch serves all the lights in the room. But what about when you're going to bed? You have to go to the front door, turn every-thing off, bark your shins and stumble back to bed in the dark.

Shoeshines

Looking well-groomed on the road is important, and I admire the European tradition of setting shoes out overnight to be shined. However, take a tip from the experience of Robert Anderson, retired CEO of Rockwell International, and carry a back-up pair of shoes.

'I was staying at the Churchill in London and put my shoes outside the door, as is the custom,' recalls Anderson. 'When I got up in the morning and went out to retrieve them, they weren't there. They were nowhere to be found. It doesn't sound like much of a disaster, but when you get up in the morning and want to go somewhere, you're stuck if you don't have your shoes. I'd only brought one pair with me. I finally had to get someone from the hotel to go out and get me some slippers so I could at least get to a store to buy some replacements. I reported the disappearance to the hotel detective, and when I got back to my room that night after dinner my shoes were back in my room.

'I was baffled. "What the hell happened?" I asked him.

'"We apologize for the inconvenience, sir," he told me. "We found your shoes down on the third floor in one of the laundry rooms, behind a pile of laundry."

'It was a very strange place indeed for shoes. "How did they get there?" I asked.

'"We have an old sheik staying with us, and he's a bit deranged. He goes around at night and steals shoes. We found about half a dozen pairs there, sir, mostly wingtips but a few tassel-loafers as well."'

Be Finicky About Your Hotel Room

Whatever your expectations when you book your reservation, when you are actually shown to the room it's up to you to make sure that you are getting what you requested. Too many business travellers are too tired to notice room details when they arrive. Often you are so relieved by the time you finally reach your hotel room that you are insufficiently meticulous about checking it thoroughly. Not me. Don't accept the room to which you are shown without a careful look around. **It will never be easier to change your hotel room than before you've slept in the bed or flushed the toilet.** This involves a careful examination of not only the room itself but the corridor, and rooms surrounding it.

The Itzhak Perlman Rule

Violinist Itzhak Perlman once came up with one of the most elegantly simple maxims for judging a hotel room from the outside. **Never accept a room if the door next to it doesn't have a number on it.** That unnumbered door is a guarantee of a less-than-restful stay. Almost invariably it leads to something noisy, such as the elevator, the dumbwaiter, the laundry room, the soda and/or ice machine, or the place where the vacuum cleaners lurk and chambermaids go to gossip.

Cleanliness Is Next to . . .

I'm particularly finicky about hotel cleanliness. In a recent Wyndham Hotels & Resorts survey, stale rooms were the leading complaint business travellers had about hotel accommodation. Unless you accept rooms that smell or look unclean at home, you shouldn't accept them on the road.

Assuming that the room passes your initial test, consider the bedding, an important component of room cleanliness (and one which is entirely out of view when you arrive). At most hotels, blankets are not changed with each new guest, and not every hotel provides fresh pillows. For all you know, they could have been in the room for weeks, or used just last night by a profusely sweating conventioneer and his dandruff-prone spouse. Even if the room appears acceptable, there are ways to make sure that your accommodations are really clean. Unless you have great confidence that this is done routinely, **call housekeeping and ask for a fresh blanket and pillow for the bed**. Ask them to replace the spare blanket and pillow in the closet as well.

The Shower Test

Unless you will be hosting meetings in your room or suite, you may find that you'll spend more of your waking hours in your hotel bathroom than anywhere else. Low water pressure in the shower was the second leading non-service complaint of business travellers in the Wyndham survey. Ignore the impatience of the bellman waiting for his tip. This room deserves considerable attention.

To me, a great hotel must have a great shower. This means a plentiful supply of hot (but not scalding) water. It also means that **the water must stay at a uniform temperature and pressure unless you yourself change it**. Most business travellers have tales of a near-death experience in a hotel shower – by either sudden scalding or the instant arrival of a new Ice Age. When you check your room in an unfamiliar hotel, turn on the shower.

The first thing to notice is whether this can be accomplished without a manual from the tap manufacturer. All too many of these high-tech taps have an all-in-one control, whereby the difference between on/off and hot/cold is a subtle adjustment in or out, left or right. There are teensy little arrows and microscopic lettering indicating which is which. I need my glasses to read, but I most assuredly do not wear them in the shower. Without them I must resort to guesswork to determine whether I'm going to freeze or broil with every turn of the knob (or stick or handle or button or dial). I'm sure some interior designer thought this looked quite modern and elegant, but to me it's a potential disaster.

Watch the shower for random fluctuations in temperature and pressure. What happens when you flush the toilet or turn on the tap? What happens when someone down the corridor or on the floor below you does likewise? In general, **be more suspicious of bathrooms in older hotels than in newer ones**. Although older hotels may have been refurbished many times, only in the most thorough renovations are plumbing difficulties resolved. **Taller hotels are potentially more susceptible to plumbing problems than low-rise buildings**. Without booster pumps, most hotels taller than eight storeys will have trouble with water pressure, particularly on the upper floors.

Who's got the best bathrooms around? The stately Biltmore in downtown Los Angeles vastly improved its water pressure in a recent facelift. The Savoy in London has shower heads on the ceiling and a supplemental water-pressure system. The Regent in Hong Kong and other Regent hotels (as well as the Grand in Washington, formerly a Regent property) are known for their large and well-appointed bathrooms, which are also equipped with shower temperature regulators.

Planning a Business Meeting away from Home

Making good use of your hotel or your chosen restaurant when you must host an out-of-town event involves careful planning. A lot of business travellers call up the hotel and say, 'I've got twenty people coming for lunch. Arrange to have a private room. Goodbye.' If that is the extent of your planning, you'll get what you deserve.

Take Advantage of Being the Host

There's a great deal to be said for being the host rather than the guest. Along with the privilege of paying the cheque, you get to decide who's invited and where you'll dine. Given the choice, I'm most comfortable in a dining ambiance that's quiet rather than noisy, roomy rather than crowded, responsive rather than difficult. Use your status as host to call the shots, but mind what shots you call.

The Three Business Meals of the Day

The first guideline to follow is **make the meal fit the occasion**. One of our executives contends that the First Rule of Lunch is *Never have a business lunch with someone you have never met before*. He figures it's as risky as a blind date. By the time the appetizer comes around and you realize that the two of you have nothing in common, it's too late. You're trapped. Business meals have always been tricky. Unlike office meetings, where you know you have gathered to discuss business, business meals are partly social, partly business – and the ratio between the two changes from meal to meal. In general, business meals get progressively less business-like as the day wears on.

Breakfast Should Bustle

Breakfast is for getting down to business. I often have two breakfast meetings before 9 a.m. You don't have to apologize for setting a specific business agenda at breakfast and getting right to it. In fact, people expect and appreciate it. Breakfast doesn't eat up time. About forty-five minutes is standard. You can be comfortable with anyone – even boring strangers – within that time frame. You also don't have to eat much, or plan too strenuously – muffins or rolls, juice and fruit and coffee and tea are about all that's required. Almost any business hotel ought to be able to make a good breakfast presentation of this sort. (If they can't, it's a very bad sign indeed. Find another hotel or restaurant for a lunch or dinner meeting, and another place to stay next time you're in town.)

Breakfast also creates momentum in a business relationship. People don't seem to mind meeting once or twice a month for breakfast – if they know something positive will be accomplished. Lunch and dinner are much tougher to schedule. I particularly like breakfast for floating trial balloons – for piquing the other side's interest with a new idea and telling them, 'You don't have to decide this at breakfast.' Best of all, issues brought up at breakfast can be followed up the same day.

The Rules of Lunch

Lunch takes time. Lunch costs money, and depending on the food and drink you consume, lunch can destroy the rest of your day. Having said that, I must admit that I am nevertheless a proponent of the business lunch. **Lunch provides the perfect balance between business and pleasure**. Like a meeting, it has a predetermined beginning and end. Enjoying yourself is not frowned upon and getting something accomplished is also approved. Lunch is also an effective shorthand of telling someone you like them, simply by the care and taste you devote to choosing the restaurant or other venue. Done well, lunch can create a friendly intimate atmosphere where your guests drop their 'game face'. People are relaxed and more revealing of themselves. This makes them more vulnerable – and more receptive to your ideas.

Not everyone is a good lunch 'date'. I also don't generally have lunch with people I've never met. I also don't have lunch with professional 'luncheoneers' – people who dine out daily, whether there's a reason to or not. Neither pleasure nor business will result from such a lunch. And I don't have lunch simply to thank someone for doing business with us.

I try to have lunch with:

- People I already know;

- People I want to know better; and
- People who need to know me better.

Important lunches should be one-on-one. I seldom have lunch with more than one person at a time (unless I'm hosting a conference). With two or more guests, the psychological dynamics become more difficult to interpret or control, defeating one of the main purposes of lunch. And I will not turn to business at the table until the main course has arrived and the waiters have departed.

Supper Is For Solidarity

Dinner is the most social of business meals. It takes place after the business day in the twilight hours that most people regard as 'down time'. It is loosely structured and open-ended. It can be festive, relaxed, informal, and revealing.

Most significantly, dinner takes time. In fact, the sheer amount of time required for dinner – anywhere from two and a half to four hours – implies that the people present know and like each other.

Frequently, business dinners involve not just the principal business clients or colleagues but their spouses as well. In short, **dinner is for bonding**. Dinner is for making personal connections, not making deals. If you're looking for a direct cause-and-effect connection between a meal and a sale, you won't find it at dinner. If your association has become sufficiently congenial that everyone feels comfortable having dinner together, don't spoil the relationship by discussing business matters at the table.

Be Precise

When you are arranging a business meal, keep these functions in mind. Because of their length, dinners seldom have to be plotted out, since neither you nor your guests are likely to be going onward to another event. Breakfasts, with their limited agenda and abbreviated time frame of an hour or less, generally take care of themselves. If you are hosting a business lunch, however, it is important to orchestrate the timing of the meal. When I have lunch served at my office, I tell my catering staff quite precisely how the timing of the meal will go. I get real specific: 'People will be arriving at 12.30, I want you to take their drink order, and at ten minutes to one I want you to have the first courses on the dining-room table. I want the service to move briskly. I want lunch to be finished by 1.30.' **Be precise with hotel or restaurant staff that is catering a business lunch or dinner for you.** Failure to accomplish this is one of the leading reasons why business lunches fail to accomplish their objectives.

When we are hosting a lunch or a dinner meeting at a restaurant in London or Paris or at a conference centre such as Chewton Glen or Turnberry, I select the menu and wine myself. I let the hotel or restaurant know that I am particular about how the meal and the meeting will go. I'm very attentive to the timing of the meal. I don't want the food being thrown at us; on the other hand, I don't want to wait. I want the wine poured delicately, no more than half a glass at a time. I literally give the schedule of the meal to my assistant and have her communicate it to the hotel or restaurant staff. If I don't do this, the meeting can be destroyed by interruptions. The moment we start getting heavily into a major topic, the waiters waltz in with the main course.

This may sound overly controlling, but I don't have any hard and fast rules. Each meeting is different. I've got to think about it beforehand and tell the staff, 'This is how I'd like it to go.' I'm amazed that a lot of executives – who otherwise want everything to go their way – don't do that.

Cover the Ends

We do table plans for all meetings, whether only IMG staff will be attending or whether there will be others present. **Never have an end with nobody at it.** A number of times you'll walk into a private room and there's nobody at the end. You've got to have balance to a table.

You also must make the most of your seating arrangements. Don't necessarily put people who like each other next to one another. No one is going to learn anything from that. They can have lunch together without me. You've got to mix them up. I routinely put two people who don't really know each other next to one another. Then they might actually talk to each other and begin to appreciate one another. It's wonderful to see how it works. The whole point is to get everybody together.

At a business lunch, people get very agitated about table plans. Everyone is always very concerned about where they will be seated. **Never leave the place cards in the dining room beforehand.** Invariably people will sneak in, have a look and try to change the seating. I have a trusted staff member place them just before they open the room. Never ever put them out earlier.

Leaving the Airport

Once you've landed, retrieved the luggage and cleared Customs, sometimes getting transportation into the centre of town can be a problem. I find that using limousines is worth the extra cost for me, since I get a lot of work done in them along the way, but I recognize that not all business travellers are in a position to have a private car, even if it would be productive for them to do so.

Peter Kuhn of my London staff has a solution that works well for him in Europe. 'If you're going to one city frequently, make an arrangement with a taxi company whereby you can call them and have them meet you. That's my budget version of being met by the chauffeur. It gives you a very big advantage. You don't have to stand in line. You get to know people who are reliable. Sometimes you can get these people to run errands for you while you are going to a meeting. Then they'll come back to get you in time to get you to the airport. It all works very smoothly. They'll run a tab for you. It's a little more expensive than just hailing a cab, but it's worth it in terms of efficiency.'

This kind of relationship can be developed in cities you visit frequently. At IMG we maintain a travel 'book' that tells our executives how to get from the airport into the city, which cab or limousine services to look for (and which to look out for). It's even easier to do in your own home town. If you have this kind of relationship with a limousine or cab company, they ought to be willing to make a stop at your office before heading to the airport to pick you up from a return trip. When they do that, they can pick up faxes, messages, or mail that you can sort through on your way back into town. If many employees in your firm do a lot of travelling, as a high-volume customer you should also be able to negotiate a better rate.

If You Have to Rent a Car

Until recently, in most major cities of the world (with the notable exception of Los Angeles), renting a car to do business has generally been unnecessary. Indeed, in heavily developed cities like London, Tokyo, Paris and New York, narrow, clogged streets and a shortage of parking spaces make a rental car an out-and-out liability. Increasingly, however, businesses are diversifying their locations from the centre of town into the suburbs. Although partially a response to congestion, high labour costs and other urban problems, the blossoming of the computer age has freed many more businesses from their dependence on the central city.

The US computer and electronics complexes in the Silicon Valley south of San Francisco, the science-research firms concentrated in the La Jolla area of San Diego, and various paragovernmental 'think tanks' in the Virginia and Maryland suburbs outside Washington, DC, are just a few examples in America of business centres that are conveniently reached by car, but are not well served by buses, trains or subways. Since almost everyone in these areas drives, cabs are generally expensive and inconvenient because there is little demand for them. Sometimes you can rent a car for a day for the price of a one-cab ride from the airport.

The Name of the Game Is Speed

All the big international rental car agencies – like Hertz, Avis and Budget – offer the highway equivalent of frequent-flyer programmes, which give preferred business users a leg up on ordinary renters. Based on surveys (and on reading their letters of complaint), the one thing business travellers want most when renting a car is speed – not that the car should go fast, but that it should be able to leave the airport fast. Thus, the primary advantage of having a perks card with a car rental agency is acceleration – the ability to get out of the airport and back in faster than other travellers, and with a minimum of hassle. The better agencies have no-wait deals – you select your own car rather than having one assigned to you. The keys are in the ignition, and the motor may even be humming. All you have to do is drive away.

Hierarchies Among Renters

As with airline Special Services programmes, the big international rental car agencies offer preferential (and all but completely unpublicized) 'meet and greet' treatment to their most prestigious clients, though this varies from country to country. All of these programmes are highly restricted. You don't 'qualify' for this status of service, the equivalent of a platinum charge card – it is conferred on you, like a knighthood, by the rental agency. And how do you get this kind of service? If you are truly a senior executive frequent renter and cultivate your personal relationships with one particular agency, your odds of becoming entitled to join these exclusive ranks go up substantially.

The Price of a Rental Car

The rental prices of the big international agencies have been inching up, in part because most travellers have gotten wise to the desirability of rejecting collision damage waiver insurance when they rent a car. With increasing numbers of drivers rejecting CDW, rental car agencies have lost one of their most lucrative profit centres, and are trying to compensate by raising their overall rates. Obviously the desirability of CDW varies from country to country, and you should never drive off inadequately insured, especially in foreign parts. Even so, think very carefully before accepting collision damage waiver insurance, which in some countries can add as much as 30 per cent to the daily cost of the car. If you are renting a car in your own country of residence, you may find that you are already covered under your own insurance policy or through a credit card. Check with the Customer Service representatives at your credit card company to see whether and in what way you are covered.

How do you get a good car at a bargain rate? Many large corporations negotiate special deals for their employees who are on the road frequently. Some big-volume travel agencies are able to get special consideration for their clients as well. What do you do if you're trying to do this on your own?

Yield Management, Round 3

This is your third clinic on yield management. Rental car prices are incredibly location-sensitive. According to recent surveys in the United States, the cost of a midsize car with unlimited mileage averages $29 in Miami, $48 in Chicago, and $61 in New York. Better rates can be had at weekends than in the middle of the week. Perks cardholders get better deals (and better cars for the money) than occasional renters.

However, these 'average' costs mask wide price fluctuations. Car rental agencies, like hotels and airlines, continually realign their prices to account for changes in season, day of the week, convention traffic, general inventory, and the need to keep up with what competitors are offering at the next counter in the arrivals terminal. **None of the big international agencies is consistently cheaper than another**. Just because Budget had the best deal in Miami last week doesn't mean that it has the best deal in London this week.

As is the case with hotels and airfares, **never take the first** quote offered. **Keep asking questions.** Find out what specials and promotions are being offered by the rental agencies. Often these are the cheapest deals around. However, you won't get the cheapest rate unless you ask for the cheapest rate, and even then the agent may not be able to find it. Like the airlines, car rental companies have thousands of rates in their computer system.

With yield management in rental car prices, just as with yield management in airfares and hotel rooms, the differences in price are not always rational from a business executive's point of view. If you want to pick up a car in one location and leave it in another, sometimes there is a drop-off charge; other times it's free. Many experienced business travellers holding confirmed reservations with one agency will walk up cold to the counter of a rival and ask point blank for the best deal. If you are on a late-arriving flight and the agency is sitting on an oversupply, you may find yourself driving off in a car a grade or two higher at a bargain price.

Some Potential Pitfalls

Travellers who try to take advantage of a bargain rate and then try to piggyback other reductions (such as discount coupons received when frequent-flyer miles are cashed in) generally find that the added discounts are not applicable to already diminished prices.

Even status car renters have to be prepared to do some old-fashioned dickering, both before picking up the car and after. It's not uncommon for bargain rates that were confirmed by phone to be unavailable or 'not in the computer' when you arrive at the check-in counter. **Always have your reservation confirmation number with you.**

One of my associates missed a return flight from New York to Los Angeles when Avis personnel at Kennedy Airport insisted he owed over $750, including a hefty drop-off charge, for a week's use of a Lincoln Town Car. Originally it had been a really great deal – the car had been rented to him at Dulles Airport in Washington, DC, with unlimited mileage and free drop-off at JFK, for $150. The New York agent insisted that her counterpart in Washington had made a mistake. The dispute continued so long that my associate was confronted with the choice of either making his plane or correcting the invoice. It was a close call, but in the end he decided that solving the $600 misunderstanding on the spot was more important than making his plane. This is a good point to emphasize, not just with rental cars but with travel in general: **When you must dispute a bill, it's a lot easier to win your case in person and before you've paid it than to try to get your money back after the fact when you're on the other side of the continent.** Watch your credit card statement when the charge does come through. Sometimes your bill will contain an unwarranted post-departure 'adjustment'.

Special, Just for You

Beware of the 'special' upgrade offered at the check-in counter. For just a nominal charge you may be offered a chance to upgrade the car you have reserved to a larger, more luxurious model. Sometimes the offer is legitimate; often, however, you are going to pay to be upgraded to the car you would have gotten anyway. Why? If the rental car agency is sold out of the class of car you reserved, it would have given you a free upgrade to the next available category (from midsize to full size, for example). If you rent cars frequently, familiarize yourself with the makes and models you prefer and what category they fit into – compact, midsize, full size, or luxury. Do you want to pay to upgrade your midsize to a full size vehicle? If possible, ask to see the car you would get without the 'special' upgrade, or at least get a full enough description of the vehicle so that you know that it exists (make, model, colour, licence number).

Don't be too quick to present any upgrade coupons, either, if you are on one of the frequent flyer programmes that includes them. If the agency is out of the car you reserved, you were going to get one free upgrade in any event. Wait till you see what car you are actually going to be offered before you offer them your upgrade. At that point you can either save your coupon for another occasion, or use it for a two-class upgrade this time. If you do upgrade to a better class of car, **make sure that the model of the car is the only thing that's more expensive.** You know that the bigger car is going to use more petrol, but check carefully to see that the cost per mile (if there is one) does not increase along with it.

Watch Your Fuel Gauge

Almost all rental car agencies maintain that they send you out of the airport with a full tank of petrol and ask you to return the car in the same condition. Business travellers, anxious to get on their way, can sometimes forget to check, either coming or going. This can be expensive. **Check the fuel gauge before leaving the airport.** I've been given cars with just a quarter tank of fuel, or less.

I've also been hit with a hefty surcharge to refill the tank on a car I returned half-empty. Although expensive, the surcharge wouldn't have been nearly so galling if the total cost hadn't implied that the fuel tank on the rented saloon held enough to run a truck. Ask the agent when you rent the car how many gallons the tank holds. **If you don't fill the car up yourself when you return it, be prepared to pay a sizeable (and perhaps illogical) premium.**

Cab Sense

There isn't a business executive alive who hasn't been ripped off by a cabbie in some part of the world. How often this happens to you as a frequent traveller depends on how highly developed your cab sense becomes. Cab etiquette and cab larceny vary from one country to another. In some cities (New York, Rome, Mexico City) cabs are infamous; in others (London, Tokyo, Stockholm) they are notoriously excellent.

In Rome, drivers often conduct themselves as if they were

auditioning for a spot on the Ferrari Formula 1 team. Fortunately, most of them are pretty proficient and you arrive
white-knuckled but in one piece. Aside from the not inconsid-
erable problems of exorbitant fares and reckless driving, the
main danger to the business traveller of using cabs is leaving
briefcases, luggage and other belongings in the cab after you
get out. It may take some practice since your primary view of
him will be largely of the back of his head, but **make a habit
of noting the appearance of your driver, his name and ID
number**. If you do leave something behind, at least you have
some information to go on. If you leave your briefcase in a
cab in New York and all you know is that the taxi was
yellow and the driver didn't speak English very well, you've
just described two-thirds of the cabs in Manhattan.

In New York, the three most frequent problems are lack of
facility in the English language, geographic ignorance, and
an industrial-strength case of Big Apple rudeness. To be fair,
you can also find salt-of-the-earth New Yorkers who will
cheerfully give you their opinion (whether you solicit it or
not) about everything from hot stock tips to local politics or
the lowdown (and point spread) on the Knicks and the Jets. If
you find yourself in a cab piloted by one of these endangered
species, sit back and enjoy it as a quintessential New York experience.

In Mexico City, the cab meter, if there is one, is an orna-
ment. In some cities, particularly in the developing world,
cabs without meters are common. If you choose to get into
an unmetered cab in any city, **negotiate the fare before you
set foot in the cab**. Once inside the cab or at your destination,
you are in no position whatsoever to bargain.

In any city, there are some common-sense ground rules
that will minimize your cab problems. **Know 'about' what
your cab ride should cost.** Ten dollars may get you five miles
in Baltimore, two miles in Los Angeles, twenty feet in Tokyo,
two feet in Zurich, and halfway to Laos in Bangkok. Guidebooks and newsletters track what a cab ride should cost in
major cities. If you are leaving a meeting in unfamiliar
territory and need to call a cab, ask your business associates

what the approximate cost might be. Be aware, however, that getting stuck in a traffic jam can be expensive (even in Bangkok), since the meter keeps running. If traffic is stalled and it's just a couple of blocks to your destination, pay your fare and walk the rest of the way. You'll get there faster, and it will be cheaper, too.

Foreign Exchange Without Foreign Intrigue

Unquestionably, western Europe is far more rational about this process than the United States. In Europe, currency exchange at a bank or other financial institution is an everyday occurrence, with rates posted prominently for all to see. You may have to shop around to get the best deal, but all your options are pretty much out in the open.

In the US, it's a chore even to discover what the exchange rate is, and many banks are reluctant to make the transaction. To add insult to injury, there's often a hefty service charge to boot. If you're trying to dispose of the last few francs left over from a trip to Paris, the service charge in the United States can be so high that you may as well not bother. But wait – do you really want to get rid of that last $50 worth of francs? Are you never going back to Paris? Is no one in your firm ever going back to Paris? If representatives of your firm do a lot of transatlantic or transpacific travel, your company may wish to set up a multi-currency 'petty cash' drawer for just such leftovers.

The amount to be maintained is not large – about enough for the fare between the airport and the hotel in town. This can be a lifesaver for redeye flyers. More than one of my associates has arrived in a foreign airport at the crack of dawn (or in Italy at almost any time, since bank holidays there are frequent), and suddenly discovered that he was technically 'broke' because he'd forgotten to bring a bit of local currency along.

It used to be the case that the worst rates of exchange were found in the airports, since exchange houses there were able to take advantage of these sorts of desperate travellers who had neglected to plan ahead and were in effect stranded without any usable currency. Now, however, all is not necessarily lost at the airport. Many airports have automatic teller machines (ATMs) linked to international networks like Plus or Cirrus. In Singapore you can get a better Singapore dollar/ US dollar exchange rate through a Plus ATM than you can by using a credit card or going through a local bank. Although the global banking network is growing, this knowledge, however, does you absolutely no good personally unless you **remember to bring a list of addresses of foreign banks with ATMs that accept your card.**

Suppose you really do want to get rid of all that left-over foreign exchange before you leave? After you **make sure you have enough to tip the hotel staff, pay your way to the airport and pay the departure tax,** empty your pockets and apply the contents to your hotel bill, and put the rest on your credit card.

Sleuthing Your City

Knowing what cabs cost is a small part of sleuthing your city before you get there. Especially if you are headed to a city for the first time, research your destination with the same zeal you employ to research a potential business partner (or a challenger).

If many members of your organization travel, make sure that everyone benefits from the experience of his or her fellow employees. At IMG we do this by keeping a book of approved hotels, cab companies and a listing of restaurants where we've had positive experiences. We also encourage well-travelled executives to disseminate any advice they've picked up on their travels that can increase an executive's efficiency or save the company money. The following is a typical memo, distributed to our worldwide executives, written by a senior executive in 1990 after a business trip to Tokyo. He had some hard-won thoughts about getting from Narita Airport to central Tokyo:

Executives travelling to Tokyo should be aware that getting from Narita Airport to central Tokyo can be trying and time-consuming. If you're not careful, it can also be the most expensive cab ride in the world. Visitors have the following four options (listed in descending order of cost-effectiveness) from Narita to Tokyo:

Airport Limousine: This is a large, very comfortable bus, with guaranteed seating for everyone, that makes frequent trips to bus terminals in central Tokyo and direct trips to many of the city's hotels. Cost: Y2100 or $20.

Train: A train called the Narita Express leaves from the airport terminal to Tokyo central station approximately every 60 minutes. This train service is by far the fastest, most reliable way to go between Narita and Tokyo. Its one-hour travel time equals the best that a bus or car can achieve in light traffic. The same trip by bus or car can take two to three hours in heavy traffic which, of course, does not affect the train. Cost: Y2205 or $21 to Tokyo; Y2310 or about $1 more to Shinjuku.

Taxi: An ordinary taxi departing from the taxi stand at Narita is convenient if you have an out-of-the-way destination or are travelling with a lot of luggage. Cost: Approximately Y17,800 or $170.

Hire Car: This is a phenomenally expensive cab ride. The vehicle is an ordinary automobile driven by a uniformed driver and covers the distance no faster than a bus or taxi and usually slower than the train. Depending on whether the driver speaks English, cost varies between $500 and $600 one way.

The savings this sort of cost-conscious advice represents, multiplied by the dozens of cities our executives visit annually, can be considerable. But it doesn't have to be so formal. Any travel insights from any returning traveller should be encouraged. Yet, for some reason, many executive travellers jealously guard hard-won knowledge gleaned in their experiences, even from their associates. **Share your travel knowledge**. If you are in a position to do so, insist that others do likewise.

What's In My 'Go To' Files

I maintain 'go to' files on cities I visit or expect to visit. For places that I know well, such as London and New York, I've kept most of the generalized knowledge of the city in my head. I find that I am much more experimental with restaurants than I am with hotels, so that much of my filing deals with eateries. My files are a collection of clippings from travel newsletters and from magazines, as well as recommendations passed on to me by friends, business colleagues, sports and entertainment personalities, reliable hotel concierges and other restaurateurs. Restaurateurs are, of course, a tough group to please. As such, when they have good things to say about a restaurant that is not their own, I pay attention.

I do, of course, keep track of extraordinary hotels that associates and staff members have told me about. Up until now, my way of sharing this information is by means of the Notes and Comments section of my monthly newsletter, *Success Secrets*. The following Gazetteer section, however, represents the accumulated 'head knowledge' and file clippings from my own travels, as well as from IMG staffers and other business executives.

Don't think this is everything you need to know, however. Follow the current travel newsletters and magazines. In the US, I have a complete set of the most current Zagat restaurant surveys, which are compiled not by reviewers and critics but by actual diners. Get a good guidebook or two. How do you know which guides you prefer? Read what they have to say about your home town. If they make your town sound like a place you've never been to and are raving about restaurants you know to be second-rate (or closed), that should cause you to suspect their input about other cities as well. However, you should know that the same individual (or team of individuals) doesn't write each volume in the series.

You should also know that for many parts of the world, travel books are outdated by the time they reach the bookstores. Don't expect the cab ride or *prix fixe* dinner to cost exactly the same at the time of your visit as it did when your guide was published, even if it's brand-new.

Monitor the weather for a few weeks before you leave. Make sure you have a decent map of the city where you're headed. Visit an international magazine stand and pick up the local paper. Check to see if there are interesting places, museum shows, or other cultural events scheduled during your visit. This can be both an opportunity and a warning. If you find yourself headed for Paris during the Paris Air Show or the spring or fall fashion showings, there won't be a decent restaurant reservation in the city. Gather as much input as you can. **If you leave for a business trip carrying nothing but this book, you haven't followed my advice.**

GAZETTEER

How to Hit the World's Leading Business Cities
– and Stay Running

Amsterdam

Relentless business growth has pushed Amsterdam well beyond its tourist image of charming merchants' homes lining concentric rings of canals. Although there is no central business area any more, location as well as physical splendour still make the **Hotel de L'Europe** the best choice for executive travellers here. A slightly more off-beat choice in a quieter setting would be the **Pulitzer**, where twenty-four interconnected canal houses form one of Europe's more unique hotels.

Best small hotel: **Ambassade**.

Best out of the way hotel: **Hotel Lauswold** in Beetsterzwaag, a luxurious country castle worth the ninety-minute drive.

Best chef, great location: **Halvemaan**.

Best seafood: **Oesterbar**.

Best Japanese: **Yamazato** (in Hotel Okura).

For gourmets: **Beddington's** and **Christophe**.

Best hotel restaurant: **Excelsior** (in the Hotel de L'Europe).

Worth the drive for dinner: **Bistro Klein Paardenburg** (fifteen minutes by car in Oudekerk a/d Amstel).

Most 'Amsterdam': **Keyzer**.

Best diversion: **Rijksmuseum Vincent Van Gogh**.

Medical emergencies

Doctors: **Central Doktersdienst**, 020/664 2111.

Dentists: **Tandarts Bemiddling Bureau**, 020/627 5815.

Hospitals: **Onze Lieve Vrouw Hospital**, 020/599 9111 and the **Vrije University Hospital**, 020/584 9111.

Business tip
Taxis can be phoned (677 7777) to any location and are remarkably quick and reliable.

Barcelona

Barcelona was a great place to visit before the 1992 Olympics. But hosting the Games dramatically forced it to become an international showcase. There are several world-class hotels here now, but the gold medal still goes to the **Ritz**. Not so far behind in tems of panache are **Condes de Barcelona** and the stylish **Rivoli Ramblas**. Newly opened is the **Rey Juan Carlos I**.

Best weekend retreat: **Hostel de la Gavina** (ninety minutes away on the Costa Brava).

Best seafood: **Botafumeiro**, **El Cangrejo Loco** (in the Olympic Harbour).

Power lunch: **Reno** and **Via Veneto**.

Best brasserie: **Brasserie Flo**.

For gourmets (and worth the effort): **Eldorado Petit** (fifteen minutes by car) and **Hispania** (forty-five minutes north in Arenys de Mar).

Best bargain dining: **Senyor Parellada**.

Best-kept dining secret: **Passadis del Pep**.

Local watering holes: **José Luis**; **Network Café**.

Best hotel gyms: **Princesa Sofia**; **Meliá Barcelona Sarria**.

Best jogging: **Carretera de les Algues**.

Best tennis: **Real Club de Tenis Barcelona**.

Best golf: **Real Club de Golf el Prat**, next to the airport.

Best diversions: Touring the buildings by the architect **Gaudi**, unique to Barcelona; the **Miro and Picasso Museums**; the **Boqueria food market**.

Medical emergencies

Doctors and hospital: **Hospital Clinic I Provincial**, 323 14 14.

Dentist referrals: **Institut Dexeus**, 418 00 00; **Amesa**, 302 66 82.

Business tip

Restaurants very rarely serve dinner before 9 p.m., and smoking cigars is a popular after-dinner ritual.

Berlin

Although I had few business reasons to visit Berlin regularly in previous decades, that is changing rapidly with reunification. With the Wall gone, Berlin will continue to pursue its rightful place as Germany's premier business and cultural centre. Hotels, already at an acceptable international standard, will surely improve. For old-world charm and crack efficiency, the **Bristol-Kempinski** has its advocates (rightfully so), but I prefer the **Grand Hotel** in what used to be East Berlin for elegance and its up-to-the-minute modernity.

Best small hideaway hotel: **Schloss Hotel Vier Jahreszeiten** (a grand villa in the exclusive residential area of Grunewald).

Best restaurant for serious business: **The Grand Slam** at Tennis Club 'Rot-Weiss'.

Best combination for food and setting: **Borchardts**.

Best German: **Heinz Holl**.

Best Italian: **Ciao**.

Best French: **Paris Bar**.

Best international meeting place: **Fofi's**.

Best Thai: **Thai Palace**.

Best Indian: **Kashmir Palace**.

Best Mexican (very casual): **Tres Kilos**.

Best fitness facilities: **Grand Hotel**.

Best tennis: **Tennis Club 'Rot-Weiss'**.

Best golf: **Golf Club Berlin Wannsee**.

Best jogging: **Tiergarten**.

Best bar: **Bar am Luetzowplatz**.

Medical emergencies

Doctors and dentists: the **American Consulate** has a list of referrals.

Hospitals: **Elizabeth Krankenhaus**, West Berlin, 25061; **Charité Hospital**, East Berlin, 2864669.

Business tip

Berliners are among the most impatient people on earth, but it's a lifestyle choice, not rudeness. So don't take the locals' haste personally. They won't waste your time with small talk and will give you a straight answer instantly.

Boston

In ambience and adherence to tradition, Boston is America's most London-like city. The obvious difference is size. Boston is one of the most compact American cities and is easy to navigate (Logan airport is only twenty minutes from downtown). Choosing a hotel here is less a question of where your meetings are held and more a question of what part of town suits you. (However, first-time visitors should keep in mind that there are really two Boston business centres now – the traditional downtown and the clutch of high-tech companies along Route 128 which circles the town. Choose where you stay accordingly.)

The perennially splendid **Four Seasons** would remain Boston's hotel of choice even if it didn't also happen to have the best location – overlooking the Public Garden and Boston Common. The **Bostonian** is a distant second, but worth it if you need to be close to Logan airport.

Boston's huge student population is reflected in the casual style of many of its restaurants, which cater more to young people and academics than the usual business clientele. That's a plus if you are tired of formal, overstuffed and over-priced dining salons.

Best hideaway hotel: **The Charles Hotel** in Cambridge.

Best Italian restaurant: **Davio's**.

Best Spanish: **Dali**.

Best hotel dining: **Aujourd'hui** (in the Four Seasons); **Seasons** (in the Bostonian).

Best American cooking: **Biba**.

Best bistro: **Marais Restaurant**.

Heartiest meals: **Hammersley's Bistro; Jasper's; Grill 23**.

Best for serious business: **L'Espalier**.

Best food-to-price ratio: **La Famiglia**.

Best franchises: **Legal Seafood** (for fish); **Morton's** (for steaks).

Best Chinese: **Mister Leung**.

Best pizza: **The European**.

Best meals in Cambridge: **Harvest; Michela's**.

Local secrets: **Jae's Bar and Grill; St Cloud's**.

Best gym: **Boston Athletic Club**.

Best jogging: **The Esplanade** along the Charles River.

Best golf: **Stow Acres** (public);
Ocean Edge; Tara-Ferncroft
(resort courses).

Best tennis: **Mt Auburn Club.**

Medical emergencies

Doctors: **Beth Israel Hospital,**
617 735 5356.

Dentists: **Massachusetts General
Hospital,** 617 726 5508.

Business tip
Don't arrive or depart from
Logan airport between 7 a.m.
and 9 a.m. and 5 p.m. and 7
p.m.

Brussels

For a city that is the geopolitical centre of Europe and the third busiest convention city in the world – executive travellers outnumber tourists four to one – Brussels has a remarkable dearth of world-class hotels. The newest additions – the **SAS Royal** and the ambitious **Conrad** – are certainly elevating local standards. My personal preference has always been the **Hilton** because of the great location, the first-rate executive floors, the 24-hour room service, the **Café d'Egmont**, which offers the best venue for a business breakfast, and the reputable **La Maison du Boeuf**, one of the best restaurants in the city.

Business entertaining here is another matter. The restaurants and cafés are superb, both at the high and low ends of the price scale. The Grand Place, Brussels' majestic town square, houses many fine restaurants in its 400-year-old guild houses. First choice here should be **La Maison du Cygne**, but it would be a pity for any visitor to ignore some of the wonderful establishments in Brussels' environs.

Best hotel value: Junior suite at **The Amigo**.

Best café: **Le Café Metropole**.

Best bar (upmarket): **De Ultieme Hallucinatie**.

Best bar (downmarket): **Falstaff**.

Best leisurely lunch: **La Villa Lorraine** (in the Bois de la Cambre).

Best truffles: **La Truffe Noire**.

Best light meals: **L'Escaller du Palais Royal** (on the picturesque Place du Sablon); **Sheltelma**.

Most dazzling dining decor: **Le Barbizon**.

Best way to impress your guests: Take them to **Bruneau** or **Comme Chez Soi**.

Smartest wine list: **La Manufacture**.

Local secrets: **La Quincaillerie** (excellent seafood at modest prices in a former hardware store); **Brasserie Georges** (seafood bistro); **L'Amandier**.

Best golf within sixty minutes of town: **Le Zoute** (an inland links, site of the Piaget Open).

Best golf in town: **Royal Golf Club of Belgium** at Ravenstein.

Best tennis: **Royal Leopold Club**.

Best gym: **Golden Club** (on Place du Chatelain).

Best jogging: **Bois de la Cambre.**

Best diversion: The medieval canal city of **Bruges**, the 'Venice of the North', sixty minutes away.

Medical emergencies

Doctors: **Referral service**, 02/ 648 8000.

Dentists: Referral service, 02/ 426 1026.

Hospitals: **Clinique Parc Léopold**, 02/230 4980; **Hôpital de Braine l'Alleud**, 02/384 6060.

24-hour help line in English: 02/648 4014.

Business tip

Make allowances for the fact that Brussels' airport is the worst in the Western world in terms of baggage claim, arrivals, departures, and efficiency.

Chicago

Perhaps I'm biased because I was born and raised here, but Chicago has always struck me as the perfect big city for business. It's large and prosperous, but easy to navigate. It has the best airport connections through O'Hare, a constantly growing line-up of solid business hotels (to handle the heaviest volume of trade shows and conventions in the US) and a rich crop of restaurants. It's also surprisingly pretty along Lake Michigan.

With my perennial favourite, the Mayfair Regent, closing this year, top hotel honours go to the **Ritz-Carlton** and its sister **Four Seasons** for service and lakeside views. Keep your eye on the newly renovated **Whitehall**, which may bring the elegance of a small European hotel back to town.

Best breakfast: **Walker Bros; Original Pancake House** (several locations).

Best dining concept: The half portions at **Gordon**.

Best Mexican: **Topolobampo**.

Best bargain: **Sole Mio**.

Best Chinese: **T'ang Dynasty**.

Best Midwestern cooking: **Prairie**.

Best Rich Melman restaurants: **Hat Dance** (Mexican); **Un Grand Café** (French bistro); **Shaw's Crab House** (fish); **Maggiano's** (Italian).

Best Italian: **Tuscany**; **Carlucci**.

Best hotel restaurant: **Season** (in the Four Seasons); **Le Ciel Bieu** (in the former Mayfair Regent).

Power lunch: **Nick's Fishmarket**.

Best burger: **John Barleycorn Pub**.

Best pizza: **Pizzeria Uno**.

Best golf: **Kemper Lakes** (amazing public course in Hawthorn Woods).

Best tennis: **Mid-Town Club**.

Best jogging: **Lakefront** along Lake Michigan.

Best gym: **East Bank Club**.

Medical emergencies

Dentist: **Chicago Dental Society Emergency Service**, 312/726 4321.

Hospitals: **Northwestern Memorial**, 312/908 2000 or **Rush-Presbyterian-St Lukes Medical Center**, 312/942 5000.

Business tip
Despite its big-city dimensions, Chicago is at heart a warm, friendly Midwestern town. A warm, friendly Midwestern attitude is most winning here.

Dublin

Dublin is the most genteel of cities, in part because it is barely industrialized and more focused on service and light industries such as computers. It is also one of the friendliest towns, and as tourism here increases, the hotels will surely improve (restaurants are already top-rate). **The Shelbourne** remains the traditional hotel of choice in town, although the newish **Conrad** and **Westbury** seem to have all the essentials that executive travellers need. The real prizes, however, are the spacious suites at **The Towers** annexe of **Jurys** and the elegant tranquility next door at the **Berkeley Court Hotel**.

Best hideaway: **The 'K' Country Club Hotel** (thirty minutes southwest in Straffan).

Best weekend retreat: **Ashford Castle** (three and a half hours away in County Mayo).

Best French dining: **Les Frères Jacques**.

Top business lunch: **Le Coq Hardi**.

For gourmets: **Patrick Guildbaud**.

Best Irish meal: **Celtic Mews Restaurant**.

Best seafood: **The Kish Restaurant** (in Jurys).

Local secrets: **Cookes Café, Roly's Bistro**.

Best match of setting and food: **La Stampa**.

Best Italian: **Kapriol Restaurant**.

Worth the drive: **The King Sitric** (seven miles away in the fishing village of Howth).

Best jogging: **St Stephen's Green**.

Best golf: **Portmarnock Golf Club**.

Best tennis: **Riverview LTC** or **Elm Park Golf and Sports Club**.

Best diversion: **The Abbey Theatre** (theatre is Dublin's greatest strength).

Medical emergencies

Doctors: Every hotel has its own arrangement with a local doctor.

Dentists: **The Park Clinic** 01/285 3666; **Dental Hospital**, 01/679 4311.

Hospitals: **Blackrock Clinic** 01/283 2222; **Mater Private Hospital** 01/384 444.

Business tip
The Irish love to entertain and
be entertained. Don't be
surprised if you find yourself
carrying out certain
negotiations on the golf course
or in a bar/restaurant. Also,
although punctuality is the rule
during business hours, after
hours is more relaxed. If you
are invited to someone's home
at 8 p.m., you won't be expected
before 8.30.

Edinburgh

Edinburgh's most charming feature for business travellers is also its most exasperating: it doesn't have an international airport. That's charming if, like me, you usually travel there from London by train or fly in from other European cities. But if you're flying from another part of the world, you have to touch down in Glasgow, fifty miles (and a £45 seventy-minute taxi ride) away.

Top-tier business hotels in the centre of town are limited to two. My first choice has always been the spacious and gracious **Caledonian**. But the recently refurbished and equally well situated **Balmoral** is a worthy rival.

Top hideaway hotel: **Prestonfield House Hotel**.

Best weekend retreat: **Gleneagles** (one hour north of town and easily the finest inland golf resort in the UK).

Best restaurant for serious business: **Pompadour** (in the Caledonian).

Best Italian: **Cosmo's**.

Best French: **Pierre Victoire** and **L'Auberge**.

Best bargain: Lunch at **Le Marché Noir**.

Best weekend brunch: **Café Royal Oyster Bar**.

Best seafood: **Skipper's Bistro**.

Authentic tavern: **The Canny Man's**.

Local secrets: **Martin's Restaurant**.

Worth the drive: **La Potiniere** (twenty-five minutes east of town; advance reservations essential).

Best golf: **Dalmahoy**.

Best tennis: **Craiglockhart**.

Medical emergencies

Hospitals: **Edinburgh Royal Infirmary**, 031/229 2477.

Business tip
Be aware that local bank and commercial holidays may differ from other major UK cities.

Frankfurt

The best travel feature in Frankfurt is its airport, which is not only Europe's busiest but is also its most convenient (only six miles from downtown). Although the **Steigenberger Frankfurter Hof** in town is a worthy hotel, in recent years I've been content to stay at Europe's best airport hotel, the amazing and enormous **Sheraton** which can accommodate any business need and meeting you can throw at its expert staff.

Best getaway: **Schlosshotel Kronberg**.

Best combination of food and knockout setting: **Brückenkeller**.

Best French cooking: **Erno's Bistro; Bistro 77**.

Best Chinese meal: **Regent**.

For special event: **Humperdinck**.

Best German cooking: **Villa Leonhardi**.

Best hotel (and airport) restaurant: **Papillon** (in the Sheraton).

Worth the drive for a meal: **Gutschänke; Neuhof; Die Gans**.

Best Italian: **Osteria enoteca; Gallo Nero**.

Best-kept dining secret: **Maschanz**.

Best gym: **Health Club in the Arabella Grand Hotel**.

Best golf: **Golf Club Niederrath**.

Best tennis: **Tennis Club Bad Homburg**, the oldest tennis club in Germany.

Best jogging: **Museumsufer**, along the Main river.

Medical emergencies

For doctor/dentist referrals, call the American (069/75304) or British (069/7204060) consulates.

Business tip

In a city devoted to banking, it's not surprising that Frankfurt keeps banker's hours. Everything, even restaurants, shuts down around 10 p.m. If you don't know your way around, get organized privately with your business contact.

Geneva

Geneva is such a prosperous city – replete with first-rate lodging and dining – that it's easy to forget it has a population of only 160,000. That smallness makes it one of the most pleasant and efficient business centres. It also frees executive travellers to move in and out of town to take advantage of scenic Lake Geneva.

With the steady flow of international executives coursing through the city, Geneva's hotels have an instinctive feel for what business travellers are looking for. Although you can't go wrong with the **Beau Rivage**, the **Hotel de la Paix** or **Les Bergues** (all spectacularly situated on the water), when in town I prefer **Le Richemond** which seems to be in a class of its own.

Top lodging just outside Geneva: **La Reserve**.

Best weekend retreat: **Royal Club Evian**, or **La Verniaz**, near Evian.

Best hotel restaurants: **Le Gentilhomme** (in Le Richemond); **Le Chat Botté** (in Beau Rivage).

Best business lunch (and for special dinners): **Restaurant du Parc des Eaux-Vives**.

Best restaurant bargain: **Auberge de Coutance; Chez Bouby**.

Best restaurants on Lake Geneva: **La Perle du Lac; Le Pavillon du Lac**.

Best dining in outskirts: **L'Escapade; Cape de la Place** (Plan Les Ouates).

Worth the drive: **Château Vieux** (thirty minutes away in Satigny).

Best watering hole: **La Coupole**.

For gourmets: **La Cassolette; Le Bearn**.

Best meat: **Le Boucher**.

Best Italian restaurant: **Chez Roberto**.

Best light meals: **Mövenpick; Le Flore** (salads).

Local secrets: **Auberge Communale** (in nearby Onex); **Le Patio**.

Best golf courses: **Royal Club Evian, Golf Club Divonne**.

Best tennis: **Tennis Club de Genève; Tennis Club Les Eaux-Vives**.

Best skiing: **Verbier/Valais** (two hours' drive or one and a half hours by train); **Chamonix** (one hour's drive, in France).

Medical emergencies

Doctors: **Association des Médecins**, 022/20 25 11; **SOS Médecins à Domicile**, 23-hour emergency service, 022/781 17 77.

Dentists: **Association des Médecins-Dentistes**, 022/732 80 05.

Hospitals: **Hôpital Cantonal et Universitaire**, 022/22 61 11; **Hôpital de la Tour**, 022/780 01 11.

Business tip
Here, more than anywhere else on earth, *be on time*.

Hamburg

In no other city does one hotel so thoroughly outdistance the competition as the **Vier Jahreszeiten** does in Hamburg. For sheer grandeur, comfort, attentive service and catering to every and any whim, this is certainly the best hotel in Hamburg, in Germany, probably Europe and quite possibly the world.

Best small hideaway hotel: **Garden Hotel Pöseldorf.**

Best restaurant for serious business: **Haerlin** (in the Vier Jahreszeiten).

Best seafood: **Fischereihafen Restaurant.**

Best traditional German feast: **Mühlenkamper Fährhaus.**

Best Italian: **Il Gabbiano** (formal); **Il Giardino** (casual).

Best Chinese: **Peking Enten Haus.**

Best bar: **Old Fashion Bar**.

Best after-hours venue: **Simbari**.

Best nouvelle French: **Le Canard.**

Local secrets: **Schlachterbörse.**

Best golf: **Hamburger Golf Club Falkenstein.**

Best tennis: **Club an der Alster Rothenbaum.**

Best gym: **Kaifulodge.**

Best jogging: **Außenalster.**

Medical emergencies

Universitätskrankenhaus Eppendorf, Martinstr. 52, 47 17 1.

Business tip

Hamburg is the most laid-back of German cities – in tradition and pace. Dynasties with several hundred years of history behind them dominate the town. Locals love to meet over lunch or dinner and they prefer to take their time. You will not impress people if you are in too much of a hurry here.

Hong Kong

Hong Kong is all about commerce and pace. It is noisy, crowded, bustling, top-heavy with atmosphere and sensory distractions. When I visit, I want the opposite extreme: a hotel that specializes in serenity and comfort.

Hong Kong has more exceptional hotels than any other city in the world. The **Peninsula** and the **Shangri-La**, on the Kowloon side of the harbour, will not disappoint the most exacting traveller. They are perennially listed among the top twenty hotels in the world. But my regular retreat on Kowloon is the **Regent**, for its sleek elegance and spectacular harbour-side vistas. On the Island side, in the financially-oriented Central area, the clear winner is the **Mandarin Oriental** for its veteran staff, unerring style and sheer opulence. (Describing these four hotels in ten words or less is a gross injustice to them; only a handful of establishments around the world rise to the level they achieve every day.)

Best restaurant setting: **Stanley Oriental**.

Best high tea: **The Peninsula**.

Best hotel health club: **The Shangri-La**.

Best Continental cuisine: **The Mandarin Grill**.

Best hotel restaurant: **Plume** (in the Regent).

Best steaks and chops: **The Regent Steakhouse**.

Best Italian: **Grissini** (also wonderful Sunday brunch).

Best venue to celebrate closing a deal: **Hugo's**.

Most fun French: **Michelle's** at the Fringe.

Best 'Yum Cha' (Dim Sum): **Luk Yu Tea House** (sit downstairs for a trip to old colonial Hong Kong).

Best Chinese (non-Cantonese): **Great Shanghai** in Tsim Sha Tsui (downmarket); **Hunan Garden** at Exchange Square.

Best Chinese (Cantonese): **Lai Ching Heen** (in the Regent).

Best diversion: **Ride the Peak Tram to The Peak** overlooking the harbour, eat outside at the Peak Café and enjoy the view, and wander through Hong Kong's wealthiest neighbourhood.

Best English pub: **Mad Dogs**.

Best indoor swim: The marble-columned pool at the **Mandarin**.

Medical emergencies

Doctors and dentists: Ask at your hotel.

Hospitals: **Hong Kong Adventist Hospital**, 574 6211; **Queen Mary Hospital**, 819 2111.

Business tip

Though taxis are cheap, they're tough to find. Do not cross the harbour via taxi (there's only one tunnel and it jams up easily). Use the *Star Ferry* or the metro instead.

London

London is so vast that it is absurd to offer a quick hit-list of its best lodging and dining. For top-tier hotels, all the guides will direct you to the Savoy, Connaught, Dorchester and Claridge's (perhaps the Ritz, Berkeley and the newish Lanesborough as well). But to hit the ground running in London, your hotel strategy should begin and end with location, not status. In other words, no matter how partial you may be to the Savoy in London's West End, if all your business activities are thirty minutes away in Knightsbridge, you're better off making friends with, say, the **Hyde Park Hotel** or the **Hyatt Carlton Tower**. I'm particularly fond of the latter. Before we opened up a London office and I acquired a home nearby, I conducted all my business from my room in the Carlton Tower or from a booth in its exceptional **Rib Room**.

London restaurants have long since shed their reputation for dullness. The London dining scene rivals New York or Paris and is even more varied and dynamic. Every cuisine can be found here.

Best classic French: **Tante Claire; Mirabelle**.

Best Indian: **Bombay Brasserie**.

Best Chinese: **Penang**.

Best Nouvelle Chinese: **Zen Central**.

Best Thai: **Khun Akorn**.

Best fish: **Poissonnerie de L'Avenue; Le Suquet**.

Best English food: **Simpson's in the Strand**.

Best game: **Rules**.

Best pub: **The Australian**.

Best cocktail hour: **Blake's**.

Best off-the-beaten-path meal: **Wilds**.

Best hotel dining: **The Connaught**.

Best tea service with view: **The Park Room** (in the Hyde Park Hotel).

Best Italian: **Santini's**.

Best Italian (downmarket): **Trattoo**.

Best burger: **Drones**.

Best presentation: **Mosimann's**.

Best steaks and chops: **The Guinea**.

Power lunch: **The Savoy Grill**.

Best weekend lunch: **Cliveden**.

Best roast beef: **Rib Room** (in the Hyatt Carlton Tower).

Best sushi: **Suntory**.

Best Spanish: **Robato's**.

Best pizza: **Pizza Express** (the Earls Court Road branch).

Best brasserie: **Langan's**.

Best private clubs: **Annabel's; Mark's Club; Harry's Bar**.

Best Lebanese: **Al Hamra** (off Curzon Street).

Most underrated restaurant: **The Greenhouse**.

Best gym: **The Peak** (in the Hyatt Carlton Tower).

Best tennis: **David Lloyd Tennis Club**.

Best golf: **Stockley Park**.

Medical emergencies

Dentists: **24-hour Dental Emergency Service**, 081/677 8383.

Doctors and hospitals: **University College Hospital** and **Charing Cross Hospital**.

Business tip
Check bills to see whether service is included – or ask – before you tip; you may be tipping twice as much as you wish or as the service merits.

Los Angeles

Los Angeles is so immense and culturally diverse that there's no appropriate symbol for the city – unless it would be an automobile (presumably a convertible equipped with phone and fax machine), which is the only suitable method to get from one spot to another here. Meetings should be scheduled with careful attention to a road map to avoid wasting time shuttling between distant corners of the city.

With my LA 'home', the Beverly Hills Hotel, now closed for a three-year renovation, my first choice for world-class service (and a relatively central location) is the **Peninsula** and the ever-splendid **Four Seasons**. For a more remote hideaway with luxurious grounds, there is the **Hotel Bel-Air**.

The Los Angeles restaurant scene is rich but volatile. Restaurants open and close with blinding speed but the following are in the midst of long runs:

Best bargain: **Opus**.

Best service: **Chasen's**.

Best Provencal cooking: **Pinot Bistro**.

Best Wolfgang Puck restaurants: **Chinois on Main** and **Granita** (thirty minutes up the coast in Malibu).

Best California cuisine: **Patina**; **Citrus**.

Best Pacific Rim cooking: **Chaya Brasserie**.

Most opulent: **Rex, Il Ristorante**.

Best pizza: **Spago**; **Orso**.

Best burger: **Fat Burgers**.

Best Mexican/Best margarita: **El Cholo**.

Best hot dog: **Tail of the Pup**; **Pinks**.

Best Chinese: **The Mandarin**.

Best steak house: **Arnie Morton's of Chicago**.

Local secrets: **Il Giardino**; **Saddle Peak Lodge**.

Best breakfast: **Patrick's Road House**.

Best setting: **Four Oaks**.

Best Italian: **Valentino**; **Campanile**.

Best golf: **Malibu Golf Course**.

Best tennis: **The Tennis Place** on Third Street.

Medical emergencies

Doctors: **Physicians Referral Service** (310 483 6122).

Dentists: **Dentists Referral Service** (310 380 7669).

Hospital: **Cedars-Sinai Medical Center** (310 855 5000).

Business tip

Say something nice about LA. Residents, who invariably have emigrated here from somewhere else, have an inferiority complex about LA. They are so used to hearing wisecracks about the surreal lifestyle they have chosen that they are pleased (perhaps shocked) when a visitor praises some aspect of their city other than the weather.

Milan

For a town that is Italy's financial centre and clearly all business, Milan is not deep in great hotels. Constant trade shows ensure that the best-situated hotels are fully booked (so reserve far in advance). The standard executive amenities (good phones, 24-hour room service, etc.) are often lacking in so-called business hotels here. And staff and service can be patchy.

My lodging strategy has always been: Don't take chances. Stick with the best (and damn the cost; you'll pay nearly as much at second-rate hotels). My first choice remains the **Principe de Savoia** for its spacious rooms and over-the-top elegance; the location on the busy Piazza della Repubblica is a nuisance only if you travel by foot. Its sister hotel across the square, the **Palace**, is no less venerable. The **Pierre** is a small, ultra-modern favourite with American executives and tourists. The brand-new 98-room **Four Seasons Milan** should join this elite if it lives up to the Four Seasons name.

If you don't dine well in Milan, you either haven't done your homework or need to get new friends. But be aware that lunch, not dinner (when Italians prefer to spend time with their families), is the optimal time for a working meal.

Best reason to commute from Lake Como: The palatial **Villa d'Este** (thirty-three miles north of Milan). A world-class resort this close to town should not be ignored.

Best by reputation: **Gualtiero Marchesi**, the Michelin three-star where nouvelle Italian cuisine was invented.

Best pasta, best waiters: **Alfio**.

Best way to impress your guests: **Santini**.

Best Bice: The original **Bice**, progenitor of super-successful clones in Paris, New York, Tokyo, etc., is here.

Best reason to drive thirty minutes to eat: **Antica Osteria del Ponte** (book far in advance).

Best Milanese cuisine: **Grand San Bernardo**.

Best takeout: **Peck**, the nonpareil gourmet food store, is also a nonpareil restaurant for business.

Best cappuccino: **Cova**.

Smartest lunch: **Biffi Scala**.

Liveliest dinner: **Giallo; Briciola; Girarrosto Toscano.**

Best pizza: **Rosy e Gabriele.**

Best golf: **Golf Club Milano** (in Monza Park).

Best tennis: **Circolo Tennis Milano.**

Best diversion: **Soccer at San Siro Stadium.**

Medical emergencies

Doctors: **American Consulate** has references for English-speaking doctors, 02/652 841.

Dentists: **Istituto Stomatologico**, 02/542 751.

Hospitals: **Fatebenefratelli Hospital**, English-speaking emergency room (*pronto soccorso*), 02/63631.

Business tip

Pan-European travellers should beware the impenetrable fog at Milan's Linate Airport between November and March which can cause massive delays. Best time to land or leave is between 11 a.m. and 3 p.m. Long-haul flights usually leave from Milan's other airport, Malpensa, where fog has less impact.

Montreal

The first thing to remember about Montreal is that it is a French-speaking city with some English-speaking citizens – not the other way around. The luxurious **Le Quatre Saisons** (Four Seasons) hotel is my lodging of choice in Montreal. The **Hôtel Inter-Continental Montreal** is the other world-class venue here. Not surprisingly, Montreal is densely populated with very good French restaurants, but the city's huge immigrant population guarantees that almost every imaginable meal is possible here.

Best Italian: **Le Latini; La Sila.**

Best seafood: **Costas; Milos.**

Best steaks: **Moishe's; Gibby's.**

Best traditional French: **Les Halles.**

Best watering hole: **Whisky Café.**

Best Chinese: **Tai Kim Lung; Piment Rouge.**

Best business breakfast: **Hôtel Ritz-Carlton.**

Best dinner in the outlying areas: **L'Eau à la Bouche.**

Best bistro: **Chez Gauthier.**

Best lunch: **Mas des Oliviers.**

Best burger: **Il Etait une Fois.**

Local secret: **L'Express.**

Best fitness facilities: **Le Quatre Saisons** Hotel.

Best tennis: **Nun's Island; Le Sporting Club du Sanctuaire.**

Best golf: **Royal Montreal Golf Club** (private).

Medical emergencies

Doctors: **Montreal General Hospital,** 514/937 6011; **Royal Victoria Hospital/Emergency,** 514/843 1610.

Dentists: **Côte-des-Neiges Dental Centre,** 514.731 7721; **Emergency Dental Services,** 514/875 7971.

Business tip

Winters are brutal in Montreal, so keep in mind the elaborate underground network that connects most office buildings and hotels downtown. (Underground is also the setting for some of the best shopping in North America.)

New York

To enjoy New York, you must first stay sane in New York. That requires a measure of tolerance – for the confusion, noise, rudeness and delays. Once you accept those conditions, you are in the world's most exciting city.

The bulk of New York hotel rooms for executives can be found in the midtown grid between 42nd and 59th Streets where most of the gargantuan conventioneer hotels I abhor can be found. Better choices can be found uptown in the quasi-residential calm of the Upper East Side. The **Carlyle**, the **Lowell**, and the **Westbury** have their proponents. At the **Mayfair Regent**, there are four telephone lines into each room, local calls are free and room service is from Le Cirque. First choice within our company's ranks, though, is the **Mark**.

I've long thought that the smartest dining strategy for New York (and London, Los Angeles, San Francisco and Paris too) is *not* to patronize a restaurant until it's two years old – when it's no longer 'hot' and you can actually enjoy yourself. I also prefer restaurants that in price and pretension are one notch below the familiar axis of Lutece, Le Cirque, La Cote Basque and the Four Seasons.

Best lunch: **Arcadia**.

Best Southwestern cuisine: **Mesa Grill; Arizona 206**.

Best bistro: **Le Comptoir; JoJo**.

Best Mexican: **Zarela; Rosa Mexicano**.

Worth going to Brooklyn: **The River Café**.

Best seafood: **Manhattan Ocean Club**.

Best steaks: **The Palm**.

For gourmets: **Aureole; Bouley**.

Best $22 burger: **21**.

Best pizza: **Tirami Su**.

Best theatre-district meal: **Orso**.

Best tapas bar: **Solera**.

Best Italian: **Palio; Le Madri**.

Best hotel dining: **Mark's** (in the Mark); **Lespinasse** (in the St Regis)

Best-kept secrets: **Rosemarie's; Zen Palate**.

Best gym: **New York Athletic Club**.

Best jogging: **Central Park** (during daylight).

Best golf: **Arrowood** in Westchester County.

Best tennis: **Grand Central Tennis; Roosevelt Island Racquet Club.**

Medical emergencies

Doctors: **Affiliated Physicians of St Vincent's,** 212/775 1218; **Central Park West Medical,** 212/775 1218.

Dentists: **Concerned Dental Care,** 212/696 4979.

Hospitals: **Beth Israel Medical Center,** 212/420 2000; **Mount Sinai Hospital,** 212/241 6500.

Business tip

Before you enter a cab, know where you're going and how to get there. The rudeness of New York cab drivers is a hoary myth – because few cab drivers speak English well enough to be rude – but they can be geographically illiterate.

Paris

There are so many *faux* Parisian establishments around the world (the type that bill themselves as 'a little bit of Paris in the heart of ——') that when I find myself actually in Paris, I aggressively seek out the quintessentially Parisian places and experiences that could not be replicated in any other city.

To hit the ground running in Paris, you must first surrender to Paris. It took me years to realize what this meant. I used to resent the high cost of everything there, until a friend taught me to think of the outrageous prices as a 'value added surcharge' for all the things that make Paris special – the sidewalk cafés, the public gardens, the richness of the architecture, the late evening light in summer. That makes the steep bills easier to bear. (Also, Hong Kong, London, Tokyo and Stockholm, among other cities, are now easily as expensive as Paris.)

Any listing of Paris's best hotels leads off with the familiar quintet – the Ritz, Crillon, Bristol, George V and Plaza Athenée. Of these five, my favourite for years has been the **Crillon** because it is not living on its exalted reputation but, under General Manager Hervé Houdre, continually surpassing it.

It is difficult to get a bad meal in Paris. If your intention is to impress a business associate at dinner, you're certainly welcome to the established temples of gastronomy – Jamin, Taillevent, Tour d'Argent, Apicius, etc. But unless you take a perverse pleasure in bragging about how much you spent on a meal, you can easily get more bang for the buck elsewhere in town.

Best weekend retreat: Gerard Boyer's **Les Crayères** in Reims.

Best distraction: **Musée d'Orsay**; people-watching at **Les Deux Magots** (on the Blvd St Germain).

Smartest hotel choices on Left Bank: **Lutetia**; **Hôtel de Saint Pères**.

Best hotel dining: **Les Ambassadeurs** (in the Hôtel Crillon).

Best bistros: **Chez Géraud**; **Benoit**.

Best cheese shop: **Barthélemy**; **Androuets**.

Best brasserie: **La Coupole**.

Best tea room: **Mariage Frères;
La Cour de Rohan.**

Fastest waiters: **Le Divellec.**

Best croque monsieur: **Café Flore.**

Best hot chocolate: **Angelina's.**

Best seafood: **La Marée; La
Cagouille.**

Best jazz/dancing: **Le Caveau de
la Huchette.**

Best croissants: **Dalloyau.**

Best 'event dining': **Le Pré
Catelan.**

Friendliest meal: **Duquesnoy.**

Most imaginative meals: **Michel
Rostang; L'Ambroisie.**

Local secrets: **Le Récamier** (also
best outdoor dining).

Best takeout: **Fauchon.**

Best English-language
bookstore/news-stand:
Brentano's; W H Smith.

Best outdoor market: **Rue de
Buci.**

Best jogging: **Parc Monceau;
Bois de Boulogne** (before dark);
Jardin de Luxembourg.

Best hotel gym: **Royal
Monceau.**

Nearest great golf course: **St
Germain en Laye.**

Best tennis: **Racing Club de
France** (for members); **Paris
Country Club.**

Best thing to do on a Sunday:
Visit Le Marais area near the
Place des Vosges. Shops are
open on Sundays as this was
once (and still is) the heart of
the Jewish quarter.

Medical emergencies

Doctors: **SOS Médecins,** 47 07
77 77, English-speaking
referrals.

Dentists: **SOS Dentistes,** 43 37
51 00, English-speaking
referrals.

Hospitals: **American Hospital** in
Neuilly, 47 47 53 00.

Business tip

Do not try to hail a taxi on the
street London-style. You must
go to a taxi stand.

Rome

Visiting Rome can offer as many frustrations as pleasures. It is a chaotic city that rewards the travelling executive who plans well ahead and double-checks everything. Front-line hotel options range from the great rooms and tradition at the **Grand** to the greenery and privacy of the **Lord Byron** or the international glitz at the **Majestic**. My favourite hotel is the **Hassler-Villa Medici**, managed by Swiss and perfectly situated at the top of the Spanish Steps.

Best reason to commute from outside Rome: **Posta Vecchia**, a beautiful hotel within the property of Principi Odescalchi in the village of Palo on the Roman seaside.

For gourmets: **Il Moro**.

Best pasta, best waiters: **Augustea**.

Best hotel dining: **Relais Le Jardin** (in the Lord Byron).

Best way to impress your guests: **Alberto Ciarla**.

Best reason to drive fifty minutes to eat: **Vissani**, brilliant Italian cooking in the small hamlet of Civitella del Lago in Baschi (Orvieto).

Toughest to book: **Felice; Testaccio**.

Best Roman cuisine: **Checco er Carrettiere**.

Best takeout: **Franchi**.

Best cappuccino: **S. Eustachio**.

Smartest lunch: **Mastrostefano**.

Liveliest dinner: **Il Matriciano**.

Best pizza: **Picchioni**.

Best golf: **Acquasanta**.

Best tennis: **Circolo Tennis Parioli**.

Best diversion: **Vatican Museum**; the beach at **Fregene** on the Roman coast in summer and in winter.

Local secrets: **Porta Portese street market** on Sunday mornings.

Medical emergencies

Doctors and dentists: English-speaking recommendations: **Salvator Mundi Hospital**, 06/586041.

Hospitals: **Rome American Hospital** 06/25671; **European Hospital**, 06/52259.

Business tip

Cooperativa Airport is a private taxi service (Tel. 65010858) that provides a punctual service with large, comfortable, air-conditioned automobiles to and from the airport to the city centre for the reasonable fixed price of L 60,000. A great way to avoid being fleeced.

San Francisco

San Francisco is my favourite city (I'm not alone in this opinion) and I go out of my way to visit it. If you want to know what the rest of America will be thinking and doing three years' hence, come here first.

Although it's hard to argue with the perennial excellence of the **Four Seasons Clift Hotel** or with *aficionados* of 'boutique' hotels who seem to gravitate to the **Prescott Hotel**, for location, staff and relative tranquility my first choice remains the **Stanford Court**, closely followed by the **Mandarin**. The **Fairmont Hotel** has finished its recent renovations and is definitely worth a try again.

As you would expect of a city that starts most of America's dining trends, San Francisco has a spectacular and seemingly inexhaustible restaurant scene, not just within the city proper but an hour away in the Napa Valley and over the Golden Gate Bridge in Marin County too. Being adventurous here rarely disappoints.

Weekend retreat in Napa Valley: **Silverado Country Club; Auberge du Soleil**.

Best hideaway resort in Oakland: **The Claremont Resort**.

Best Mexican: **Margaritaville**.

Power lunch: **The Big Four**.

Toughest table to book (but worth the effort): **Postrio**.

Best brasserie: **Stars; Bix**.

Best Sunday brunch: **Perry's; Green's**.

Watering hole: **Washington Square Bar & Grill**.

Best California cuisine: **Square One; One Market**.

For gourmets: **Zuni Café** and **Chez Panisse** (in Berkeley).

Best French: **Masa's**.

Worth the drive: **The Lark Creek Inn**.

Best local ambience for a casual meal: **Fog City Diner**.

Best Italian: **Donatello**.

Best burger: **Hamburger Mary's**.

Dining in Napa: **The French Laundry; Mustard's Grill; Tra Vigne**.

Best gym: **YMCA** (financial district); **Club One**.

Medical emergencies

Dental: **San Francisco Dental Office** provides 24-hour emergency service.

Hospitals: **San Francisco General** (415/821 8200).

Business tip
September to November is the best time to visit, but schedule early to beat the convention and trade show rush.

Stockholm

The dominant element in Stockholm is water (and not just because it rains a lot here). The city sits on a string of fourteen islands in the Baltic, so everything beautiful and interesting here is either near or on a body of water. I'm not sure where Stockholm picked up the reputation for being a cold, bland city, but it is a false impression. I've been visiting Stockholm regularly since the mid-1970s heyday of our client Bjorn Borg and always do so with eagerness. Everything here is expansive and slightly larger than normal scale – like a restaurant with vaulted ceilings, oversized chairs and the tables spread far apart. I never feel cramped in Stockholm. Yet with its centralized business area, it is an easy town to navigate.

Most of Stockholm's hotels fall into the standard international executive class – reliable and efficient. By far the best is the **Grand**, marvellously situated on the water and in the heart of everything. The **Diplomat** is an up-and-comer among executives who yearn for a less hectic atmosphere.

Best hideaway hotel: **Victory Hotel** (a de luxe, antique-filled, one-of-a-kind jewel in Stockholm's Old Town).

Best weekend retreat: **Grand Hotel Saltsjöbaden** (a gorgeous nineteenth-century 'castle' just ten miles away on the Baltic).

Best restaurants open on Sunday night: **Bistro Jarl** and **Östergök**.

Best for serious business dinner: **Paul & Norbert**.

Best seafood: **Wedholms Fisk**.

Best burger: **Eriks** (downstairs).

Best business lunch: **Eriks** (upstairs).

Best game dishes: **Den Gyldene Freden**.

Best hotel dining: **Grands Veranda** (in Grand Hotel).

Small jewel: **Min Lilla Trädgård** ('My Little Garden').

Best-kept secret: The **Leijontornet** ('Lion's Tower') restaurant in the Victory Hotel.

Best golf: **Ullna Golf Club** (thirty minutes from town).

Best tennis: **Royal Tennis Club**.

Best gym: **Sturebadet**.

Best jogging : **Djurgården park**.

Best diversion: **A boat trip to** one of the islands (e.g., Utö or

Sandhamn) in the Stockholm archipelago.

Medical emergencies

Doctor: **City Hälsocentral**, 08/ 20 69 90.

Dentists: **Senkt Eriks Sjukhus**, 08/54 11 17 (8 a.m. to 9 p.m.); 08/44 92 00 (nights).

Business tip

Unless you are a passionate sailor, obsessed with everything nautical, do not be lured into booking a cabin on any of the boat hotels anchored in Stockholm's harbour; the novelty will wear off very quickly.

Sydney

Sydney is the most nonchalant international business centre. With its breathtaking habour and beaches, it is a perfect combination of San Francisco and Rio de Janeiro. Yet there was a time in the 1960s and '70s when I hated visiting Sydney. The hotels were ancient, the food was terrible, international phone calls were impossible to complete, and other than the friendly citizenry, some nice golfing and pleasant weather, there was little comfort or joy to be found.

Fortunately, no city in the world has transformed itself more dramatically for the business traveller in the last twenty years than Sydney. Qantas, the national carrier, is one of the world's great airlines. There's a healthy choice of hotels that cater to executives, and the restaurant scene is vibrant.

The **Regent**, which continues to merit its reputation as the best hotel in the Southern Hemisphere, is my first choice here, though it is getting a healthy challenge from the **InterContinental** and two relative newcomers, the **Ritz-Carlton** and the ambitious **Park Hyatt**.

Top business restaurant: **Kables** (in the Regent).

Best wine list: **Treasury** (in the InterContinental).

Best tourist trap: **Doyle's on the Beach.**

Best Italian: **Tre Scalini; Darcy's.**

Best Chinese: **Imperial Peking.**

Tastiest/healthiest cuisine: **The Pier.**

Best harbour setting: **Bilson's.**

Best garden setting: **Lucio's.**

Best Sunday lunch: **Bather's Pavilion** at Balmoral Beach.

Local secrets: **Café Nouveau; Five Doors; Bayswater Brasserie; Claudes.**

Best jogging: **Botanical Gardens** alongside Sydney Harbour.

Best golf: **NSW Golf Club.**

Best tennis: **White City; Paddington; Rose Bay.**

Best gym: **The Hyde Park Club.**

Best diversion: **Darling Habour; Berowra, Hawksbury River.**

Medical emergencies

Doctors: **Executive Health**

Medicentre, 02/276 963;
Women's Medical Centre, 02/
231 2366.

Dentists: **Dental Emergency
Services and Central Dental
Laboratory**, 02/211 1011.

Hospitals: **St Vincent's Hospital**,
02/339 1111; **Sydney Hospital**,
02/228 2111.

Business tip
Australians do not always tip
for services provided and are
sometimes perturbed by visitors
who insist on tipping (especially
in excess of 10 per cent) because
it tends to ruin the system for
them.

Tokyo

Tokyo may be the toughest city on earth in which to hit the ground running. It is sprawling, like London, but the unfamiliar language and local customs make it a challenge for Western executives who do not do their homework.

Again, like London, there are many top-notch hotels here, but choosing one should be dictated by location. Though people I respect swear by the modern opulence of the **Seiyo Ginza** and the unalloyed excellence of the **Hotel Okura**, for service and convenience, I remain loyal to the **Capitol Tokyu**. **Keio Plaza**, in the heart of Shinjuku, caters marvellously to foreign executives and business groups.

Tokyo has more bars and restaurants than any city in the world. Western diners will notice an interesting irony in the restaurant scene here. Though Japan may block imports of Western-made technology and consumer goods, that has not stopped Tokyo from aggressively importing restaurants and dining trends from the West. Some of the best restaurants I've tried in recent years are Tokyo outposts of proven winners from America, Italy and France.

Best classic French: **De Roanne; Hiramatsutei; Apicius.**

Best Italian: **Enotecca Pinchiorri.**

Best hotel dining: **Keyaki Grill** (Capitol Tokyu); **Attore** (in the Seiyo); **La Belle Epoque** (in the Okura).

Best Chinese: **Toh-Ka-Lin.**

Local secret: **L'Eau à la Bouche; Second.**

Best American franchises: **Spago; Trader Vic's.**

Best French franchises: **La Tour d'Argent; Maxim's.**

Best Italian franchises: **Bice; Sabatini; El Toula.**

Best sushi: **Kyubei; Nakata.**

Best pizza: **Tant Tant** (in the Tokyu Department Store/Main Building).

Best golf: **Kuni Country Club** (public – Prince Hotel).

Best tennis: **Shinagawa Prince Hotel; Tokyo Hilton.**

Best jogging: **Imperial Palace; Akasaka Palace.**

Medical emergencies

Doctors: **Tokyo Medical &**

Surgical Clinic, 03/436 3028;
International Clinic at
Azabudai, 03/3582 2646.

Dentists: **Yanagisawa Dental
Clinic in the Capitol Tokyo Hotel**
(03 581 4511); **Tokyo Clinic
Dental Office**, 03/3431 4225.

Business tip
The Japanese do not tip for
services rendered, save for a
chambermaid in an inn or for
special appreciation. A 10 per
cent service fee in hotels and
restaurants is usually included.

Zurich

Zurich is *the* city that most closely approximates the 'hit the ground running' ideal. It may be the easiest city in the world to conduct business in. It is prosperous, compact, easy to move around in and, as a major financial centre, has a healthy respect for the primacy of commerce.

In a nation as reliant on tourism as Switzerland is and as obsessed with cleanliness, order and efficiency, the excellence of Zurich's hotels should not be a surprise. Pride of place in my heart will always go to the **Dolder Grand**, an otherworldly retreat a few minutes from the centre of town which, besides having its own golf course, tennis courts, ice-skating rink and sublime gardens, is also a state-of-the-art business hotel. The **Baur au Lac**, though indisputably one of Europe's great hotels, surprised me that it doesn't have 24-hour room service. If you're an early riser don't expect coffee before 6 a.m. This is its only deficiency.

Best summer hideaway: **Ermitage** in Küsnacht (fifteen minutes away on Lake Zurich).

Weekend retreat: **The Parkhotel** at Witznau (this placid chalet rivals Villa d'Este; closer to Lucerne than Zurich, but worth the forty-five-minute drive for extended stays).

Best business lunch: **The Grill Room** (in the Baur au Lac); **Brasserie Lipp**.

Best dining bargain: **Bier-Falken**.

Best restaurant on Lake Zurich: **Petermann's Kunststuben**; **Savoy Grill**.

Restaurants worth the drive: **Witschi's** and **Sihlhalde**.

For meeting over drinks: **Pacifico** and **Kronenhalle**.

Best Italian: **Gala**; **Academia**.

Best gourmet, best pasta: **Tübli**.

Best light meals: **Nouvelle Thai**; **Königstuhl**; **Blaue Ente**.

Best Swiss food: **Rosaly**.

Best beers: **Bierhalle Kropf**.

Best golf: **Zumikon Country Club** (in a suburb of Zurich).

Best tennis: **Grasshoppers Club**.

Best skiing: **Laax** (a drive of one and a half hours); **St Moritz**.

Medical emergencies

24-hour free medical and dental

emergency service:
Notfälldienst, 01/261 61 00.

Hospitals: Accident department
of **Zurich Universitatsspital** 01/
255 11 11.

Business tip
As in Geneva, always be
prompt.